The Myth of Japanese Efficiency

In memory of my grandfather, Dan Coffey

The Myth of Japanese Efficiency

The World Car Industry in a Globalizing Age

Dan Coffey

Leeds University Business School, UK

Edward Elgar

Cheltenham, UK • Northampton, MA, USA

Published by
Edward Elgar Publishing Limited
Glensanda House
Montpellier Parade
Cheltenham
Glos GL50 1UA
UK

Edward Elgar Publishing, Inc.
William Pratt House
9 Dewey Court
Northampton
Massachusetts 01060
USA

A catalogue record for this book
is available from the British Library

Library of Congress Cataloguing in Publication Data

Coffey, Dan, 1966–
    The myth of Japanese efficiency : the world car industry in a globalizing age / Dan Coffey.
        p. cm.
    Includes bibliographical references and index.
    1. Automobile industry and trade—Japan—Management. 2. Automobile industry and trade—Production control—Japan. 3. Toyota Jidosha Kabushiki Kaisha. I. Title.
    HD9710.J32C635 2006
    338.4′7629222—dc22
                                                    2006012794

ISBN-13: 978 1 84542 041 3
ISBN-10: 1 84542 041 1

Typeset by Cambrian Typesetters, Camberley, Surrey
Printed and bound in Great Britain by MPG Books Ltd, Bodmin, Cornwall

Contents

v

1. Introducing the myth of Japanese efficiency

The basic method of producing automobiles changed very little between 1913, when Henry Ford introduced the moving assembly line, and the 1970s, when a radically new system of production began to emerge in Japan. (Dicken 2003: 364)

Fordist practices came to be seen as limiting, because they were suited to the manufacture of large quantities of standardized goods . . . shifts were occurring in global consumerism: the mass markets which had made Fordism so successful were being supplanted by 'niche markets' for innovative, high quality goods. (Giddens 2001: 384)

The new system was based on the development, application and diffusion of new principles of production and organizational capabilities that enabled Japanese manufacturing enterprises to compete on more comprehensive performance standards combining cost, quality, time and flexibility . . . failure to adapt to, or counter, the new production system would lead to industrial decline. (Best 2001: 37)

1.1 INTRODUCTION

The past few decades have seen a concerted movement, visible in and running through academic studies, teaching literature, policy statements and business commentaries of otherwise diverse opinion and hue, to proclaim that radical changes in the world's car manufacturing and assembly sector have led the way in transforming production potentials in factory systems more generally. The point might reasonably be ventured that a similar movement is discernible in an earlier generation of responses to the first appearance of car manufacture and assembly on a massive scale in the Highland Park factories of Henry Ford. The iconography of the continuously moving conveyor belt, and of workers tasked with successively adding parts in a large number of discrete and individually repetitive operations to produce a finished product, is for this reason indelibly associated in the popular mind in the West today with one particular industry; and if the car industry is again cast as a leading industry that meters the pace and direction of change in industry and in industrial society more generally, then this is how it was before. But the radical change which is the subject matter of this book is, we will argue, of a qualitatively different type,

1

because its terms are more obviously myth. The change in question pertains to the alleged appearance in Japan – and evident from the early 1970s – of a new way of organizing the manufacture of complex goods: this we challenge. We argue, for example, that the 'lean and flexible' production now popularly associated with the Japanese car assembler Toyota is unacceptable if viewed in historical and empirical terms and seriously assessed as a manufacturing model, but that its success as a story is one that may shed light on cultural responses to global stresses.

This book sets out to establish its propositions by means of a series of studies combining case work, historical review and accessible but rigorous modelling to assess received views on Japan's impact on the world car industry, with particular regard to process flexibility, resource productivity and the organization of work. It first establishes a systemic non-correspondence between what is said and what can be demonstrated on behalf of the Japanese production model, as purportedly exemplified in the car industry by Toyota and others, and then asks a different question: how can particular institutional responses to and policy evaluations of the Japanese phenomenon be understood, if what is claimed to be true is not true? While broached in this book from the viewpoint of the attendant stresses of globalization, deeper issues are also noted, pointing to unresolved questions for future research of interest as much to cultural anthropologists as to economic and business analysis.

1.2   THESIS AND SCOPE

To avoid misunderstandings at the outset, it is not intended to argue that Japanese car assemblers are inefficient – there is no question of denying their successes, or capabilities in design, assembly, marketing and distribution. Neither do we wish to understate their individually unique attributes, not only in comparison with global competitors, but also in comparison with each other; and it is not the intent of this book to deny their intrinsic interest as manufacturers and corporations. Nor is it suggested that related issues of organization, industrial relations, or corporate strategy become any the less interesting because of positions set out in this book. What this book is concerned with, however, is asking why success should appear hand in hand with the wholesale construction of a set of counterfactuals about an industry.

In this regard, the 'sense of the myth' with which we are concerned is neatly, if cumulatively, encapsulated in the passages cited at the outset of this introductory chapter. First, there is a purported awareness amongst industrial observers of the emergence of a novel type of production system – circa the 1970s – with its point of origin in Japan. Second, there is a manifest belief amongst commentators that the purported shift in production potentials has coincided (serendipitously) with a pronounced change in patterns of global consumerism. A now very large literature exists extolling the contrasting characteristics of the old and the new forms of production – inflexible versus flexible, task work versus team work, low trust versus high trust, integrated versus de-integrated – underscored by claims of a great leap forward in the potential efficiencies of manufacturing resource use. Moreover, there is a pervading sense that what is described in the car sector has a more general relevance; that what has been 'witnessed' in the making and selling of cars is of fundamental significance. The proposal that a 'new system' emerged in the 1970s, to which failure to adapt, or counter, would mean inevitable decline (Best 2001: 37) is a vision that encompasses more than just car assembly; indeed for many commentators – perhaps most particularly those employed in the study of the social sciences, although by no means exclusively – it is one extending from industry to industrial society writ large.

These commentators propose that changes supposedly observed in the world's car industry exemplify, in a particularly 'vivid' form, changes apparent more generally in the organization of production; that is to say, and as already noted, the car industry is held up as the industry which measures a more general transformation:

> We concentrate on organizational and social change because the 'mass production paradigm' or, more simply, 'Fordist paradigm' dominated management philosophy for more than half a century and it is only late in the twentieth century given way to a new style of management thinking and organization . . . The most spectacular example of the redesign and reorganization of a production process and the associated network of subcontractors was of course the 'lean production system' of the Japanese automobile industry. The worldwide exports of cars and consumer electronics were probably the most vivid evidence of Japanese technological strength for large numbers of people all over the world. In the United States especially the reversal of their prolonged dominance in the archetypal mass production industry was bound to make a very deep impression. (Freeman and Soete 1999: 138, 151)

The words are from a reputable survey textbook of industrial innovation by two well-known economists, Chris Freeman and Luc Soete. The value of this passage, as an illustration, follows from its representative quality. A 'Fordist paradigm' in the 'mass production' industries is said to have dominated (Western) 'management philosophy' for more than 50 years, exemplified in the car industry certainly, but also clearly not regarded by the authors as being exclusive to it: indeed, the car industry is selected in this context only as providing the 'most spectacular' example of a break from this past, evidenced by the supposed emergence of a distinctive 'lean production' in Japan; the transition from the old to the new is located 'late in the twentieth century'. Moreover, in this same passage the appearance of the new 'system' is explicitly and confidently associated not only with a period of organizational change in this and other industries, but also with 'social change' more generally: in this connection, the fact that the writers are economists writing for economists is nicely indicative of a wider assurance on this point – there is no hint here of any intended controversy. Changes purported to have occurred in the organization of Japanese factories in one particular industry (cars) are in this way duly held to be reflective of a more fundamental transformation in industrial society: Japan's car assemblers appear here in a double role, playing a part as both agents and emblems. A similar sweep of association can be found in any number of texts appearing in the course of the past 20 or so years, produced from within and without academe by writers who must in many cases struggle to find much else by way of common ground.[1] We will presently consider a number of such works for their general propositions, and for the detail of positions set forth on particular aspects of the organization of manufacturing activities in the industry which constitutes their chosen point of departure.

Considered as a set of constituent studies, the present book could be read as a contribution that dissents from the current conventional wisdom on a number of critical points pertaining to developments in the world's car industry, *sui generis*. As instances we might note, in anticipation and as examples, the following propositions:

(a) It will be argued that the assumption that Toyota and other Japanese car assemblers led a break from 'Fordist' mass production of standardized models is historically counterfactual, and that this branch of manufacturing history has been subject to a collective process of fictionalization – Japanese car assemblers were laggards not leaders when they first introduced 'flexible' assembly systems in the 1970s, while contrary to assertion they have since typically eschewed customization strategies.

(b) It will be shown that the major global productivity survey of the 1980s which informed the idea of a distinctively 'lean' production system in fact gave more support to the opposite thesis, namely that Toyota and other Japanese car assemblers were at this time struggling to transform operatives' working time into output.

(c) It will be suggested that the 'reorganization of work' in the 1990s in Toyota's factories might best be interpreted in a complementary way – as potential evidence of undisclosed problems with unplanned line stoppages, and worker discontent.

Read at this level, the contribution could be interpreted simply as one involving a compilation of evidence that vitiates statements like that offered by Freeman and Soete in the passage cited above, and in the passages cited in the epigraph to this chapter. This does not mean, of course, that the contribution is a negative one. In the course of considering the merits and demerits of

claims made by and on behalf of Japanese assemblers in the world's car industry, the studies presented also contribute in a critically positive way to the
study of manufacturing activities in that sector: on the delineation of flexibility, the role of automation, the organization of work. In a similar way, there is
much in this book that is relevant to debates on policy formulation, whether
within state agencies, business corporations, or trades unions. Viewed solely
at this level, therefore, the contribution would be a positive one, if critical. But
at a different level it is hoped that the anomalies uncovered and explored in
this book will be of positive interest to academics and others adopting a wider
purview, and with particular regard to the cultural contexts within which a
myth, or a set of myths, about production – the factory, the business, the
consumer – can gain currency or grow.

This theme is tentatively explored throughout the constituent studies that
make up the first half of the book – counterfactuals are highlighted, confirmation biases noted – and then expanded upon *vis-à-vis* globalization, the sepa-
rating interests of Japan and Japanese transnational corporations and the
resurgent confidence of Western capitalism. In addition to drawing out some
possible connections between the emergence of a particular narrative about
Japanese manufacturing prowess on the one hand, and development in the
international political economy on the other, over the relevant period, some
speculative comments are offered in conclusion and in the spirit of free
commentary as to the possibility of a different kind of study, one that seeks as
its subject matter the meaning of myths about production – of production
fantasies.

The constituent parts of what, for summary purposes, is referred to in this
title of this book as the 'myth of Japanese efficiency' have evolved over a
period of decades. For example, in works written over the course (say) of the
past ten years, it is commonplace to see Toyota described as a 'lean and flexible' producer. But the view that Japan's car assemblers, led by Toyota, were
proving to be highly flexible operators in the organization of the interface
between factory and market gained serious currency amongst Western
commentators in the middle 1980s. By contrast, the words 'lean production'
gained currency only in the following decade, primarily in the context of
economies in resource use for *any* given set of products. These considerations
are not the same, and one advantage of the book form is that it is possible to
deal with themes in a way which gives space in which to signal chronology
and development. From the viewpoint of a study dealing with material generated by processes of myth-making this is an important consideration: the
significance of the distinction between 'lean' and 'flexible', for example,
hinges not only on chronology, but also on the role in each case of corporate
promotion. By the same token, it is similarly possible to consider emergent
strands that point to further evolution of the commentaries on 'Japanese'

manufacturing efficiency as the relative fortunes of the Japan's domestic economy have waned comparatively. Similarly, some space can be given to assessing branch developments: for example, that lean production is a capitalism-friendly answer to global warming, that it represents the future of military procurements and that it is the material basis for socialism.

But this book is neither written as, nor is it intended to be, a critical literature review. Works cited are chosen either for their representative quality, or as seriously intended contributions to literatures pertaining directly or indirectly to its subject matter. Since the book is partly intent on addressing an existing body of recorded opinion from the viewpoint of the light this might shed on processes of myth-making about production, this inevitably means that works cited may be cited for this reason. But in many cases the intent will be to suggest a different interpretation of carefully garnered observations, rather than to dispute them; and even where outright disagreement is unavoidable, this need not entail a wholesale dismissal – the goal rather is to highlight and contrast a gulf between what is believed and what evidence will allow. In many cases, a great deal of carefully researched and important material stands alongside tacit assumptions and assertions which (it will be argued) are ill-founded: inasmuch as space allows, an attempt is made throughout to discuss in discriminating terms. At the same time, this study – or set of studies – is not intended to be a treatise. There is no pretence at an exhaustive coverage of the literature, although it is naturally hoped that nothing has been missed that would invite a serious change in position. Since not everyone agrees on every topic, even when they hold some views in common, works are cited strictly in the context of the topic covered in the relevant chapter.

While the organization of the book, and the complexity of its subject matter, precludes an initial literature review, some notable literary milestones can certainly be listed. In the first substantive chapter of this book (Chapter 2), for instance, reference is made, for purposes of literary comparison, to Abernathy (1978). The thesis advanced in this remarkably focused and powerfully written work in many ways established the template for the 'crisis of Fordism' narrative relied upon by so much of what has since been written about changes in industrial society and the impact of Japanese production methods in the car and other industries. This, it will be recalled, was that the car industry had become (by the 1970s) a mature industry, locked into a particular form of volume production based on large capital investments requiring stable markets in which to sell identically-specified products replicated in very large quantities, suppressing moreover any internal impetus for radical changes in product design: 'innovation gives way to standardization as a competitive tool, product diversity to economies of scale' (see Abernathy ibid.: 11). The overall prognosis was therefore bleak: it was predicted, a position later abandoned by its author, that resource productivities were for this reason reaching secular limits. The thesis of declining investment opportunities for further productivity growth in turn became the foil against which the first MIT survey of the world's car industry tested the likely impact of 'Japanese' production methods in the car industry – as well as new microprocessing technologies (see Altshuler et al. 1984: 135); but our interest is less with this, since it is *not* our contention that global myth-making about the historical progress of a major industry, one moreover that is the subject of close scrutiny by large bodies of professional industry observers, is explicable in terms of the misleading effects of cleverly written but misdirecting studies. Rather, our interest in citing Abernathy will be one of comparison, from the viewpoint of highlighting the suddenness of the change in precepts and perceptions that is a marked feature of the fictions that provide our chosen subject matter.[2] For the main part items cited with critical intent are employed in much this sort of illustrative way, although at some junctures a more detailed assessment is required and given of empirical propositions, such as, for example, the MIT-based survey work reported in Womack et al. (1990).

From the viewpoint of literary milestones, therefore, it is certainly possible to list publications that appear in retrospect to be 'major events', either because of their subsequent following, or because the approach taken within captures in a particularly succinct or apt way a relevant shift in precept and perception. We must certainly also include here Ohno (1978), a hugely influential book which appeared propitiously in Japan in the same year that Abernathy was published in the West, and which accredited Toyota with inventing an alternative type of production system characterized by a hitherto unanticipated flexibility. The status of this work is such that it will make an appearance in almost every chapter of our own book. On the side of social science, Piore and Sabel (1984), appearing in another propitious coincidence in the same year as the first MIT survey, is also notable for its status: very clearly influenced by developments believed to be underway in the making and selling of cars, the thesis presented here is one of a new 'industrial divide'. Works like these generate their own following – amongst works appearing in this earlier period one might also include Aglietta (1976, 1987), a neo-Marxian treatise with a distinctive political economy – each makes reference to a notion of industrial 'Fordism', albeit in individually distinct ways, and each is regularly cited in connection with a purported transition to a new type of industrial system organized around a new type of production. But the issues we are concerned with, considered progressively, seem to point towards something more than the mere substance of 'key' publications.

So far as issues of operations management are concerned, any account of a manufacturing process encounters an obvious difficulty, lucidly explained in an elegant review of the issues involved in the interpretation of artifacts in the history of technology, by Robert Gordon (1993: 75): 'Technology, particularly mechanical technology, involves a large component of nonverbal thinking that is not easily recorded in words or even by drawings . . . the instructions for assembling many toys and household appliances illustrate this problem'. The particular context for this comment is the difficulties entailed in setting out accurate and comprehensible descriptions of the work of artisans, but the general sense is true: it is not easy to describe, succinctly and with a fair degree of accuracy, even a simple manufacturing process, perhaps even especially 'familiar' processes.[3] In the following chapters pains have been taken to acknowledge the particularly telling phrase, or apt description, that makes the task of exposition and analysis easier. The approach as a whole is to combine this in places with a more 'formal' representation of production variables, in the form of simple models. Like any model, these are not intended to be literal descriptions of concrete instances, with all details appended, but rather aids to communication that help pinpoint key relationships and dimensions. At the same time, no attempt is made to build up *a priori* constructs, step by step, since the result would be unreadable. The formal is textually integrated with the informal.

So far as history is concerned, the position adhered to is that it is possible to identify departures from material evidence and, on the basis of sudden changes in precept and perception that seem to pass through a literature without notice or comment, to pose questions that can be subjected to further investigation, and can in particular be tested against material evidence. The comparative samples of past and present observations on the content of the world's car industry are selected to illustrate themes being progressed in individual chapters, to indicate sudden changes in precept or perception that merit further study, or to provide corroboration for statements in the text. At the same time, these parts of the chapters complement the parts which develop the case on the basis of other forms of evidence, whether analytical or empirical.

1.3 CHAPTER CONTENTS AND PROGRESSION

While it is hoped that the book as a whole develops an integrated perspective on its subject matter, each of its chapters is also written so as to make an individual contribution on points of substantive interest and controversy. The chapter sequence reflects, nonetheless, the overall progression of the main thesis of the study.

Chapter 2 ('Wide selection: a myth encountered') can be viewed on one level as dealing with important issues of operations management. To this end, it broaches the question of comparative flexibility in assembly operations from the particular viewpoint of the 'width' of selection offered to prospective customers. In this context, the point of departure is the number of alternate model specifications that can be identified for complex products (cars) that will be built up (once selected) on the same production lines, in a single integrated assembly process. The chapter considers and rejects the claim that Japanese assemblers, led by Toyota, obtained a comparative advantage in the market place owing to more flexible assembly processes. It observes, with supporting illustrations and historically grounded comparisons, that, contrary to what is now a commonly held view in the literature, Toyota and other Japanese car assemblers have typically eschewed rather than promoted customization strategies in the selections offered to prospective customers seeking to buy cars. And in this part of its argument the chapter concludes that, when simultaneous account is taken of the comparative widths of model selection offered to customers, stock–flow ratios in production and the lead times on new customer orders, much of the evidence advanced to support the notion of a Japanese-inspired breakthrough in the organization of more flexible assembly operations falls to the ground.

At the same time, there are deeper issues. The presumption that Japan's assemblers stole a march over Western rivals – allegedly confined to 'Fordist mass production' – by being leaders in the introduction of mixed-assembly systems is counterfactual: in this sphere of operations, Toyota in global terms was an historic laggard, not a leader. Indeed, the assertion that the mid-1970s saw a decisive break in manufacturing practices in the car industry, with its epicentre in Japan, relies on a series of counterfactuals. Chapter 2 makes the case for assessing some of the most glaring in cultural terms: it highlights the re-imagining of production practices hitherto conceived of as having evolved in the West as more recent innovations conceived of in Japan; their allotted role within this revisionist process as harbingers of change; and an accompanying narrowing of precepts *vis-à-vis* consumer sovereignty.

Similar themes are considered in Chapter 3 ('Production malapropisms: the BMW–Rover Group controversy), which is again intended to serve a dual purpose. Its vehicle is a study of an ill-fated experiment in just-in-time production at a British car plant: it considers afresh – albeit with a rather particular focus – the controversy that has periodically erupted in the UK over the ill-starred fate of the Rover Group, following difficult periods of collaboration with the Japanese firm Honda, ownership by the German firm BMW, divestment, shrinkage and re-launch as MG Rover, receivership and threatened liquidation, and a possible reprieve from China. Doubts about Japanese flexibility in car assembly naturally also raise doubts about the status and meaning to be accorded to the words 'just-in-time' production, when invoked to imply some historic distinction for Japanese assemblers in the car industry. Broached as an essay on further issues pertaining to operations management, this chapter explores these themes while setting out complementary evidence which shows how a poorly conceived proposition about manufacturing efficiency can undermine a vulnerable company's ability to realize its intended objectives in the market place. It also contains material of some potential interest to historians of the car industry as well as to compilers of case studies in business strategy: against a recent view that the ill-starred Rover Group was briefly revitalized by (Honda-fed) Japanese production practices, a success squandered by the German firm BMW which misread the market for British brand cars, the contra-proposition advanced is that the German firm's plans were undone, at least in part, as a consequence of prior misadventures involving a homegrown attempt to engage in 'Toyota-like' production. But again, there are deeper issues, not least the tacit assumptions made in controversies of this type about 'national' – British, Japanese and German – manufacturing attributes.

Chapter 4 ('Lean production: the dog that did not bark') steps back from the operations aspects of manufacturing 'flexibility' to consider instead resource use at the level of labour productivity at different measured levels of plant automation. More specifically, it looks again at the findings of the MIT-headquartered International Motor Vehicle Programme (IMVP) studies on productivity in car assembly plants throughout the world car industry; these studies are perhaps best known in the context of their public dissemination, in the late 1980s and early 1990s, as definitive proof of the emergence of a new and superior 'lean' production paradigm in Japan: in fact, it was in this connection that the words lean production were coined and popularized. The sheer scale of the IMVP studies – not so much unsurpassed as unapproached since – and the apparent enormity of their impact on thinking about Toyota-like production methods, demand that they be properly addressed as an empirical contribution. The tack adopted in this regard differs somewhat from other commentaries: leaving details to the chapter itself, the proposition advanced is that, if taken seriously, the IMVP studies are better interpreted as having set out compelling evidence that labour in Japanese assembly plants was utilized no more 'effectively', and possibly less so, than labour elsewhere. After considering some implications, and comparing this rereading of the data with existing critiques, the stage is then set for a second reassessment, focused on the 'reorganization of work' at Toyota.

This reorganization is taken up in Chapter 5 ('Back to the future: the reorganization of work at Toyota'), which considers some widely noted experiments at Toyota with the organization of work on its car assembly lines. These commenced in the late 1980s, as a response to growing problems experienced at this time in Japan in recruiting and retaining workers, notwithstanding that it was precisely at this time that the standard interpretation of the IMVP studies was elsewhere feeding the beast by proclaiming the millennium in the organization of operations at Toyota. After an initially nonplussed reaction from Western commentators, these changes have largely been assessed since as representing either a continuance of a distinctive production model, or a 'next' step towards some even higher form. In this chapter, the contra-position set out, based in part on a re-assessment of the data collected by factory visitors, and on comparisons with some strikingly similar antecedent experiments in the factories of Western assemblers some 20 years earlier, is that the changes might be more fruitfully considered from the viewpoint of comparative line-stoppage rates under different forms of work organization. This provides an entirely consistent perspective not only with the data generated by first-hand observers of the Toyota experiments, but also with the reassessment of the IMVP studies in Chapter 5: by the late 1980s, things may not have been as commonly supposed at Toyota's plants. The discussion is extended to touch on the question of 'team work' in the car industry.

If the first set of chapters explore some substantive problems *vis-à-vis* the production methods and practices that have been identified with a Japanese-led revolution of production potentials in the car industry (and beyond), the next set out an alternative prospectus on what insights might be gleaned *vis-à-vis* globalization controversies.

Chapter 6 (Rivalrous asymmetries and the Japanese myth') deals with three overlapping issues. First, it considers the mounting tide of reaction to Japanese import penetration in Western markets through the 1970s and into the 1980s, taking as its vantage point the disturbing effects of a newly emerged world power (Japan) making inroads into markets hitherto dominated by Western oligopolies operating in a highly rivalrous sector. Second, it considers the wider political context that permitted Japan both to develop its manufacturing industries and to access Western markets shielded from other entrants, while at the same time blocking Western corporations seeking to access Japan. Third, it addresses some of the ways in which the malaise that afflicted the Japanese economy in the 1990s has been reflected in the shifting nuances of the debate on Japanese production methods, and their 'transforming' effects on Western economies. One question considered in these contexts is whether myth making about the Japanese contribution to manufacturing organization might be at least partly explicable not only by reference to the cultural stresses occasioned by changes in the global economic order, but also by the policy imperatives of some of the principal affected parties. In this regard it is interesting to observe that while leading business commentators remain publicly assured of the reality of a Japanese-led 'lean' revolution in manufacture, the terms of the debate on Japanese production methods have turned in a way which serves to dismiss in every other regard the potency of Japanese economic and social institutions *vis-à-vis* a Western or (more specifically) an Anglo-Saxon model. And in this context the chapter explores the twin themes of durability and plasticity.

In developing these issues and themes this chapter necessarily makes the point that for some corporate players and state agencies there is considerable political utility in the notion of a shift towards a more productive (and consumer led) type of manufacturing organization, quite apart from what can be gleaned from empirical evidence. Since large corporations and their state sponsors are important forces, this might be expected to impinge on the production of 'knowledge' and 'truth' in ways which are both fairly direct and rather unsubtle. But at the same time, it is clear that there are corporate critics – both within and without academe – who have bought into the view that a radically unpleasant set of production practices have swept outwards from Japan across the globe, and that the challenge for workers, and for workers' representative bodies, is to resist 'lean production'. An interesting question is the extent to which vocal critics of 'Japanization' have endorsed a poorly founded set of claims concerning manufacturing practices at the cost of a more realistic assessment of the discontents of globalization and the problems facing industrial workers.

Chapter 7 ('Rethinking lean thinking: substance and counterfeit) further explores this and other issues by means of a critical review of the most recent edition of a best-selling book on 'lean thinking' (Womack and Jones 2003). The book in question, *Lean Thinking*, ascribes an iconic status to Toyota MC as the leading exemplar of lean practices in production. The chapter observes that the metaphors employed in books of this kind ('pull', 'flow', 'perfection') *vis-à-vis* supporting production concepts mirror in a simple way the terms of what is now more generally believed about developments in industry. At the same time, this chapter notes a separate and distinctive use of metaphor running through the text, associated with a thoroughgoing 'unitarism' in the attitude recommended to managers seeking to apply the tenets of lean thinking to workplace organization. In this context, the proposition considered is whether lean thinking, as expounded in the specimen text, is best viewed as a substantive project that draws on the experiences of Japanese car assemblers in order to evolve 'best practice' recommendations for manufacturers, or as a cultural counterfeit that owes little to Japan but which has become a convenient vehicle by which to promote quite separate agendas. The chapter expands on the issues of substance and counterfeit to explore another sub-text: the peculiarly insulting status accorded 'German' craftwork by 'lean thinkers'.

The final chapter, Chapter 8 ('The totalizing myth: Japanese efficiency as a cultural fiction'), draws together the separate parts of the preceding chapters, and makes the case on the basis of the whole for a reassessment of the Japanese phenomenon in the car industry in terms of a fantasy about production, or a production fantasy. Following a brief reprise of relevant aspects of earlier chapters, this chapter first considers the myth of Japanese efficiency from the viewpoint of its 'totalizing' features, before speculating on where further investigation of the phenomenon might lead. On the first point, it is argued that the myth structure is complete, in the sense that attendant details relating to production are consistently interpreted in a way that sustains the terms of the myth; and totalizing, in the sense of inferences now being drawn.

ACKNOWLEDGEMENTS

Acknowledgement is due the Economic and Social Research Council, which funded some of the research underpinning the thesis advanced in this book (principally via ESRC Award H5246006494, but also via earlier ESRC funded doctoral research). I am also pleased at this juncture to acknowledge the assistance in preparing this manuscript of Dr Carole Thornley, who read and discussed every word: in addition, it was she who first suggested I enter a factory environment to see to what extent it differed from expectation, and who recommended a wider purview. I should also acknowledge here Professor Keith Cowling, who supervised this first factory visit, and whose views on the matter of political economy have influenced the perspective adopted in this book on issues of corporate strategy and accommodation in the global economy. Dr Giuseppe Calabrese, editor of the *International Journal of Automotive Technology and Management*, also provided me with the opportunity to edit a special issue (Volume 5 No. 3) with a particular focus on questions of product supply and product management, and a number of passages reflect the perspectives set out by various writers who contributed to this issue. Other influences are acknowledged at appropriate junctures in the main text. As per normal apologies to readers in such matters; all errors and omissions remain wholly the author's own.

Thanks too are due the team at Edward Elgar for their considerable encouragement and superb professional assistance, not least to Jo Betteridge, Nep Elverd, Emma Meldrum, Francine O'Sullivan and Emma Walker, as well as to all of those others involved in the processes of editing, production, marketing and distribution.

NOTES

1. Freeman and Soete are economists. Dicken, cited at the outset of this chapter, is a geographer and the author of a deservedly best-selling textbook *Global Shift*, which has as its intended focus the 'reshaping' of the global economic map of the 21st century (see Dicken 2003). In this book the world's car industry appears twice, both in a dedicated chapter ('Wheels of Change') dealing solely with this sector, and in a chapter on purported changes in the organization of production processes more generally (rather revealingly entitled 'Technology: the Great Growling Engine of Change'). Much space is given here to a contrast made between 'Fordist' and 'post-Fordist' production principles, and to the supposed impact of Japanese innovation in the car industry as the exemplary instance (see, in particular, ibid.: 105–15, 363–9). The next work cited in the epigraph is also a standard textbook. Giddens is a sociologist, but again the car industry is chosen in his *Sociology* for its emblematic features: much

space is again given to the 'Fordist'/ 'post-Fordist' contrast (in the chapter dealing with 'Work and Economic Life') as an important theme in advanced industrial economies. Following preambles on the factory division of labour, and Taylorism, the factories of Henry Ford are selected as providing definitive illustration of the 20th century extension of the principles of 'scientific management'; the example is established both as a specific ideal and as a general indicator of wider societal trends in the organization of consumer goods production, and then is propelled forward by 50 years, to the 1970s, and 'a new era of capitalist economic production in which flexibility and innovation are maximized in order to meet market demands for diverse, customized products' (see Giddens 2001: 383–5). This development in turn is linked (in part) to Japanese production methods. Students are also informed that some commentators use 'post-Fordism' as a shorthand term by which to express an intent to explore a plethora of (somehow) related issues, like 'party politics', 'welfare programmes' and 'consumer and lifestyle choices' (ibid.: 386). In this text, Japan's car assemblers are identified as the agencies by which a transformation is realized in a particular industry, but an industry which is expressly selected for its revelatory character. Many other such examples could be given from across the academic divisions, even if only considering textbooks.

2. In keeping with this approach little space is given over in this book to textual exegesis *vis-à-vis* the works of individual contributers to the relevant literatures. There would no doubt be much to recommend this for a number of cases: for example, upon re-reading the first MIT survey of the world's car industry published as Altshuler et al. (1984) (op. cit.), an engaging prospectus that leaves a palpable sense of imminent transformation in a major global sector, under new rules of the game partly ushered in by the Japanese, it was hard not to be struck by the extent to which it seemed to capture the US *zeitgeist* of the period. While not all of the contributors were American, the sense of decline and foreboding on the one hand, and the search for imminent change on the other, remind one of 'Morning in America'.

3. This no doubt accounts in part for the heavy reliance on metaphor in much of the literature that provides the subject material for this book, and for the willingness of audiences to bestow legitimacy on arguments concerning concrete matters of manufacturing practice which are conducted in these terms. Notwithstanding some of the criticisms made in this book, this is understandable, at least up to a point. Even something as simple as a 'car' is not easy to describe briefly or precisely: for example, the *Concise Oxford English Dictionary* defines a car as a 'powered road vehicle designed to carry a small number of people', a definition that requires an already well-developed consensus on what the class of object entails, because if a car is not a bus, then neither is it a motorcycle. In a number of places we will suppose some common and shared understanding of concepts, true in every book of this type.

2. Wide selection: a myth encountered

The assembly of motor vehicles has come a long way since Henry Ford's pioneering days at Highland Park. The customer of the 1950s could choose among engines, body styles, colors for both exterior and interior, and even hubcaps. He could designate what he wanted in the way of accessories – radio, heater, air-conditioner, for instance – and the car combining his preferences would roll off the assembly line in company with others representing different assortment of choices. (Rae 1965: 200)

Last year a Yale University physicist calculated that since Chevy offered 46 models, 32 engines, 20 transmissions, 21 colors (plus nine two-tone combinations), and more than 400 accessories and options, the number of different cars that a Chevrolet customer conceivably could order was greater than the number of atoms in the universe. This seemingly would put General Motors one notch higher than God in the chain of command. This year, even though the standard Chevrolet never accounts for less than two-thirds of Chevy's sales, Chevy is offering still more . . . indicating that while they may not be increasing their lead over Ford, they are pulling away from God. (Higdon 1966: 97)

With the unwinking sincerity with which the publicity machine speaks to its master, the consumer, a Ford advertisement in October 1969 explained revealingly, that with all the different versions and options '. . . YOU end up with a car that has the features you decided to have. For the price that YOU decided to pay. The choice is yours. Not ours. That's the whole point of our policy of offering so many cars and so many options. A motor car is too big a thing to shove down someone's throat.' (Bannock 1973: 240)

2.1 INTRODUCTION

One of the most striking assertions that reverberates through the voluminous literature that accredits the Japanese car industry with contriving a revolution in production methods, albeit one ostensibly not apparent until the 1970s, is the notion that up to this point car manufacture and assembly in North America and Western Europe was dominated by a 'Fordist' model of 'mass production'. In context, these are words intended to invoke factory systems that were individually limited, whether by basic know-how or prohibitive cost, in their ability to build a range of different model specifications using the same equipment and on the same production lines. Putting to one side the particular choice of words – 'Fordist mass production' – used to convey the idea of large-scale factory systems with operations limited to volume manufacture of more or less homogeneous goods, what is at issue is a definite hypothesis about the actual parameters of the systems of factory organization which grew to maturity in the automotive industry in the decades after World War II, sometime after the pioneering achievements of the Ford Motor Company and the Model T. What is seemingly proposed is that a factory observer, let us say in the 1950s or 1960s, or perhaps later still, watching finished cars emerge in large quantities – 'in the mass' – from the final build sequence of a 'typical' Western assembly plant, and with North America included, would have noted that each car was either exactly alike in every detail or, if differentiated, then only in some very limited manner and degree. Further to this, it is maintained that car assemblers in Japan, led by Toyota, were in the vanguard of world developments by achieving a facility – evident from the 1970s – to provide prospective customers with a menu of choices from a large number of different model specifications for cars assembled on the same production lines, in a 'mixed' or varying sequence. This notion is prominent in what, for short-hand purposes, we might call the transformation myth.

Briefly, we will set out the following propositions:

(a) Contrary to repeated assertions that Japanese assemblers revolutionized volume car manufacture by being first to break from 'Fordist mass production', via the introduction of mixed-assembly production methods that would allow different specifications of car to be built up on the same assembly line in a varying sequence, we argue that in this sphere of operations Japanese firms were historic laggards, not leaders.

(b) Contrary to claims that Japanese assemblers place a particular premium on allowing customers a 'wide selection' of choices on individual car specifications, we note that the evidence shows that Japanese firms have typically eschewed variety of this kind.

(c) We find no basis for judging Japanese assemblers to be more flexible either now or in the past than their Western counterparts, once the data generated by comparative assembly lines on product stocks and lead times is reinterpreted in light of point (b).

If these propositions are considered only in their negative aspects, then their initial input to the thesis explored in this book is essentially this. First, we reject one of the most prevalent misconceptions about the Japanese contribution to car manufacture and assembly *vis-à-vis* the development of mixed-assembly production systems, on grounds that the received view in question is both historically and geographically counterfactual. Second, while it is undoubtedly true that the delineation of 'flexibility' in complex assembly operations will always be contentious, there are compelling grounds for rejecting any assertion

that car assemblers in Japan – led by and including Toyota – have ever demonstrated an historic and empirically-supported advantage in their comparative
ability to manage the interface between factory and market, as judged by the
management of finished product stocks for completed cars and lead-times
from order to delivery on new sales. At the same time, viewed positively, this
chapter sets out an approach to production modelling that can be used to
generate criteria by which to rank assembly systems in terms of their greater
or lesser efficacy in managing finished product stocks and customer orders,
and in a way that takes a fuller and more accurate account of the stylized facts
of the world's car industry; by investigating how differences in the range of
model specifications built up in a factory process could reasonably be
expected to impact on other key variables, we are in a better position to then
consider further issues, including the organization of component part supply
and the content of the famous Toyota 'just-in-time' system.

These points relate to what we might think of as the operations side of the
equation. Claims made on behalf of and, as we will see, by Japanese car
assemblers, with regard to comparative manufacturing prowess, could be
addressed solely in these terms. But as we also suggest, there are aspects to
these claims that demand the attention not so much of the operations research
specialist or business historian, as the cultural anthropologist. In this regard,
the second main intent of this chapter is to highlight some of these aspects.

2.2   WIDE SELECTION

Since much of this chapter is concerned with the ability of assembly systems
to accommodate a mix of model specifications, it is useful to adopt some
terminology. The phenomenon with which we are concerned has been aptly
described in the literature as the practice of 'wide selection'. Haruhito Shiomi
(1995: 38) employs this felicitous expression to refer to situations in which
alternatives exist for individual model features selected by buyers of cars –
such as, for example, car body or engine types, colours, or options – which are
then built up in the same production facilities: the selections made by
customers determine the particular mix of model specifications that roll off the
assembly line. Where 'wide selection' is practiced by an assembler, prospective customers are provided with a choice from a range of permissible end-
product specifications for cars that will be built up in a single integrated
assembly process.[1] The myth which provides subject matter for this chapter
commences with the proposition that Japanese car assemblers stole a march
over their Western rivals by learning first how to practice wide selection.

A distinction must be drawn between the practice of offering a wide selection of model specifications for cars built up in a single integrated assembly

process, and product variety achieved via the separate assembly of discrete car lines in distinct assembly processes. The classic example typically given of the latter is General Motors' production and marketing strategy in the 1920s, when the American company established a multidivisional structure to manage its several distinct car lines – the Chevrolet, Pontiac, Buick, Oldsmobile and Cadillac – each separately assembled. For instance, Banri Asanuma (1994: 121–3) uses the GM example to contrast variations between car lines made in separate production facilities with 'orderable variations' *within* car lines built in a *single* production facility. Historically, of course, there is some overlap: White (1971, 26–7), writing more than 30 years ago, could note that the GM plant at Fremont, California, was in 1967 assembling models from no less than four differently 'badged' car lines or 'makes' – the Chevrolet Chevelle, Pontiac Tempest, Buick Special and Oldsmobile F-85 – all on the same production line, aided in this instance by a shared body-shell. White also describes the production at this time of 'two totally unrelated cars' on a single line at Pontiac's Michigan 'home plant', while an interesting example, of some apparent complexity, is also given for a second Michigan plant, this time managed by Ford (ibid.: 27, 316). But allowing that on some assembly lines operations are liable to be more complex than on others, the key point for wide selection is that a mix of different model specifications is built up on the same production lines, regardless of how these models are badged or labelled: 'The assembly process is made . . . complex by the fact that rarely do two identical cars follow each other down the line. Cars of the same make will be of two- and four-door varieties, hardtop and regular sedans, with or without optional extras like automatic transmissions, power brakes, power steering, and radios' (ibid.: 27–8). And so forth.

It should be evident from the dates of these examples that the practice of offering customers a wide selection of model specifications is not such a recent phenomenon in Western car assembly plants, or, more specifically, in North American plants. Even a cursory acquaintance with the enormous body of contemporary descriptive writing generated by the industry can establish this, as witnessed by the examples displayed in the epigraph to this chapter. The first is from Rae (1965) on the history of the American car in an entry to the *Chicago History of Civilisation* series; it has been selected because it highlights the conspicuous interest shown in a mid-1960s history to the rapid evolution of the US car industry in the preceding decade towards manufacturing and marketing strategies based on the 'assortment of choices', for target customers, that could be generated from the outputs of a single consolidated assembly plant. The second is a passage from an article that first appeared in *New York Times Magazine* at around this time, which jokes about a competitive expansion in model specifications; the same passage, we might add, is also quoted to good effect by L.J. White (above) in a chapter dealing with durability, styling and proliferation (see Higdon 1966, op. cit.; also White 1971: 189). The third, penned by an author to whom we will return, strikes a somewhat sourer note. It describes a Ford advertising campaign from the late 1960s, this time not in the US, but in the UK. Again the availability to prospective customers of choices from a very large number of different model specifications is very much to the fore – in the preceding line to this passage its author speaks of 'millions of custom-built specifications' (Bannock 1973, op. cit.: 240).

Now on this basis the correct conclusion would be that insofar as wide selection is concerned, Japan's car assemblers, including Toyota, are historically late arrivals. And this should not in itself be a matter of controversy. For example, Shiomi (1995, op. cit.) reports that Toyota launched its first 'full line' of cars, embodying the practice of wide selection, only in the mid-1960s, following some local experimentation by its consignment assemblers in the assembly of a mix of model specifications. This full line comprised '48 different combinations of engine, body and transmission' which expanded 'with the inclusion of different interiors, exteriors, and paint colours' to yield (initially) 332 finished model specifications: and it was launched in 1966 (see ibid.: 38). An exactly matching date sequence is also provided by Asanuma (1994, op. cit.), supported by references to Japanese industry sources and company histories for Toyota. These dates are in turn consistent with other timelines given for the Japanese car industry.[2] Since by the mid-1960s mixed assembly and wide selection (if we retain this term) was already a well-established practice in the North American factories run by Ford and General Motors, and indeed increasingly an aggressively marketed feature in their sales campaigns, the order of innovation is clear.

But this is not how it is routinely portrayed today. The dates pertaining to Toyota's first steps towards mixed assembly and wide selection are not themselves at issue: what is remarkable is that it is precisely on the basis of the sort of dates shown above that there has been a major movement over the past 20 or so years to proclaim that mixed-assembly systems only appeared in the car industry following the pioneering efforts of Toyota from the early 1970s, spreading outwards from Japan first to North America, and then to Western Europe. Today Toyota is hailed as the world shaker, and Japan is identified as the epicentre of a new industrial revolution which took shape in the form of innovative mixed-assembly systems and the introduction of novel wide selection practices. The preceding era has been repackaged as a kind of antithesis to the new one: Japanese achievements of 30 years ago are now contrasted not with a then actually existing state of affairs, but rather with a contrasting precept – 'Fordist mass production'.

In this context it is instructive to note a rare recent study by an historian of the car industry which looks at how some of the perceptions about the sector's past have been remoulded in recent decades in the academic and business press. In this carefully researched contribution to industrial historiography, Lyddon (1996) observes a change in the way in which commentators elect to employ the words 'mass production'. Whereas most recent commentary makes the term more or less synonymous with volume manufacture of a narrow range of model specifications, the phrase has previously been employed in quite different ways. Of particular interest in this latter regard are some instances taken from the supposed heyday of Fordist mass production. For example, Peter Drucker, writing in the mid-1950s, could argue that the 'essence of genuine mass production' was that it created 'a greater diversity of products than any method ever devised by man', owing to the possibilities for combining parts differently to form a 'large variety' of finished goods (Drucker 1955: 85–7, in Lyddon ibid.: 82). In these passages, Drucker, a famous managerialist, is describing a trend within industry in general, but the spirit is wholly in line with many enthusiastic descriptions given of car assembly plants at around this time. For an earlier generation of commentators the 'mass' in mass production could refer simply to an overall production volume, rather than to a uniform production content.[3] A change in the usage accorded a familiar set of words – mass production – marks, from one point of view, the shift in perception which has elevated Japanese car assemblers at the expense of their Western counterparts, *vis-à-vis* the first appearance of wide selection.

While there is a diminishing return to simply adding further descriptions of car assembly plants in the post-World War II years in order to vitiate this myth, Lyddon does provide several which are worth noting in addition to those given above. In the mid-1950s, and in keeping with Drucker's musings, descriptions are given of car assembly plants in North America which express their authors' astonishment at finding factories that can 'run for more than a year', and at 'maximum rate', without being obliged to produce two identical cars. These words are taken from Walker et al. (1956). Lyddon quotes from the relevant passages as follows:

> three distinct 'makes' of automobiles, each with many models and styles. Each body is painted with one of forty-five distinct colors . . . There are over one hundred twenty-five separate accessory specifications . . . the possible combinations are 'astronomical' . . . the schedules are so contrived as to permit each car in sequence to be preceded or followed by a car of completely different type, instead of a 'run' of similar models. (Walker et al. 1956: 7–8, in Lyddon ibid.: 83)

Lyddon also cites a similar, if slightly more restrained, account from a leading UK source at this time. F.G. Woollard, a significant figure in engineering of manufacturing processes in the 20th century, disliked the term 'mass production' because of its potential for trivializing the organization of the 'new' processes involved in the manufacture of complex product assemblies. In respect of Austin Motors' car assembly plant in the mid-1950s, Woollard refers to its 'flexibility' in coping with changes in chassis and body, 'colour and trim', and options like heaters and radio (Woollard 1954: 172; see also Lyddon 1996:78, 83).[4]

There are, in fact, two aspects to this issue. The question as to historical precedence in the introduction of mixed-assembly systems *per se* is clearly one; here it is the contention of this chapter that the move to award precedence to Toyota and Japan represents a recent and perhaps culturally significant transformation of precepts, wholly inconsistent with a massive body of prior evidence, but all the more interesting for it. This is one issue. A quite separate question is what car assemblers actually chose to do (or have done) with their facility to mix model specifications on the same production lines, judged from the viewpoint of their revealed strategies as car sellers, as well as car makers. On this second issue, even a cursory inspection of the literature of the past 20 years will convince that there is a firmly embedded notion, and largely amongst the same body of commentators, that Japanese car assemblers favour marketing strategies based on model 'customization'.

The point here is that an assembler may possess the facility to mix model specifications on the same assembly line, but elect not to use it in a way which makes much demand on that facility *vis-à-vis* the provision of 'build-to-order' selections. But what now seems commonly supposed is that not only is mixed assembly in the car industry an innovation that should be properly attributed to the example set by Japanese assemblers, but that these assemblers *also* elected to use this facility to 'customize' products. We have seen this association already, in the introduction to this book. Giddens (2001) identifies a supposed shift away from 'mass production' methods in the 1970s with a need to meet market demands for 'diverse' and 'customized' products, a shift purportedly exemplified by Japanese manufacturing practices in the car industry (ibid.: 385); car manufacture on the Japanese, or Toyotan, or 'lean' model is, for Dicken (2003), almost indistinguishable from production geared towards 'mass customization' (ibid.: 108). And some assumption of this kind is evident also in Shiomi (1995, op. cit.), and Asanuma (1994, op. cit.); in both cases, Toyota is perceived as an assembler with an historically demonstrated comparative advantage in offering customers 'minor' as well as 'major' product variations. To take a related example, Benjamin Coriat (a French writer) cites the same data on the same Toyota car line in much the same way to establish the emergence – 'under the pressure of the Japanese' – of a 'new regime of variety' in the car industry (Coriat 1997: 244–7).

The list can be easily extended, even if restricted to writers who are prominent in their own fields, but who have no particular research connection with the car industry. Michael Porter, in collaboration with Hirohito Takeuchi and

Masakamo Sakakibara, gives testament to a predilection on the part of Japan's 'lean' producers towards 'a wide line of models offering multiple features', based on 'standard products' with 'a wide range of options' (Porter et al. 2000: 70); an eminent authority on international economic relations, Robert Gilpin, also highlights the provision of 'customized products' as one of the defining features of the manufacturing practices associated with Japanese car assemblers (Gilpin 2000: 167); and returning to Japan, the late Yasusuke Murakami, the 'Japanese Weber', is on record as crediting Japanese car makers with the 'prototype' for small-lot production of differentiated products in a previously 'mass production' industry (Murakami 1996: 331). A similar emphasis on the potential for 'custom-built' cars as one example of changes sweeping this and other industries 'late in the twentieth century', and for reasons closely associated with developments in Japan, is evident also in Milgrom and Roberts (1990: 511–12), two leading economists intent on exploring the implications of the 'new' manufacture.

A particularly apt illustration is given by B. Joseph Pine's (1999) *Mass Customization*, a well-regarded contribution to the literature on manufacturing strategy *vis-à-vis* customized products, and a winner, moreover, of the Shingo Award for Excellence in Manufacturing – so named after Shigeo Shingo, one-time head of Toyota industrial engineering.[5] In Pine's study Toyota is cited as an 'excellent illustration' for companies seeking to develop market strategies based on the manufacture of a large number of individually differentiated products – hence 'mass customization'. The passage continues thus: 'Although it is not yet in a position to truly mass-customize automobiles, the company [Toyota] has come a long way from copying American mass-production techniques to fully embracing the tenets of Mass Customization as its way of doing business. It did this through continual incremental improvements over thirty or forty years' (ibid.: 137). The general presumption here is the same as that already noted as an interesting counterfactual, namely that while American mass production was intrinsically unsuited to the manufacture of different model specifications, a great transformation became evident in the car industry around the mid-1970s as Toyota began to 'proliferate model variety' in its factories. But the specific assertion is that, over and above this, Toyota's assembly plants have been both well-equipped and increasingly disposed to capture markets via mass customization.

But in fact the opposite is true. If the claim that Toyota stole a march over Western competitors by advancing on Fordist mass production constitutes an historical counterfactual, this association between Toyota and mass customization compounds the difficulty: Japanese car assemblers, as can be seen illustrated below, have typically eschewed this sort of strategy, an observation which raises further issues.

2.3   WIDTHS OF SELECTION: MODEL SPECIFICATION COUNTS

The theme of mass customization brings us to a topic of long-standing interest within the car manufacture and assembly sector. This is about how one interprets the very large differences that can be observed in the sum totals of the alternate model specifications that can be calculated when comparing car lines. In many cases car assembly plants must accommodate situations where the number of feasible model specifications significantly exceeds the expected lifetime volume of sales, but since this is not always the case the issue naturally arises as to what such differences mean for assembly plant operations. An interest in this question sits barely concealed beneath the surface of commentaries of 40 years ago, and there is still today an undoubted fascination with this dimension of manufacture. Shiomi (1995), for instance, appears to visualize the 'overall' width of the selections offered prospective customers by car assemblers in these terms, as clearly do other writers. And mass customization is in turn also linked to a significant width of selection in this sense, which is to say, with many optional features.

Indeed, a common tactic employed by writers proposing to argue that the main impetus in the world's car industry towards the adoption of custombuilding strategies has come from Japan, via the competitive examples set by Japanese car assembly plants, has been to simply express astonishment at the total number of alternate model specifications that can be counted for car lines built by firms like Toyota. For example, Kaplinsky (1988), to impress upon readers the extraordinary achievements of Japan's car assemblers, confessed himself 'bemused' by the 'bewildering range of alternatives' offered to consumers in the 1980s as a consequence of Japanese advances, as instanced by a Toyota range available in no less than 'five body types', and with an options list sufficient to generate 'more than ten thousand potential variations' (ibid.: 456). And this example is not unrepresentative, if judged against publications of the past 20 or so years: a similar disposition can be found in most of the other works cited in this chapter that have appeared in this period. But where this more recent literature goes amiss, however, is in asserting that very large specification counts are both a recent phenomenon, and one associated with Japan. As will already be clear, the orders of magnitude quoted by Kaplinsky are in fact rather small beer – astrophysicists in the 1960s were after all apparently amusing themselves by comparing car specification counts in North America with God's handiwork (see above). But historical precedents and orders of magnitude aside, the topic is an important one.

First, if the total number of model specifications between which customers can select is large, we can ask how the practice of wide selection is actually managed. And if there is some considerable variation across assemblers and car lines as to the overall width of the product sets from which customers make selections, we can ask how this impinges on other dimensions of car-making that are relevant to the measurement of assembly plant performance, and the appraisal of comparative degrees of system 'flexibility'. Before considering this, however, we must first obtain a realistic picture of the stylized facts of the world car industry – and of the companies that favour customization strategies.

Exposition of the number of potential variations that can be generated on the specification of a car, given the features and options lists which are presented to customers, is invariably informal, so much so that discussion of the orders of magnitude that can be arrived at when making a model specification count risks incurring incredulity: for this reason, an explicit and preliminary account of the arithmetic properties of the calculation, which is not in itself difficult to undertake, is helpful. Here we follow Coffey (2005a), which explains the very large numbers that can be generated when counting specifications on a car line via an assessment of the 'largest' feasible number that could potentially be calculated if the assembler imposed *no* restrictions on choice combinations for marketed features. The largest feasible model specification count in this formulation is denoted by ρ:

$$\rho = C_e \times C_i \times 2^{C_2} 3^{C_3} \dots N^{C_N} \tag{2.1}$$

Here we use C_e and C_i to denote respectively the total number of available exterior and interior colours. Provided no restrictions are placed on matches, making colour choices available on a car would simply scale up proportionately the total number of end-product specifications: for example, if there are ten exterior colours and two interior colours then a total of $10 \times 2 = 20$ exterior and interior colour combinations ($C_e \times C_i$) is defined for every vehicle. The rest of this formula is derived as follows. First define an alternatives list as the list of permitted alternatives for some stated feature: for example, if both left-hand-side drive and right-hand-side drive cars are built, then this provision makes a list with two entries. With no restrictions this would double the total number of potential specifications, because every car built could be in either left- or right-hand drive. If there were a total of C_2 lists each containing two entries then the number of specifications would multiply by 2^{C_2}, on the grounds that every one of these lists would double the possible combinations: this gives the next element in the formula. The same logic of simple multiplication extends to the inclusion of longer lists of alternatives: for example, if cars could be built with a manual sunroof, electric sunroof, or no sunroof, this makes a list with three entries, which would in turn raise specifications by a factor of three. If then there were C_3 lists with three entries then specifications would multiply in an analogous way by 3^{C_3}: this gives the next element, and so forth. In this formula the number of distinct lists each containing j choices is therefore represented by C_j (for $j = 2, \ldots; N$), covering all attributes other than colours.

What this shows is that the relationship between the alternatives offered for individual model features and the overall width of selection can be presented in what are quite literally 'exponential' terms. It is evident from (2.1) that the total specification count, in the absence of restrictions on combinations, can be expressed via a formula in which a series of integer valued exponents attach to positive whole numbers (≥ 2), that are then multiplied out to give the total count. A little experimentation will confirm that even apparently modest lists of choices on individual model features may generate surprisingly large numbers of possible combinations. On some car lines, the total number of different model specifications defined by available choices will be very large indeed.

In practical terms there are usually restrictions on combinations. But when inspecting changes over the past ten years in overall widths of selection as defined by model specification counts, there is evidence that where significant lists of optional features are available for cars that will be built to order in the factory, assemblers' restrictions on permissible choice combinations are getting fewer: a possible reason for this may be that this greatly simplifies the design of choice menus for internet ordering.[6] But in any event, restrictions on cross selections of product features are easily dealt with from the viewpoint of counting. Given the format in which cars are usually marketed it is generally possible to configure choices to use a formula similar to (2.1). If restrictions are imposed on cross-selections of product features, the restricted specification count will be smaller than the largest feasible count with no restrictions. Consequently, if we denote the restricted count by $\rho*$ we would necessarily observe that:

$$\rho* \leq \rho \qquad (2.2)$$

Over time, the differences between these magnitudes have tended to fall. But in the samples of our own calculations for car lines presented in this chapter, all restrictions on feature combinations imposed by assemblers have been fully incorporated in the count.

Some illustrative counts are given in Table 2.1 for samples of ranges marketed in the UK, taken from the author's own calculations: the examples given, chosen in order to be indicative of a wider context, are divided into two sets, each separated by a ten year period. Before continuing, it is perhaps worth pausing to note that each of the car lines sampled in this table was marketed as a set of model 'derivatives' – a set of packaged specifications – with additional variation permitted, if at all, via selections on colours and 'options': this is a standard industry practice, and here we follow the assemblers' own formats.[7]

Table 2.1   Comparing overall width of selection for selected ranges

(i) Company	(ii) Range	(iii) All specifications
1991/1992:		
	Whole range:	
Honda	Concerto	17
Toyota	Corolla	568
Ford	Escort	2722
Vauxhall (GM)	Astra	19656
Rover	200/400	63072
VW	Golf	30629888
BMW	3 Series	18.5×10^{12}
April 2003:		
	Saloons only:	
Honda	Accord	130
Toyota	Corolla	54
Ford	Focus	1053360
Vauxhall (GM)	Astra	12947904
	Saloon derivative:	
(MG) Rover	45 Series 1.6 16v	1078832
BMW	*3 Series 3l6i	5.3×10^{11}

Note: * Excluding 'communication' options, but including 3l6i SE.

Source: Coffey (2005a).

From the table it is immediately apparent, and in confirmation of a point already made, that specification counts, once all colours and options are included, can range from mere double digit figures to quite significant and surprising orders of magnitude: this reflects the simple algebra of counting, since what matters is the number of possible choice *combinations* of marketed model features, rather than the number of model features *per se*. Note in particular that whereas in both instances the sampled Toyota and Honda car lines possess feature and option lists sufficient to generate only a relatively small model specification count, the German car manufacturer BMW markets ranges which yield, quite literally, billions of specifications: it is with this sort of difference in mind that we must broach questions of plant operation. The differences are in fact principally a consequence of the optional features made available to buyers from each car line: the Toyota Corolla, for instance, has always been marketed in the UK with little or no choice of options, whereas the options list for the BMW 3 series (as with colours) is very extensive. The importance of the options list is emphasized in the progression shown in the table, which commences with entire car lines with few options and hence low specification counts, and finishes with single model 'derivatives' with many options and hence high specification counts. There are also discernible trends which are again illustrated in the table's selections. In particular, while in the UK the Japanese giant Toyota has, if anything, cut back further on customer options over the past ten years (from a comparatively low base) the trend amongst competitors like Ford or GM has been towards more extended options lists. This last point is illustrated in the table for the Ford Focus and GM Astra saloons, which in April 2003 had options lists sufficiently extensive to generate over one million and over twelve million specifications, respectively. The importance of the options list is also illustrated in the last entries for the more recent period, with separate counts for individual (saloon) derivatives marketed by (MG) Rover and BMW at that point: the lone MG Rover derivative generates more than a million specifications, and a lone BMW derivative (circa) 530 billion.

If placed in historical context – and here one might again point to the redoubtable Yale physicist who calculated some 40 or so years ago that there were more Ford and GM model specifications than atoms in the universe – it is clear that car assemblers, in North America and Western Europe at least, if not exactly in Japan, have for some considerable time been practicing, on some car lines, a form of wide selection that generates a total number of alternate model specifications greatly in excess of conceivable sales. If this were made the defining criterion for 'flexibility' in assembly plant production, then Japan's car makers have always demanded less of their factory managers than Western counterparts. Latecomers rather than leaders in the introduction of mixed-assembly systems, the specification counts generated by typical car lines built and marketed by Toyota and other Japanese firms have always been small beer, if this is what one is interested in knowing.

This is not to deny changes over time. Expanding from a very narrow base indeed, and following tentative first steps in the 1960s, the number of model derivatives offered by Japanese assemblers in their production and marketing packages has certainly grown so as to be a match for rivals' offerings, allowing as always for fluctuations over time and variations as between individual car lines and assemblers and for the fact that the number of car lines and their market positioning similarly vary. However, the specification counts generated by a car line is also sensitive to the length of the options list: and while the 1980s did see some local extension in the provisions made by Japanese assemblers in some of their overseas markets *vis-à-vis* North America and Western Europe, encouraged perhaps by quotas that encouraged added options as a way of increasing revenues for a quantity-constrained volume of sales, the 1990s saw retrenchment.[8] For example, Toyota's response to tougher trading conditions (see Bernstein 1997: 435; also Rhys 2005) in this more difficult period was to cut back on 'available options', a consistent decision given its prior history as a car maker, since these were never very extensive to begin with.

2.4   DELINEATING FLEXIBILITY: STOCKS, LEADS AND WIDTH

So much has been made in the literature of the past 20 or so years about the supposedly superior 'flexibility' of Japanese car assembly plants in building cars, that it is reasonable to consider the implications of this further. Indeed, at this juncture we are already in a position to dismiss the simpler type of claim in this regard as untenable: Japan's car assemblers did not lead the world industry out of an earlier epoch of 'Fordist mass production'; in the sphere of mixed assembly they were global latecomers, not leaders; Japan's car assemblers do not, and have never, placed a premium on 'mass-customization'.

To make further progress on the appropriate delineation of flexibility and the design of a comparative and empirically operational performance measure requires that we identify some of the other variables upon which we might expect width to impact. In this section we consider the effects of width on two variables: (i) finished product stock, and (ii) lead times from order to delivery on new sales to customers. The particular significance of these variables is that they are frequently cited as assembly plant performance indicators, and in contexts which often invoke direct associations with manufacturing flexibility. In order to derive a criterion by which to gauge comparative flexibility that takes simultaneous account of each variable we must first posit a broadly applicable working model of how a volume assembly plant might actually accommodate width of selection.

2.4.1   A Working Model

The obvious outlines of such a model commences with an assembler that schedules a core set of 'standard' specifications for production ahead of sale, with the balance of units built over immediate sales held as finished product stock. This is reflected in assemblers' marketing formats, and it will do no great violence to what is envisaged here if one identifies these standard specifications with a car line's model derivatives, scheduled in quantities (and colours) that reflect past sales compositions, with a default selection on optional features where these exist. If in addition to their selections from this core set of standard specifications customers are indeed allowed to choose 'factory-fit' options from an options list, these enter into the master schedule as *substitute* specifications: these cars are built to order. In other words, the assembly process operates as a system of prior scheduling, with substitution for options: at a broad level, this should not be too controversial as an application to volume car assembly, and something much like this can be found in practically every serious description of operations. Where we differ from much of the recent literature (as, for example, from Liker 2004: 121–2) is in maintaining that this is neither a recent practice, nor one first conceived of in Japan: descriptions of this broad type are as old as the practice of offering cars with factory fit options.[9]

Occasionally, attempts are made to develop a more formal terminology. For example, Banri Asanuma (1994, op. cit.) draws a distinction between the *basic* part of a car, encompassing features like 'body type', 'engine type', 'transmission type' and 'grade of luxury', and the *secondary* part, comprising 'options' and 'colours'. In Asanuma's lucid account, the following description is given of how a 'flexible' assembly system works: the final mix of the basic features in cars built is 'fixed' in the production schedule prior to the mix of secondary features, which can be varied at a later stage to accommodate customization through selection by customers of factory-fit options (ibid.: 127). While developed principally with reference to a (mistaken) assumption that Toyota is particularly adept at customization, this is consistent with the working model we intend to employ. Using Asanuma's terminology, what we call standard specifications, scheduled for production ahead of sale, incorporate the default selection on secondary features: for instance, if cars are scheduled for production in advance of sale with fabric seat covers but never with leather seat covers, then fabric is the default selection and leather the factory-fit option. A factory-fit option is conversely a choice on some secondary part of the car that will only be scheduled for production after an order is placed for this specification: a sale incorporating a leather seat cover (in our example) would then be 'built to order'. The line of demarcation might, of course, be drawn differently in different plants: for example, what is a factory-fit option for a car line built in one plant may not appear as a choice in a car line built at another, or it may be incorporated in one or more of the standard specifications.

For present purposes, however, since the substance is the same, it is sufficient from the viewpoint of terminology that we simply distinguish sales of cars that are sourced from a set of standard model specifications – scheduled to build in advance of sale – from sales of cars that incorporate factory-fit options, and hence must be built to order in the plant.

2.4.2   A Trade-off Curve

With this 'working model' in place, in essence a simple and stylized depiction which is reasonably consistent with intuition and observation, we can consider how the following variables could be expected to relate to each other: product stocks, lead times and width. In doing so, we will assume that the stylized assembly plant is one in which a car line is produced that offers – from the viewpoint of a prospective customer – a non-negligible set of choices both at the level of model derivatives and in the options list: there is an appreciable width of selection in both standard specifications and factory-fit options. We treat this as given initially, to better consider product stocks and lead times.

Figure 2.1 displays a curve in two dimensions, labelled W^0. The anticipated average lead time across sales of all cars built in our stylized assembly plant from order to availability is displayed on the horizontal axis, and denoted by T. This lead time is an *average* in the sense that it comprises the (sales-weighted) lead time both on orders sourced from standard specifications and orders routed through the assembly plant. In the absence of further complicating factors, from which we abstract at this point, T can be expected to rise with the share of sales routed through the plant to incorporate factory-fit options:

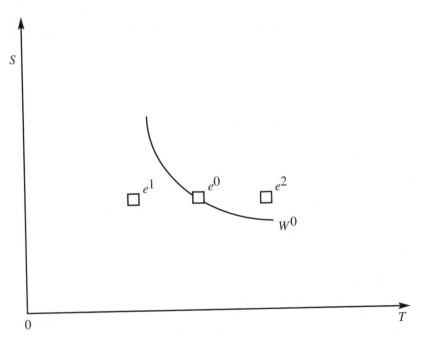

Figure 2.1   A trade-off curve

these cars are only built to order, never to stock – so the customer has to wait.[10] Conversely, the expected ratio of product stock held to current production in this period by the plant is displayed on the vertical axis, and denoted by S. This variable is a stock–flow ratio, which will rise or fall with proportionate changes in finished product stock. If stocks are initially adjusted in line with anticipated demand for cars incorporating factory-fit options, S will be lower the higher the expected share of sales to be built to order. Thus provided that initial stocks are proportionately reduced *vis-à-vis* the (given) expected production rate, a rise in the share of cars built to order will reduce S while increasing T. Hence curve W^0 is a locus of possible product stock and lead time outcomes for the plant: its negative slope identifies an implicit trade-off, given the operating parameters of the site. Note that our analysis to this point is constructed in *ex ante* (or before the event) terms. The actual point at which the plant will expect to find itself on the curve in the period in question will turn in part on prices. With the options list given, the lower the prices charged for customization the further down the curve – reading from left to right – the assembler will expect to be: all else being equal, the expected outcome will be that as prices on options fall more people select them.

2.4.3 Manufacturing Flexibility

All points on the curve W^0 are equally efficient in a manufacturing sense. For example, a point like point e^0 is no more or less efficient in this sense than any other point on the same curve, given the set of choices in both standard specifications and factory-fit options. So far as efficiency in an operations or manufacturing sense is concerned the assembler could only be reasonably judged to have 'improved' performance if it were able to achieve, via some reorganization of operations and for the *same* width of selection, a point beneath the initial trade-off curve, for example, point e^1. From this we can infer another criterion by which to gauge an improvement in manufacturing flexibility: all else being equal, a new state could be ranked as more flexible (in an operations sense) than an old state provided that it permits a point to be reached below the old trade-off curve. For example, if there were no other disturbing changes to be considered, a reorganization of plant operations that meant that a point like e^1 was now attainable could be called an efficiency improvement. On the other hand, a corresponding move to a point like e^2 would imply the opposite.

The difficulty in applying this sort of criterion to comparisons between assemblers which practice strategies based on model customization and assemblers (like Toyota) which do not is that like is not being compared with like. If the point e^1 in the preceding example were attained only by eliminating (or sharply curtailing) the options list from which customers could previously select, then this would hardly comprise evidence of a manufacturing improvement: not only would T fall automatically as the increment to the average lead time arising from built-to-order models disappeared, but the curve itself would change in shape and position (shrinking to a point as options disappear). In fact a comparison between two states differing significantly in width of selection would probably find an expected difference for this reason alone in both S and T, since what is being compared involves a non-commensurate set of specifications and hence choices. Since the curtailment of the options lists for factory-fit selections by Japanese assemblers has more often than not been severe, even when judged against 'volume' competitors like Ford or GM, it would take a considerable act of faith to directly interpret differences in lead times or stock–flow ratios as evidence of a qualitatively superior manufacturing machine. There is non-commensurability of a type which vitiates simple inferences, even if other difficulties are ignored.

2.4.4   An Example

An illustration may help. The possible significance of width was first borne in upon the author when carrying out assembly plant logistics research in the UK-based auto assembly sector in the early part of the 1990s. Figure 2.2 provides an example. A spread for a small number of car lines, each assembled separately from the others, is given from this period, with variables defined as follows. Financial provisions made against products held as stocks were divided through by expected (forecast) annual sales, to obtain a stock–flow indicator for each car line under 'normal' working conditions; this was then matched, for each range, against the actual lead times on deliveries for cars incorporating factory-fit options, measured from sale to receipt in the UK, over a common two-week interval (in the figure, this data is normalized so as to only show relative positions within the sample). The use of year ahead forecasting data as a basis for gauging *anticipated* stock–flow ratios was an attempt to mitigate the problems posed by relying on historical accounts-based data, given the well-known difficulties caused by shocks to demand (see below). From the overall shape of the distribution there is some suggestion of a 'trade-off' between the stock–flow and lead-time indicators, and it would certainly be tempting when confronted with data of this sort to propose that sites be ranked as more or less efficient depending on whether or not they appear to lie below or above the 'curve'. But the overall 'width' of selection for these car lines ranged from the relatively modest (a few thousand specifications), to the more substantial, with a tendency towards an increase in the size of the options lists as one moved from left to right through the distribution (this being less obvious in the main 'body' of points, but becoming marked for the car lines making up the 'tail'). It was puzzling over how best

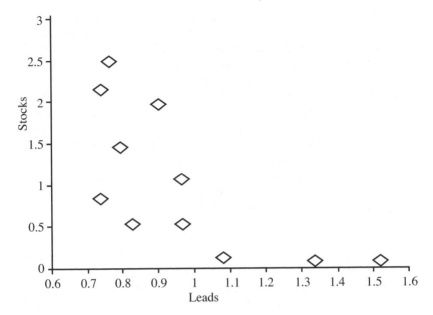

Source: Coffey (2005a).

Figure 2.2 Stock–flow ratios and factory order leads

to interpret data of this kind that first suggested the significance of a simultaneous assessment of not only product stocks and lead times, but also width of selection.[11]

2.4.5 Extant Studies

This brings us to our main point. A great deal of data – comprised of both anecdotal observation and more systematically collected material – has been amassed to suggest that both product stock to production flow ratios and customer order lead times have at times been markedly lower for Japanese-built cars than for rivals' products. This has been duly interpreted both as 'proof' of claims advanced by, and on behalf of, Toyota and other Japanese assemblers of a distinctive just-in-time production system, and as an empirical demonstration of its practicable benefits. For example, and here we select from the systematic end of the spectrum, Delbridge and Oliver (1991a, 1991b), in a well-known pair of studies, present data on stock turn (a stock–flow proxy) compiled from company accounts, and on customer order lead times, which seems to confirm an 'advantage', if this is the right word, to Japanese car assemblers on these variables. This data is then presented simultaneously – and with some perspicacity – in Oliver and Wilkinson (1992: 320–22), as evidence of a real manufacturing breakthrough in Japan: if all else were equal, and accepting that complications are posed by demand shocks, seasonality, and export ratios, a simultaneous reduction in both stock–flow ratios and customer order lead times could be indicative of an efficiency gain of the sort described above in Figure 2.1; such data would be suggestive of organizational differences generating points 'below the curve'. The problem with this inference, other complications aside, is that it neglects differences in width. This is not to say that Delbridge and Oliver ignore this issue; but what they assume is that Japanese assemblers excel in offering wide selection via customized products: Toyota-like organization is recommended as providing a type of 'flexibility' that 'may provide a company with a crucial competitive advantage where market environments are unstable, *and where there is a premium on customized goods*' (ibid.: 33, emphasis added).

But again, this is not so. By analogy with the simple exercise in comparative statics in point (iii) above, it must be asked if, all other complications aside, what the Delbridge and Oliver data reflects is not the benefits of a more flexible Toyota-like production regime, but rather the eschewal of width. A reduction in stocks and leads with a wider selection of models could be indicative of a potential sea-change in a manufacturing sector: but a reduction in stocks and leads with a markedly restricted set of products *vis-à-vis* the model specification count is certainly not.

2.4.6 Demand Shocks and Capacity

One other point deserves mention in this connection. In debates over productivity comparisons it has been argued that Japanese car assemblers benefited in the 1970s and 1980s from higher rates of capacity utilization than Western competitors, and that allowances for this should be made in comparative analysis. Masahiko Aoki, a Stanford economist, has responded with the view that this misses the point: the reason why these differences in capacity utilization existed can and should be accounted for in differences in the modes of organization employed to make and sell products. Accrediting Toyota with a 'superior ability to fine-tune for minor product variations' – in other words, to 'customize' the product – Aoki (1988: 8–9; 1990: 4–5) has argued that capacity utilization will have been higher as a result of what is therefore a definite Japanese innovation. Like so many other commentaries, Toyota is contrasted in this account with a model of 'Fordist mass production', with factories consigned to homogeneous goods manufacture. We can see why Aoki's proposition is not a tenable one: Japanese assemblers certainly did not win market share in the 1970s and 1980s via a superior organizational ability to keep pace with customer tastes and preferences via generous lists of optional features, and consequently their high rates of capacity utilization cannot be explained in this way. For present purposes the relevance of this observation is as follows. Conditions which generate a high rate of capacity utilization in a factory are also conditions liable to 'improve' factory performance with respect to the size of product (and part) stocks relative to production; if we cannot credibly include amongst these conditions the assumption, as per Aoki, of a superior sales performance achieved via customization, this becomes a critical factor to consider when assessing the data. In addition to the effects of a restricted options set, a proper assessment of the sort of descriptive statistics compiled by Delbridge and Oliver (above) also require that judgements be made about the effects of a high demand relative to capacity.[12] Once the real differences in width are admitted or noticed, this important complicating factor can no longer be discounted or ignored as a criticism of received wisdoms in this area.

2.5   THE MYTH OF JAPANESE FLEXIBILITY: A BIGGER CONTEXT

One part of this chapter is concerned with establishing the fact of the historical and empirical fictions that support the recasting of Japan's car makers as first-movers in the development of mixed-assembly systems, and specialists in mass customization. Another part is concerned with exploring some issues relevant to manufacturing operations: while there are good grounds for considering width of selection when addressing questions of flexibility as this pertains to the interface between factory and market, there is no discriminating basis upon which to stake a compelling claim that Japanese firms like Toyota have at any time demonstrated a qualitatively improved way of organising this interface, judged at least from the perspective of manufacturing efficiencies in assembly. Both parts are hardly unrelated, and it is the connections between the two as much as the fact of the historical revisions and empirical suppressions evident in the relevant bodies of writing and commentary which suggests material meriting further study. Since it is our view that this type of study is of the sort perhaps best undertaken by a cultural specialist, we conclude this chapter – the first of the studies making up this book – with some broad observations.

At one remove it would be interesting enough if the only issue raised was the construction and wholesale acceptance on the side of Western observers of a counterfactual story that sees home-grown developments recast first as the invention and then as the particular provenance of 'outside' forces which threaten 'domestic' industries: if one were to think in this context of the mixed-assembly initiatives and wide selection practices of North American car plants in the 1950s as a home-grown development, the 'outside' forces would be constituted in the factories of Toyota and the other Japanese assemblers. But even at this level, and here we make points that we return to in later chapters, a little reflection must point to deeper issues. European penetration of North American markets over the same period hardly excited this sort of response (and vice versa), while Japan's industrial renaissance in the post World War II era hardly counts as an 'external' event', outside of and beyond the reach of US policy influence and control. Moreover, we must remember the peculiar status given to the car industry amongst those commentators who have seen in the rise to eminence of a firm like Toyota evidence of changes and wonders: as observed in the introduction to this book (in Chapter 1), Japan's car assemblers are allotted a double role in narratives which depict Toyota as a harbinger of a 'post-Fordist' state, cast therein both as agents and emblems, realizing a fundamental transformation in an industry that has also been specifically selected for its revelatory aspects. The historical and empirical counterfactuals entailed by the inventions which provide metaphor and sustenance for such narratives point to more complex matters than making and selling cars.

It is notable that whereas an earlier generation of writers was liable to express a mixed bag of views on the implications for consumers of changes in the organization of manufacture that involved 'wider' selections of line-of-product specifications, in more recent comment opinion has quite discernibly narrowed. It has now become almost axiomatic that this sort of 'flexibility' in production is a *sine qua non* of consumer sovereignty in the market.

So far as past criticism of big business in the car industry is concerned, factory observers – as long ago as the 1950s – were commenting on the 'astounding' potential of a Ford or General Motors to mix model specifications on the same assembly lines; but in addition to the impressed and the enthusiastic, the post-World War II era also saw the growth of a particular kind of criticism of this kind of manufacture, the spirit of which might best be summarized in the phrase 'make fewer, but better'. A particularly apt example is provided by Graham Bannock, cited in the epigraph to this chapter. Head of Economics and Market Research at Rover (in the UK) from 1962, before moving after merger with Leyland to work first at Ford UK, and then as Manager of the Product Development Group of Ford Europe, Inc., Bannock's subsequent career inverts the traditional path of poacher turned gamekeeper. A car industry expert to the core, but inspired to better things by both J.K. Galbraith and Ralph Nader, Bannock resigned to turn his hand, quite effectively, to corporate criticism (see Bannock 1973, op. cit.: for career details, see ibid.).

Possessed of first-hand knowledge acquired at a senior operating level of product development in the car industry, and consequently displaying both a considerable ability as a connoisseur as well as an offended sense of aesthetics[13] (perhaps heightened by a manifest distaste for the disdain with which he perceived customers to be held by the corporate giants of the car industry) Bannock advanced the following thesis. The post-World War II dominance of the US domestic market by Ford, GM and Chrysler had coincided with a 'quite astonishing degree of technical stagnation' in product development (Bannock 1973: 225–6). Instead, the giants (or 'juggernauts') had turned to an impoverished product engineering-cum-selling strategy characterized by two distinctive strands: first, the then widely-criticized practice of the US oligopolists in introducing annual styling changes to their car lines – annual model changes in the 1950s and 1960s were decried by economists of the day as wasteful of resources and an anti-competitive selling strategy,[14] and second, the practice of marketing what we are calling a wide selection of models, based on different selections of major and minor product features in the same car line. Bannock's pitch, based on his own experiences as a senior Ford figure in European product development, was that while developing the 'build your own car approach' further than any other manufacturer in Europe, offering (our term) a wide selection of models, Ford was also establishing a situation whereby customers could choose between an enormous number of individually poor designs: 'American car-buyers have been conditioned to want the appearance rather than the reality and it is clearly the intention of Ford that the European consumer should be conditioned in the same way' (ibid.: 239). By abandoning, as a matter of a shared commercial policy – that is to say, as a *strategic* choice – fundamental innovations in product design, and promoting instead 'conventional designs' sharing 'an almost identical technical concept', the giant US firms had stripped American consumers of the real range and variety of competing designs still found in Europe, but this was being obscured in the language of choice and variety offered by the mixing of model attributes. Bannock's gloomy prognosis was that smaller manufacturers offering a rich variety of basic designs with fewer car lines and a narrower set of specifications would be replaced by larger manufacturers offering a uniform policy on basic designs offset by the illusion of choice generated by 'millions of custom-built permutations' (ibid.: 240).[15] Bannock took the view that misguided state policy, mergers, and the 'American example' would prove the undoing of Europe's consumers (ibid.: 225–6) – offered customization but no choice.[16]

What is important for present purposes is that a critic of big business 30 years ago could identify wide selection with a *loss* of consumer sovereignty. In raising this issue we are not concerned so much with framing a particular answer – for example, smaller car firms in Europe (like BMW or Mercedes Benz, or the niche Porsche) have attempted to maintain a quality cars image partly on the basis of 'craft' and 'customization' – as with noting that the question itself is one which has largely dropped from view. The reinvention of an industrial history in itself is an interesting development. The language used to describe the advances made in the 1950s and 1960s in American run car plants since the factories of

Henry Ford – 'assembly of motor vehicles has come a long way since Henry Ford's pioneering days' (Rae 1965: 200); 'the Model T days of "any color as long as it's black" and very little assembly line variation have passed into history along with the Ford Model T' (White 1971; 28); 'Ford have, in fact, developed the "build your own car approach" further than any other manufacturer in Europe, a far cry from Henry Ford's famous "any colour you like as long as it's black"' (Bannock 1973: 239) – is almost textually interchangeable with later papers extolling the ability of Toyota and other Japanese car makers to run a mix of model specifications on the same line. But in addition with the process of historical revision has come a dulling of critical edge: historical reinvention has been overlaid with a more unambiguous sentiment of 'progress'.

Another point is the relationship between a generation now of writing and discussion on trends of purportedly global significance, and the career trajectory of a single manufacturing firm, Toyota MC. This question is complicated by Toyota: much of the initial impetus for an association between flexibility, wide selection and Toyota came not from outside observers struck by an empirical observation, but from one Taichii Ohno, at various times a Managing Director, Senior Managing Director and Executive Vice President of Toyota. In a book published in Japan in the late 1970s, and heralded abroad long before its English translation, Ohno claimed to have been *personally responsible* for overseeing a revolution in car assembly, one that transcended a 'Ford-style' system. Ohno, no doubt a very capable manager and director, drew his own contrast with Toyota, by claiming first credit, and in no ambiguous terms, for the act of building a mix of model specifications, using his 'own' system for controlling materials movement in the plant (Ohno 1988: 35–40). In publicity terms, this has proved a distinctive and abiding coup, and judged from a Toyota perspective, no mean one. The claim has fed directly into the revision of industrial history which has seen Toyota elevated as the car maker that first practiced wide selection. Judged solely from the perspective of a private corporation, and of Taichii Ohno's contributions to that company, there is nothing reprehensible about this. One part of the job, one might guess, of an Executive Vice President of a successful company is to boost its profile, and to explain its progress in terms calculated to add to the glamour success brings: there has always been a place for 'bunk' delivered with gusto in successful business dealings.[17] But the response given in the West can hardly be comprehended in these terms: there are deeper issues.

2.6 CONCLUSIONS

The issues which have been the subject matter of this chapter are significant on at least three levels. Perhaps their most interesting aspect, in the broadest sense, are the processes of historical revisionism which have not only seen the car industry used as a source of metaphor and example by which to describe wider changes in economy and society, but on the basis of a wholly fictionalized account of its internal transformations. Japan has been 'invented', if the word is appropriate, as a prime mover in the introduction of assembly systems capable of building a complex mix of differentiated products on the same production lines; and this is taken to signal both a new sovereignty of the consumer, and a decisive break with a hitherto dominant form of production: 'Fordist mass production'. But for the industry in question dates, locations and supplementary assumptions are contrary to fact: it is not the case that Ford and GM were, in the 1950s and 1960s, still focused on volume replication of homogeneous product in factories ill-suited to product variety, and it is not true that Toyota and Japan were epicentres, circa the 1970s, of a transformation in this sphere; nor have Japanese assemblers in this industry ever practiced marketing and production strategies predicated on mass-customization, or minor product variation. It is a question for cultural anthropologists to consider why – if changes are abroad in a wider societal context – contemporary observers should not only seek to draw analogies with, or even construct explanations by direct reference to, changes in particular industries, but do so in a way which posits a set of historical and empirical counterfactuals.

So far as the narrower question of the comparative efficiencies of Japanese car assembly is concerned, the lessons are more straightforward, if no less important for that. If flexibility in manufacture and assembly is defined at the level of the production unit – in this instance the car assembly plant – then the lessons are twofold. If what matters is 'width' of customer selection as measured by the number of model specifications that can conceivably be constructed from a list of product features and alternatives, and on the assumption that the selections made will be built on the same production lines, then the great Japanese car assemblers, including Toyota, must be held to be less flexible than rivals. If instead the position taken requires simultaneous consideration of related variables, then again it remains the case that there is no evidence that the Japanese leader has achieved any comparative advantage in the management of finished product stocks or customer order lead times, given the qualifying observation that it has typically eschewed customization strategies.

There has been a marked interest in issues of wide selection in car assembly for at least the past five decades, since mixed-assembly systems first drew significant volumes of commentary from industry publicists and analysts, in North America and elsewhere. The number of permissible model specifications that can be generated on car lines assembled in one production unit has enjoyed a considerable longevity as a recurrent and absorbing topic of speculation for successive generations of researchers. We have argued, on the basis of a positive study of the delineation of flexibility for an assembly plant offering a substantive width of selection, that there is no evidential basis to date by which to infer that Japanese firms have at any time developed a superior organizational capacity to manage the manufacturing interface between factory and market, as judged by 'width', reliance on product stocks, and lead times to custom. This is a myth.

NOTES

1. We should perhaps note that in some cases where an assembly plant practices wide selection individual customers may not face the full set of choices from the outputs of that line, such as, for example, where cars are built in both left-hand and right-hand side drive to be sold in different national territories; such cases, however, represent a wholly natural extension to practical application of the term wide selection, and this is a qualification on meaning that we can reasonably take as granted in the discussion that follows. In this chapter we also assume for brevity that cars are built up on conventionally arranged assembly lines: some departures are discussed in a later chapter.

2. For example, Takahiro Fujimoto provides an account for Toyota which seems to be consistent with Asanuma's historical précis. Toyota is said to have begun its move towards a 'full line' of products in the 1960s (although the detail given focuses on the number of basic car platforms rather than on intra-car line variety) (see Fujimoto 1999: 41–2). Elsewhere, Fujimoto sets out a comparative timelines for the evolution of car assembly at Toyota *vis-à-vis* Ford which squarely presents the Japanese firm as the first mover to a higher form of 'flexible mass production'; in keeping with so much of the recent literature, the transition point in North America is then dated to the 1970s, and ascribed to Japan's competitive pressure and example (ibid.: 51–3). The number of Western texts to make similar claims is legion: Toyota is accredited with triggering 'a new trajectory of industrial growth' by learning to process 'different models' on the same lines, a development which became evident to Western observers in the 1970s (see Best 2001: 37; also Best 1990: 143). This is essentially the theme projected in the larger part of the works so far referred to in this book.

3. It is not difficult to find independent supporting examples which confirm Lyddon's comments on the narrowing usage of 'mass production', in the context of car assembly. D. Gharel Rhys, in a highly-regarded study of the economics of the UK car industry published at the onset of the 1970s informed readers that a 'mass production industry' like the car industry could attempt to 'cater to all tastes' by providing engine, gearbox and performance variations, combined with variations in body and trim (Rhys 1972: 52). By contrast, most recent studies are typically at pains to define mass production as the *absence* of any such provision: 'The principle of *not* catering to any customer's individual demands in production planning is one of the keys of the mass production system' (Kinch 1995: 107–8, emphasis added). The word association here is motivated, as in so much of what has been written in the past few decades, by the 'early Ford system', but in a way which then generalizes and extends without qualification. Other, more subtle, examples are considered below.

4. Woollard is perhaps best known for his contributions in other areas: 'the automatic transfer machine which was invented between 1923 and 1925 by H. Taylor and F.G. Woollard in association with James Archdale and Co. Ltd. . . . was installed in the engines branch of Morris Motors Ltd. at Coventry, but was ahead of its time' (Carter and Williams 1957: 77). But his status as an engineer is hardly in doubt, and his views at this time obviously merit attention. Indeed, we can usefully add to this particular example. In 1955 the UK's Austin Motors Company issued a pamphlet boasting that by 1934, following progressive developments over a ten year period, the company had so 'elaborated' the Austin range that its customers could choose from 'forty-four separable models based on nine alternative chassis', and a 'grand total of three hundred and thirty-three different cars' once account was also

taken of the wide range of colours and equipment also listed. The pamphlet is cited in Maxcy and Silberston (1959: 109), a much referenced if little read book, with the comment that there was 'no doubt that the trend was away from standardisation'. The dating of the pamphlet is interesting, given preoccupations in North America at this time with product variety.

5. See Shingo's (1989) own account of process organization at Toyota: it is perhaps worth noting that in this account Shingo makes no reference anywhere to mass customization.

6. The impact of on-line selling in both the car and other industries is a burgeoning area of research, but a fuller assessment that goes beyond this observation lies outside the scope of this chapter.

7. The precise terminology employed in this format is less important than the concept. In general terms, a car line derivative (or its equivalent where a different nomenclature prevails) entails a complete model specification that is defined, labelled (or 'badged') and marketed by an assembler in abstraction from any further variation that might be allowed via selections on options (or colours). As we will see in both this and the following chapter, the distinction between a car line derivative and the choices that are defined around a car line derivative bears an intimate relationship with the way in which production is organized: the marketing format reflects factory logistics. One obvious question of interest is whether car lines that are marketed with a larger number of derivatives proffer fewer options to customers, and vice versa. While one would hesitate to lay claim to any simple patterns at this level, when comparing regions, firms, or plants, this does not seem to be the case. For example, while at the start of the 1990s (we refer again to Table 2.1) the Toyota Corolla was sold in the UK with more 'badged' derivatives than the BMW 3 Series, this position was reversed ten years later: in fact, the BMW 3 Series, at this latter juncture, incorporated saloon, coupe, convertible, touring and compact derivatives, and was a quite substantial import at this level. More generally, an inspection of model availabilities across the UK found no obvious aggregate evidence in either period of a 'trade-off' between the number of car line derivatives marketed by the major car assemblers at body and/or engine level, and the overall size of the options lists. Hence a large specification count need not imply a car line that is more truncated at the derivative level.

8. So far as comparative practice in the global industry is concerned, we might add that exceptions to the 'Japan equals customization' thesis have cropped up occasionally. Cusumano (1985), for example, notes the findings of a North American consultancy contracted in the early part of the 1980s to compare Ford specifications with Japanese domestic specifications: the conclusion duly reached was that total specification counts in Japan were small – '32 for the Honda Accord, 384 for the Toyota Terel, and 786 for the Corolla' (ibid.: 193). A few years later, Krafcik (1988a) arrived at a broadly consistent conclusion when considering global trends in the *later* part of the 1980s: Japan was ranked as most 'restricted' in total specification counts, with North America occupying an intermediate position, and European (luxury) firms offering 'billions' of specifications. Interestingly, at this time Krafcik was of the view that 'customization' strategies would tend to disappear as Western firms copied companies like Toyota, a quite different reading of the industry. This has not happened: rather, Japanese assemblers, after some expansion in options lists, have tended to historical type, while a number of their competitors continue to market 'customization'. Of more interest, however, is how little discussion Cusumano and Krafcik (in every other respect frequently cited and influential figures in car industry research) managed to elicit on these points.

9. Jeffrey Liker, (2004) another Shingo prize winner, suggests a pleasing term: instead of thinking of a system of prior scheduling with substitutions as a 'build-to-order' system, one might think of it as a 'change to order' system. But while a descriptively apt phrase, Liker approvingly quotes a Group Vice President of Toyota Motor Sales speaking in a way which suggests that Toyota has only just recently developed this facility, ahead of the game *vis-à-vis* Western assemblers. The problematic status of claims from Toyota is further considered in the next section. It is perhaps worth noting that not all car assembly lines which the present writer has visited organize scheduling in quite this way. Although the exceptions have been for highly priced specialist vehicles even here the differences (which we do not explore) would not upset the analysis set out below.

10. For simplicity we assume that the lead time on orders incorporating factory fit options is unaffected by the particular selection of options, given the available set of options. Similarly at this juncture we assume that the lead time on a standard specification is also uniformly defined.

11. The stock–flow proxy calculated for this small sample is probably not too far removed from the ideal *ex ante* measure implied by the preceding analysis: the lead times are, however, *ex post*, and are based solely on cars routed through the assembly plant as built-to-order specifications – the lead time on cars sourced from finished product stock is not included in the averages (if it were, it would reduce the average time elapsing in each instance, albeit to certainly varying degrees). We might note that these car lines were also marketed overseas to varying extents, an important complicating factor if one were to attempt to draw hard inferences about relative efficiencies from the data presented. But this is not our intent: rather, the data is interesting precisely because it is suggestive of the need to isolate a number of variables, and in controlled circumstances, before seeking inferences.

12. If demand falls relative to capacity we can expect a number of effects. If the fall takes the form of a shock, product stock to production flow ratios will rise, at least initially; and so far as materials held as work-in-progress are concerned, as long as demand is depressed then on most measures of turnover the assembly plant's 'performance' will 'suffer' in a sustained way (a low rate of demand will also affect customer lead times, albeit in a more ambiguous fashion). The importance of this point is that if we question the data presented in studies like the Delbridge and Oliver papers on grounds that the wrong assumption has been made about comparative widths of selection, we must also question it from the viewpoint of differences in demand relative to capacity. The proposition offered by Aoki that more 'flexible' assembly accounts for higher rates of Japanese sales relative to capacity must also be discounted: demand and capacity issues are independently important factors. The significance of this point will naturally vary with the periods for which data is obtained.

13. Connoisseurship is used in this context in its proper sense, namely an ability to distinguish objects on the basis of form in order to discriminate in place and time (see Prown 1993: 4–5); as one would expect, Bannock (1973) displays an expert's knowledge of developments in product design. So far as an offended aesthetic sense is concerned, Bannock makes much of the American car in the 'fat fifties', the 'persistent tendency to enlargement', 'US automotive elephantiasis'; for Bannock this partly reflected considerations that included easier design, styling and manufacture, but interestingly also a deliberate intent by oligopolists to make 'options' (obtainable at a price) essentials for the North American consumer – power steering and power windows, for example, luxuries in a smaller car, becoming 'necessities' in 'unnecessarily large cars' (ibid.: 227).

14. In 1962 Fisher et al. published their famous study of the costs of automobile model change: taking 1949 as their base year, they found that had cars with the same base year specifications been built in subsequent years, but with the falling production costs made possible by advances in technology, the saving in resource expenditures over cars actually built in the late 1950s would have amounted to around 25 percent of the average purchase price of a new car at this time. Radical economists (see, for example, Baran and Sweezy 1966: 131–8) were quick to cite these calculations as evidence of the enormous waste generated by the sales effort in the US car industry, exemplified in styling changes. Their point was that a large part of the production effort embodied in an automobile consumed resources for purposes of rendering the product more saleable rather than more serviceable. This wastage was compounded by additional expenses, like extra fuel consumption or obsolescence of parts. In the same year as the above study, Menge (1962) published a paper arguing that the extra costs imposed on firms by annual model styling changes was an anti-competitive tactic, since smaller organizations would be unable to shoulder the burden. If recent years have seen a narrowing of perspectives on the separate question of wide selection, the treatment of model change over time has also seen a discernible narrowing: analyses of the car industry that used to commence with corporate strategy now more frequently look to measure corporate 'efficiency' *vis-à-vis* rapid model changes.

15. A comparison between Bannock (1973, op. cit.) and Abernathy (1978), discussed in the introduction to this book, makes interesting reading, both for their similarities and differences. In

Bannock, stagnation in design is a consequence of market structure and the corporate strategies shaping that structure; and a loss of choice to the consumer comes from market concentration of sales amongst giant firms each offering a very wide selection of similarly unremarkable goods. In Abernathy, stagnation in design is assumed determined by the hard economics of existing production methods, which it is proposed were (in the 1970s) unable to do more than manufacture single model specifications in individually large quantities. Both posit a North American industry characterized by stagnation and absence of choice, but both books are otherwise worlds apart.

16.   Entailed in this thesis is a presumption that flexible assembly of a mix of model specifications is a quintessentially American phenomenon, imported via the transplants of Ford and GM into Europe in the 1960s; without committing to this (see, for example, note 3), it does offer a hypothesis for investigation more consistent with the evidence than the unconvincing claim that Toyota was the first car maker to mix models on a single assembly line. It may be that historically-directed studies for some European countries (see, for example, Abelshauser 1995) uncover little evidence to directly challenge the notion that 'wide selection' first appeared in the 1970s for this reason.

17.   'Claude Hopkins, whose genius for writing copy made him one of the advertising immortals, tells the story of one of his great beer campaigns. In a tour through the brewery, he nodded politely at the wonders of malt and hops, but came alive when he saw that the empty bottles were being sterilized by live steam. His client protested that every brewery did the same. Hopkins patiently explained that it was not *what* they did, but what they *advertised* they did that mattered. He wrote a classic campaign which proclaimed "OUR BOTTLES ARE WASHED WITH LIVE STEAM!" George Washington Hill, the great tobacco manufacturer, once ran a cigarette campaign with the now-famous claim "IT'S TOASTED!" So, indeed, is every other cigarette, but no other manufacturer has been shrewd enough to see the enormous possibilities of such a simple story. Hopkins, again, scored a great advertising coup when he wrote: "GETS RID OF FILM ON YOUR TEETH!" So, indeed, does every toothpaste' (Reeves 1961: 55–6, cited in Baran and Sweezy 1966: 129). Ohno's descriptions of the 'mix' of model specifications being built on a Toyota assembly line is perhaps best understood in these terms. There are, however, in this case, other issues, which we shall come to in later chapters, not least an extraordinary claim that Toyota does not plan its production schedules *vis-à-vis* throughput compositions in assembly.

3. Production malapropisms: the BMW–Rover Group controversy

Let's All Be Beastly to the Germans
– with apologies to Noel Coward

3.1 INTRODUCTION

Our contention is that Toyota and other Japanese assemblers have been the beneficiaries, if this is the right word, of a possibly quite significant cultural process in which the history and substance of a major world industry has been fictionalized – a process that clearly transcends our immediate interest in the car industry, but investigation of which must naturally first be concerned with that industry. At the same time, there has been a great deal of experimentation undertaken in the West over the course of the past 20 or so years with production methods associated with Japanese car manufacture. The purpose of this chapter is to suggest that one corollary to a wider process of myth making about an industry may be a failure on the part of investigators considering the outcome of associated experiments to ask disobliging questions, or draw awkward inferences.

The illustration employed for this purpose is a case example. It is not by any means proposed that we generalize from the specific details of this example; rather we consider these details in the context of the wider themes explored in this book. The distinction is an important one, because while our chosen example sheds some light on the vicissitudes of what was the British Rover Group in its relationships first with the Japanese firm Honda, and then with the German firm BMW, thereby indirectly contributing to the rumbling debate on the 'death' of the 'British'-owned car industry, this is incidental to the main objective of this chapter as set out above. The first reason for choosing this particular example, and at this juncture in the book, is that its specific details raise issues that resonate with the subject matter introduced in Chapter 2 (at a later stage, once further headway is made with material, we will consider the specific details of a quite different case example, based on developments at Toyota in Japan). The second reason for selecting what for shorthand purposes we can call the BMW–Rover Group controversy as an illustration is that this case has generated a requisite body of specific commentary of the sort which this chapter requires as data. Our express aim is to illustrate how awkward questions might pass unasked in contexts informed by a global process of myth-making: extant (and specific) commentary is essential to this purpose.

Since in this instance the requisite case-specific commentary exists, some advance notice of content will be useful in elucidating the approach taken in this chapter. Following a period of ostensibly successful collaboration with Honda, Rover Group was acquired by the German producer BMW, an acquisition that ended badly. Prior to this acquisition, Rover was involved in substantial experiments in emulating what its executive directors took to be essential features of Japanese-style manufacture; the experiment upon which we will focus was neither superficial, nor one that can be easily understood as an exercise in nomenclature intended to conceal the pursuit of some different agenda. Our contention is that this experiment, an attempt to put in place a 'just-in-time' product supply regime, badly misfired: it undermined an attempt to develop a market strategy based on customization and build-to-order selling. This contention is informed by the findings of participative field research carried out by the author within the Rover Group just prior to the BMW acquisition, focusing (in part) on the impact of this experiment. In contrast to this view, critics of the BMW acquisition have, however, tended to assert something quite different: prior experiments with production methods linked to Japan are referred to as things almost axiomatically successful. A contrast of views highlights the sort of questions that might reasonably have been asked of the data pertaining to the BMW–Rover case by subsequent investigators, but which were not. The possibility that an experiment with (purportedly) Japanese production methods could end badly is not one which looms large in commentaries of the past 20 years. Instances where an attempt to introduce just-in-time product supply destroys the sort of flexibilities required to progress intended market strategies are likely to pass without comment.

The organization of this chapter reflects its intent. First we set out some key propositions contained in what is certainly viewed as the most authoritative account to date of the differential experiences of Rover Group *vis-à-vis* first Honda and then BMW, researched and published after BMW divested itself of the Group. We then set out opposing propositions taken from our own earlier (largely unpublished) field study of the impact of Rover Group's experiments with Japanese production practices prior to the BMW acquisition, which contrast markedly in some relevant aspects. It is how one interprets the silence in later commentaries on the points raised in our own earlier study that then becomes the basis upon which to illustrate the point that we intend to make, namely that the wider assumptions which frame commentaries on the impact of production-related experiments may actively discourage certain types of question occurring.

3.2   THE BMW–ROVER GROUP CONTROVERSY: THE END OF THE ROAD

The story of the British car industry, up to and including the formation of the Rover Group, is well-rehearsed at the level of elementary narrative details concerning structure and ownership, and these need not unduly concern us here except to the extent that they provide the backdrop against which later developments are typically judged. In the words of one observer of the industrial politics of this period, from an apparently promising position in the early 1960s the British industry passed through two phases: a period of 'unambiguous', if relative, decline in car (and commercial vehicle) production when compared to the world's major producers, followed by a series of 'spectacular and continuing defeats' for government policy in this sector (see Wilks 1984: 67). Without wishing to debate the points at which a 'crisis' becomes discernible, the accompanying sentiment, generally acceded to, is that between 1960 and 1980 the British motor industry as a whole passed through 'stagnation, decline and crisis' (ibid.). A number of smaller assemblers and component suppliers drew together under larger umbrella organizations; and in 1968 BL was created with the merger of British Motor Holdings (BMH) with Leyland Motors, a stepping stone, at least in the conventional wisdom of the time, to the creation of a 'national champion' (see ibid.: 96). But the difficulties of the British industry continued: reformation saw British Leyland Ltd. under public ownership in 1975, to become BL Ltd. in 1978. There followed, and still under the auspices of public ownership, a period of retrenchment, closures and fragmentation, and a hiving off of sections to foreign transnationals expanding in Britain.[1] The main feature of this period – informing all subsequent debates – is perhaps best understood if viewed in its broader terms: a steady shrinkage of the 'British' owned car (and vehicle) industry.

In 1986 the reduced business had become Rover Group plc, and in 1988 it was made a wholly owned subsidiary of British Aerospace plc (BAe), when the government of the day sold its majority shareholding in the car maker: this made Rover part of what was then Britain's largest manufacturing and engineering organization. In 1989, a single trading company was created by a merger between the Group's constituent parts (Austin Rover Group Ltd. and Land Rover), with a formal change of name to Rover Group Ltd. The next change of ownership took place five years later with a controversial sale of assets in 1994 to the German producer BMW. This was controversial partly because of the loss of a domestic firm to foreign ownership, but perhaps as much so because it occasioned a break with the Japanese firm Honda, which had previously engaged Rover in a number of joint ventures (commencing with BL in 1978) and had acquired a stake in the British company's equity: against public expectation, the BMW bid was preferred.

When news broke on 14 March 2000 – little more than five years later and via a Bavarian newspaper – that BMW was now proposing to break up the Group and dispose of most of its assets, there was a furore, energized both by the earlier controversy over the BMW acquisition, and by an immediate crisis for one of Britain's major manufacturing sites, the Longbridge car assembly plant at Birmingham in the UK's West Midlands. This site figures prominently in 20th century histories of British manufacture, not least because its struggles have frequently been viewed as emblematic of struggles in British industry as a whole, both internal and external: its industrial relations history has been complex and frequently sharp, while its perseverance over a long time within a shrinking domestic manufacturing sector has taken it through the ups and (mainly) secular downs of Britain's post-World War II industrial heritage. A crisis loomed for this site, because with the remaining major facilities either retained by BMW or disposed of via other companies, it was the Longbridge plant that initially failed to find a buyer. After much uncertainty the site was controversially re-established under the auspices of a new company, MG Rover: the MG Rover Group collapsed in 2005, in circumstances that have again generated considerable heat. At the time of writing, production at the Longbridge site is halted but there are hopes of a bail-out (in some form) from China.[2] Our concern in this chapter, however, is not with this, but rather with the earlier period, from the point where the Rover Group Ltd. was launched in 1989 through to its time under BMW.

The principal issues are (here) as follows. From 1989 the Rover Group site at Longbridge was engaged in experiments with Japanese manufacturing methods, the chief of which involved an attempt to implement an 'aggressive' just-in-time product supply regime, while actively attempting to reposition sales in up-market segments *vis-à-vis* main competitors Ford and GM. This period was characterized by apparent success, and an improved external reputation. BMW's failure with the site has since typically been treated in the UK as a bad example of an interloping firm – and what is worse, an interloping German firm – ruining an increasingly successful British venture and, in particular, undoing good work learned under Japanese (Honda) tutelage. We are interested both with this take on events and with the reality of the Rover Group experience with 'Japanese' production methods – the findings of its 'experiment'. A study published at the height of the controversy following BMW's disengagement with the Rover Group, written by Brady and Lorenz (2001) and entitled *The End of the Road: BMW and Rover – A Brand Too Far*, develops an overall thesis about the BMW–Rover Group controversy that provides a useful point of departure on these issues.

The Brady and Lorenz study draws on first-hand interviews with senior management figures in both Rover and BMW, as well as other relevant parties. It contains interesting details on the backroom negotiations leading up to the BMW acquisition of the Rover Group from BAe, and on why BMW rather than Honda emerged as the preferred bidder, and is no doubt in many ways a model of interpretative reporting (one of the book's authors is in fact an experienced business broadsheet editor). On the substance of Rover's previous relationship with Honda, Brady and Lorenz are also notably free of sentiments about the 'high trust' relationships which Japanese firms are so frequently said to foster with partners, perhaps because time was spent talking to some of the parties involved in contexts that would naturally dispel any predispositions to flattery. What we are interested in, however, at least for present purposes, is the account given both of BMW's ambitions for, and failures with, the Rover Group, and how in this connection Brady and Lorenz portray the Group's earlier experiments with 'Japanization'.

So far as BMW's ambitions for the Group are concerned, the account is convincing. The German firm feared the prospects of increased pressure in the quality car market, not only from American and Japanese producers, but also from Rover Group itself. Size was also an issue, with concerns that as a smaller firm BMW would soon find itself 'too small' for the world market; like its rival, Mercedes-Benz, the German firm was for this reason already planning to move into market segments 'occupied by Rover'. The strategy, as described by Brady and Lorenz, was thus for BMW to 'widen its product base to become a "full-range" manufacturer, building small cars and four-wheel-drive vehicles as well as its traditional models' (ibid.: 6–7). But rather than risk diluting the BMW brand the German firm planned to acquire the Rover brand (and facilities) instead. The aspiration was therefore that BMW would expand, and acquire a potential rival, without undermining its status as an exclusive brand (ibid.: 14–15).

> [T]he new Rover . . . would pursue the 'creaming off' strategy which targeted the top end of each and every market segment. According to BMW's market analysis, only 20 per cent of consumers in the premium segment worldwide would consider buying a BMW. The other 80 per cent were not attracted to the sporty, dynamic driver's car image of the ultimate driving machine. Rover was to be something different. (Brady and Lorenz 2001: 25)

Rover was thus intended ('ultimate driving machines' apart) to be an additional brand in the portfolio, an acquisition that would build a marketing platform consistent with the German firm's emphasis on a quality image without encroaching on the BMW brand identity. The intended strategy, moreover, tallied with the Rover Group's own attempts – evident since the launch of new car lines in the late 1980s – to locate its sales in higher price bands compared with those of its main competitors like Ford:

> [The BMW] grand design completed the strategy that had driven Rover's ostensible revival in the late 1980s. Under Sir Graham Day, then chairman, and Simpson [his successor] Rover had attempted to position itself at the upper end of the market segment. The strategy was widely seen as having been modelled on that of BMW itself. (Brady and Lorenz 2001: 15)

We might summarize by saying that BMW aimed to expand its portfolio by acquiring another (relatively) small firm, in the shape of the Rover Group: this choice was motivated in part by Rover's own efforts to emulate a BMW type market strategy.

With respect to reasons for ultimate failure, Brady and Lorenz are equally definite. The position taken and asserted at every turn in the course of their study is that this was always a doomed strategy, for the simple reason the BMW had badly overestimated the existing strength and potential appeal of the Rover brand. This is the point made in the subtitle of their study ('A Brand Too Far'), and while other supplementary reasons are given for the failure of the acquisition, this is the principal thesis guiding their assessment. BMW, anxious not to dilute its own brand identity, failed to appreciate the 'depths' to which the Rover brand – 'a sick brand' – had 'plunged':

> BMW's concern was how much elasticity existed in their brand and how best could that elasticity be used in relation to Rover? It was the classic branding debate which occurs with all mergers and acquisitions (M&As) and one which is, of course, best resolved before the acquisition. Does the appeal of expanding volume outweigh the threat of diluting the predator's brand? It was a debate . . . which would taint the whole of BMW's ownership of Rover . . . If more thought had been given to the weakness of the Rover brand and less to the strength of the BMW brand, perhaps the brand too far would not have been attempted. (Ibid.: 39, 170)

The question naturally arises as to how BMW could get it so wrong. On this point the tack adopted by Brady and Lorenz splits in two broad directions. First, a great deal is made of the (allegedly) mistaken judgement of Hans Pischetsrieder, the then Chair of BMW, criticized throughout for overestimating Rover's potential. Second, and for immediate purposes the point that we wish to single out, Brady and Lorenz argue that BMW had been fooled by the temporary improvement in Rover's fortunes as a result of improved production methods learned under Japanese tutelage: short-term gains realized on the production side of the equation via more efficient practices had served to mask from outsiders the long-term decline in the viability of the Rover brand. Honda, whatever its demerits as a business partner, had at least saved the

Rover Group from extinction by contributing both on the product side, and on the side of 'manufacturing know-how':

> Only the Honda connection had been making Rover at least minimally viable. In terms of manufacturing – discipline, attention to detail, production quality – Rover cars had learned a lot from the Japanese. But for BMW even the Honda influence on Rover was a mixed blessing. Unlike the Japanese with their emphasis on 'kaizen' – continuous improvement – the German manufacturing bible laid down hard and fast rules for what constituted premium quality. The Ronda (as jokers labeled the Honda-ized Rover) was [a] way to inculcate a culture of quality into each and every process, including management, rather than simply by increasing inspections. The approach was perceived as incompatible with typical German industrial culture . . . Even more significant was the fact that the good news of more enlightened management and efficient processes had managed to obscure the underlying news of a bad brand. So, BMW found that it had bought a company with deep-seated problems. (Ibid.: 30)

And if the 'good news' of more 'enlightened management and efficient' processes had obscured the 'underlying news of a bad brand', German practices undid even this.

It would be going too far to reduce this to a simple aphorism: Japanese production methods good, German interference therewith bad. But while Brady and Lorenz are careful not to put too much store in the notion that Honda was a munificent business partner, it is nonetheless explicit that the view which they take is that changes at the level of the organisation of manufacturing practices accounted for Rover's short-term revival. Further to this, they propose that BMW misinterpreted the basis of this revival, confusing the ostensible returns to a marketing strategy modelled on BMW's own with the immediate benefits being obtained from Japanese-style management practices, themselves incompatible with the Germanic industrial culture. In a nutshell, production practices had improved under Japanese influence, but the Rover brand itself was 'bad'.

3.3   THE LONGBRIDGE EXPERIMENT

With this proposition in mind we now turn to the observations made by the present writer on the progress and impact of Rover Group experiments with 'Japanese' production methods in the period between 1989, when the corporation was reconstituted under the Rover brand-name as part of its relaunch, and 1994 when it was unexpectedly acquired by the German car maker BMW, in preference to the Japanese firm Honda. It is the possibility of so doing that gives this chapter its unusual methodological flavour: whereas the views recounted in other sections of this chapter are (in a sense) posthumous, the observations summarized here were recorded contemporaneously with the events described in this section and are based on research that included work undertaken as a participant researcher stationed alongside regular corporate employees in marketing, distribution and manufacturing logistics, punctuated by periodic excursions to the corporate finance and product engineering divisions of the company. The larger part of this research was conducted over a period of several years, on a full-time basis, and with a particular – although not exclusive – focus on the context, content and impact of a major experiment in 'just-in-time' product supply at the Rover Longbridge site.[3]

This site was chosen for study at the time because it was here that most effort was made to commit manufacture in a thoroughgoing way to just-in-time part deliveries. The site, moreover, was also the plant selected for the launch of Rover's new marketing strategy, evolved – as Brady and Lorenz remark in a passage cited above – with the aim of positioning new models built by the Group in higher (niche) price brackets. It is worth noting too that the Longbridge built cars launched in connection with this strategy quickly became the Group's single biggest revenue generator: the site was thus of pivotal importance *prior* to the BMW acquisition, and its subsequent fall from grace when the German firm later disposed of the Group would for this reason be of interest even if it were not for the fact that it was at Longbridge that Rover engaged most thoroughly in experiments with what it considered to be a 'Japanese' production regime.

Our first main point of disagreement with Brady and Lorenz – who in this regard assume a direct connection between Rover and Honda *vis-à-vis* plant management practices – is that when working at Longbridge we observed that the reorganization of the product supply function at the site prior to the BMW acquisition owed little to Honda. In particular, the decision to build cars while implementing a just-in-time parts delivery policy was taken via the time-honoured principle of top-down decision making, but there was no evidence – from documents, interviews, or participant observation – of any impetus, assistance, resistance or even advice from Honda, which was generally perceived amongst Rover managers there as typically uninterested in the detail of how its erstwhile British partner actually organized production at its own facilities. An executive level desire to emulate not only the success but also the public example of Japan's ascendant assemblers seemed to play the major part in the decision, with some local encouragement from nearby business schools perhaps playing a minor role.

Our second is more fundamental. We propose that Brady and Lorenz are correct in identifying an intended shift at the British firm in the late 1980s towards a new product marketing strategy, one moreover based on a policy of 'up-market' sourcing of sales modelled in part on the example of the German firm BMW with respect to product–price positioning, as a template for future development. But by contrast with Brady and Lorenz who maintain that 'Japanese' production techniques helped sustain Rover in this period, we now propose that the strategy intended on the side of the market was almost immediately *undermined* at the Longbridge facility by the attempt by factory managers to implement the separate decision to adopt 'just-in-time' product supply.

So far as strategy in the market place was concerned, by the late 1980s the Rover Group was indeed embarked (and just as Brady and Lorenz indicate) on a strategy aimed at repositioning products at the upper ends of the market segments to which they were intended to sell. The new strategy was in fact launched in earnest in 1989, to coincide with the formal change of name – to re-establish the 'brand' – to Rover Group Ltd. The decision to turn the company's manufacturing and commercial strategies away from the volume tranches of the domestic market, and to orient product and sales policies towards a more 'up-market' sourcing of sales was embodied in the price-positioning of a new car line launched in this year in the lower-medium-size segment of the car market. The new line-up was marketed as two distinct series, the Rover's 200 and 400: the 400 series comprised variants on a 4-door saloon, the 200 series 3-door and 5-door hatchbacks. It was intended to broaden sales over the existing marque by expanding the range of models offered compared to what the company had previously offered (the line-up also expanded shortly thereafter to include coupé and cabriolet models). These cars were assembled together on the same production line at the Longbridge site, together with the Honda Concerto, and it is these cars which accounted for the strategic significance of that site in the year's prior to the BMW acquisition as the Group's biggest revenue generator.

It would certainly be legitimate to describe the Rover strategy at this time as one of niche market positioning, although we must be clear on our context of application. But there is no question of envisaging 'niche marketing' versus 'volume selling' in this case as if what were at stake involved a contrast between mixed-assembly and 'Fordist mass production', since this would involve historical error (see Chapter 2), and trivialize complex issues *vis-à-vis* the actual evolution of market structure in the UK. The difference must be understood in the first instance as a difference in *pricing*: each model 'derivative' that was marketed was (list) price positioned at the upper end of the price range for other lower-medium-size cars matched by body style and engine class. The marketing division within the Rover Group, when planning the launch of the 200 and 400 series cars, envisaged the lower-medium segment as comprising four sub-segments. At that time 5-door hatchbacks took almost one half of all industry sales to the UK lower-medium segment as a whole, including imports as well as domestic production.[4] Cars in this stream were 'typically' (list) priced beneath 4-door saloons, which were viewed for this reason as the backbone of the size segment's 'luxury' stream; sales of 3-door hatchbacks and sports cars were bi-modally distributed, with a cheaper 'bottom end' stream and a more expensively priced 'top end' stream. Rover cars sourced from the 200 and 400 series were launched so as to be positioned in the upper end of the price brackets in each of these four sub-segments relative to competitors' models. But in each sub-segment (with the exception of the more specialist sports car stream) the market's 'volume' sellers – led by Ford and GM – also offered model variants from competing series: the difference being in the first instance one of market positioning, rather than any implied judgement on capacities for mixed-model assembly as such.[5] While not wishing to understate the nuances of the market structure, the market corresponding to each sub-segment attracted (broadly) differentiable customers, and by expanding across each the marketing division envisaged capturing not only the older male drivers hitherto buying into the Rover marque in the lower-medium-size segment, but also younger drivers, car enthusiasts and second car purchasers – as well as women drivers – with sufficient income to buy into the Rover series, given the intended structure of prices.[6] The initial intent was also to encourage customization via a build-to-order programme based on a steadily expanding list of factory-fit options, a strategy explicitly modelled in this instance on the successful BMW 3 series: BMW was considered a benchmark.[7]

This in essence is the same 'creaming off' strategy Brady and Lorenz in their recent study have attributed to BMW regarding its subsequent aspirations for the Group, and in this regard there is no need to question or doubt their judgement. So far as car assembly at the refurbished Longbridge assembly site was concerned, the 200 and 400 series comprised the most logistically complex car line then offered by Rover from the viewpoint of production operations: it was intended that the cars from each series would be assembled together on the same refurbished line, mixed with the Honda Concerto – a separately badged, stylistically differentiated, and somewhat less diverse range with engineering features that overlapped partly, but by no means completely, with the Rover line-up.[8]

But if the 200 and 400 series model launch from Longbridge in 1989 both anticipated and encapsulated the German car maker's own vision for the Rover Group, it was in the production of this car line that the most aggressive attempts were also made to organize a 'just-in-time' product supply regime *vis-à-vis* component parts. The 'vision' entailed in the directive (from above) to factory managers (down below) was interpreted as essentially involving a more minimal reliance than hitherto on intermediate stocks of component parts and sub-assemblies as buffers to the later stages of car assembly, in itself hardly inconsistent with business school 'wisdom' of the day, then or since. R.J. Schonberger, an influential North American business consultant and author of a best-selling text that was widely cited in the 1980s, described just-in-time production as entailing a 'dock-to-line movement of materials received from suppliers and lot-less bufferless production and material movement within the plant' (Schonberger 1982: 34) – and something like this appears to have been envisaged by Rover executives.[9] But so far as the just-in-time product supply regime is concerned, a mere statement of the aspiration fails to capture, or properly convey, the imaginative effort this then imposed on production managers tasked with its concrete realization. The executive direction to organize production so as to move parts to factory fit points on a just-in-time basis led to the formation of a new logistics unit, and the planning and management of an interlocking set of policies on delivery scheduling, transport and handling. The previous route to material handling and storage at the site – based on bulk, or at least bulkier, delivery, decanting, storage, track-side delivery and consumption – was abandoned, and steps were taken to reduce plant-side inventories and storage allowances.

For reasons of transport economy small-fit parts, consisting in the main of low value added items with large volume turnover rates – various clips, fixings, studs, screws, wheel-nuts, nutserts, bulbs, badges, hinges and pins – continued to be ordered in bulk and held in stocks on sites adjacent to the Longbridge assembly plant. Soft materials for trim manufacture also retained their own delivery routes – calico, threads, labels and webbing; each was deemed to require separate treatment as a particular item. For each of these a single consolidated delivery covering several or more weeks' production was deemed practicable and more frequent deliveries were deemed impracticable. But as itemized bulk and robustness increased, concrete initiatives were taken: radiator grills, clamps and brackets, hand-brakes and clutch-cables, finishers, hoses, lamps, fuel filters and the like were delivered on a more frequent basis to a distribution centre, often several times a week; individual loads were then consolidated into a 'mixed part' delivery to be despatched from the centre to the nearby Longbridge site 'just' as needed. For the remaining items the system employed was one of timed deliveries: instrument packs, insulation pads, wire harnesses, spoilers and plastics, and complex high-level sub-assemblies like door casing and steering wheels came by this route.[10] Even here, however, a complex network of warehouses and distribution centres was employed to provide a sort of 'halfway' house for suppliers with factories that were distributed not only across the British mainland, but in Europe and even (via Honda) in Japan. These sites, scattered around the Longbridge plant in the general Birmingham area, gave suppliers the facility to ship parts out from their own factories in greater bulk than that reserved for ultimate 'small-lot' conveyance to the car assembly plant, while providing some scope for final collation and checking before delivery plant-side: final despatches from this warehouse and distribution centre system typically involved single truck deliveries carrying two to eight hours worth of parts for assembly. To receive parts 20 purpose-built loading decks were constructed around the trim and assembly section of the Longbridge factory, bringing the previous total up from 10 to 30, while civil works were undertaken to improve vehicle access to the site. The rate of handling activity for parts brought in this way to the factory increased concomitantly. The task of coordinating and operating the new system fell on the newly founded Longbridge logistics unit, as did the burden of cost control in the new product supply regime.

Remarkably, there seems to have been no anticipation of the possibility that this route to product supply would prove less than conducive to the successful execution of the strategy intended for the product. Less surprisingly, this quickly became self-evident, so much so that inside of two years from launch a series of meetings from representatives of the product supply and product marketing sides of the equation – and meetings attended by the present writer – were held (throughout 1991) to 'iron out' difficulties. The effort of coordinating the movement of inbound parts and timed deliveries to maintain the requisite degree of synchronicity with the assembly-line production sequence was made more difficult with each addition to the complexity of the car line, and at the same time the new logistical structure for parts handling and tracking made the identification of rising costs with component part variation a pressing and visible concern.[11]

It is again perhaps remarkable that nobody suggested at this point – the suggestion was not one that was even in the air at the Longbridge site – that the 'just-in-time' route to product supply be reconsidered as a possible debacle in the making: instead, pressure mounted from the product supply side of production on the 200 and 400 series car line for revisions to the product strategy launched in 1989. That this should have been the response was perhaps remarkable for yet another reason, inasmuch as there was no disagreement at the site as to the demands of the just-in-time system. It may well be that this turn of events reflected longer-standing tensions between the marketing and production side of Rover Group operations, or already existing differences of opinion between parts of the corporation *vis-à-vis* commercial strategy, or both: but whatever the underlying animus, 'just-in-time' product supply at Longbridge quickly became the stick by which factory managers could effectively beat the marketing division.

A veto was applied to the launch of some of the planned additions (although not all) to the car line-up for the 200 and 400 series models; several existing models were deleted; model styling differences and feature content became a proper subject for public debate; and perhaps of most symbolic resonance in view of the subsequent acquisition by BMW, the demand was advanced that factory-fit options be eliminated, or severely restricted – and the build-to-order customized car policy was killed almost at birth.

None of this occurred in a vacuum. The pitch delivered from the Longbridge factory site, to the effect that cost control required a veto over certain types of variety, resonated with growing concern over the developmental costs of the new product strategy. In the particular and exemplary case of the 200 and 400 series, while initial market-share results were promising, gross margins generated were still insufficient to cover developmental costs and other overheads while leaving an accounting profit greater than zero: the new car line was in fact 'loss-making' in this sense, even while generating the largest revenue by car line for Rover Group models, its premium price policy notwithstanding. This was blamed internally, at least in part, on the 'exorbitant' charges levelled by Honda for its part in the venture – principally via the pricing of the engines it supplied to the car line and the poor terms of its buyback for the Concerto models assembled alongside.[12] But the upshot of this period in the life of the Longbridge facility is that the years leading up to its acquisition by BMW not only saw developmental work scaled back, but also a production regime established which proved profoundly inimical to the execution of the new product strategy launched in 1989 – itself modelled on the German firm. Before considering this further, it will be useful to briefly revisit the topic of 'flexibility'.

'Flexibility' Revisited

In the preceding chapter it was proposed that the most fruitful way to consider the related topics of mixed assembly and wide selection in the car industry is via a simple model of prior scheduling of main product features with 'substitutions' for options. It was also suggested that the question of 'flexibility', as this pertains between factory and consumer, might be reasonably broached via an assessment of the operating parameters of the manufacturing system with respect to (expected) stock–flow ratios on the one hand, and lead times on 'factory-fit' orders on the other, qualified by a simultaneous consideration of the width of selection actually offered prospective buyers at the level of the product. A perspective of this kind is readily utilized in connection with the Longbridge experiment in opting for what was decided instead should be 'just-in-time' product supply. The growing complexity of the car line for the 200 and 400 series models would no doubt have slowed response rates in accommodating customer demands for factory-fit options, thereby extending – all else being equal – lead times on those orders. But the elimination of stock cover for a swathe of parts, combined with the effort to maintain synchronicity between assembly-line production and incoming 'just-in-time' parts deliveries, served to eliminate any vestiges of flexibility from operations, and the time it took for orders for model specifications incorporating factory-fit options to be substituted into the production schedule was steadily

Table 3.1   Composition of factory order lead times by stage (Rover Group)

(i) Lead time stages	(ii) Average composition (% total)	(iii) JIT comparator (% average length)
A – sold/submitted	18	–2
B – submitted/off-assembly	56	+33
C – off-assembly/passed sales	5	–66
D – passed sales/despatched	5	–20
E – despatched/delivered	16	0

lengthening against the Rover Group average.[13] It was in this connection, just two years after the 1989 launch, that the marketing division was issued with demands from the Longbridge site to drop its 'build-to-custom' policy.

Table 3.1 illustrates the situation at this time regarding factory-order lead times, defined as in the previous chapter (see Chapter 2, section 2.4) from the point where a sale is made by a dealer and a vehicle received by a customer when the dealer has to order direct from the factory, because a matching specification cannot be found in existing product stock. The various stages comprising this lead, as measured at this time, are in the accompanying key: a sale is made and an order submitted to the factory (stage A); the order submission is received by the factory and a matching vehicle scheduled into production (B); the car rolls off the assembly line and is submitted via the sales department (C) to a despatch point for transport (D); the completed order is delivered to the customer (E). The share of each stage in the average lead time for Rover cars as a whole is presented in the second column of the table: the significance of the speed with which an assembly plant slots substitute specifications into the master schedule for factory-order lead times is demonstrated in this instance by the fact that for all car lines built by the Rover Group stage B was easily the longest lead element. At this time, and for the Group as a whole, the time elapsing between the point where an order was received by the relevant plant managers for a factory-fit model specification and the point where a matching car rolled off the assembly line accounted for over half of the total lead time from customer sale to customer receipt (about 56 percent). The last column then compares the time elapsing in each stage for the 200 and 400 series car line with the same for Rover Group cars as a whole, expressed as a percentage increase (where positive) or decrease. For Longbridge cars built via the just-in-time route, the absolute length of stage B was in fact about one-third again as great (+33 percent) as the average for the Group: despite some limited offsets in other stages, and allowing for a

Table 3.2   Comparative plant parameters for pre-production lock-in

(i) Sample site	(ii) Pre-production lock-in
Rover Metro (Longbridge)	Post paint-shop
Mazda 323 (Hiroshima)	Just under 1 month
Honda Civic (Suzuku)*	Just over 1 month
Rover 200 and 400 (Longbridge)	2 months
Toyota Corona (Tsutsumi Nagoya)	3 months

Note: *Exterior paint colours also fixed at this point.

complex car line, responsiveness in the factory was lost, a loss expected to become increasingly problematic. (The figures displayed in Table 3.1 are calculated for data compiled two years after launch.)

What is also of some interest, and in this light, is that at around this time Longbridge dispatched a fact-finding team to Japan, to investigate scheduling and distribution in factories organized by Honda, Mazda and Toyota.[14] Amongst information obtained was data on pre-production 'lock-in' for a sample of sites: this is displayed in Table 3.2 for a sample of car lines, including Longbridge-built cars. The 'lock-in' in question pertains to the point at which the assembler in each instance permits no further variation – excepting (perhaps) for exterior colours – in the scheduled production mix, measured backwards from the planned completion date of the finished car. For example, at the Rover Longbridge site, and in addition to the 200 and 400 series assembly line, assembly operations included production of the 'metro', a smaller car built in parallel in the same factory complex (together with the 'mini'). Production managers for that line were able to make final adjustments – albeit of a very minor nature – to specifications right up to the point where painted car bodies emerged from the paint-shop: since parts were held on site in stock, the only constraints were those of model configuration, so that last changes could be made regarding some minor features and options if compatible.[15] By contrast, in the case of the 200 and 400 series car line, even minor variations were ruled out at a far earlier stage in the scheduling process, with a much earlier 'lock-in'. Whereas in the case of the metro this came right at the point where cars were fed to assembly, this came several months in advance of expected completion on the 'just-in-time' line.

So far as Japan was concerned, the visiting team found – without surprise – that Japanese car assemblers typically eschewed building to 'custom'. By historical standards at the Longbridge site the lock-in to production schedules came early at all of the plants visited, although still later than that inflicted on the 200 and 400 series car line as a consequence of the logistics of the just-in-time product supply regime. The one exception here, however, was Toyota, which was distinguished not only by its eschewal of substantive choice at the level of customer options, but also by the rigidity of its factory scheduling parameters: at the Tsutsumi (Nagoya) site, the production schedule for the Toyota Corona, for example, was reported as fixed three months out from the dates at which the finished cars were expected to roll off the assembly line. While the number of car line model derivatives (marketed specifications ignoring colours and options) was typically larger for Toyota car lines than at Rover Group as a whole – although by no means exceptional when judged against large Western car assemblers – it could hardly but be inferred that if Toyota in Japan, with suppliers close by, worked rigid production schedules, it was not reasonable for Longbridge to divest itself of inventories while simultaneously attempting to adhere to a marketing policy of customization.

The data is interesting for another reason. In the preceding chapter attention was drawn to the claim that Toyota – unlike Fordist mass producers in the West – is notable for its ability to avoid rigid production schedules. This claim has typically been advanced in connection with the assumption that Toyota has been a world leader in mixed-model assembly, to which is often added the statement that as a consequence of just-in-time procurements, mass-customization is also the order of the day.[16] While it is not proposed that the data in Table 3.2 be generalized, it is nonetheless consistent with what global evidence suggests is actually true of Toyota and other Japanese firms: late-comers to the world of mixed assembly, curtailing width of selection at car line level by eschewing (in comparative terms) any hint of model customization, it is hard to see what role would be played by less rigid scheduling parameters *vis-à-vis* feature substitutions.

3.4   PRODUCTION MALAPROPISMS

The comparative procedure employed in this chapter is an unusual one, inasmuch as we compare contemporaneous and participative observations made by the present writer on the consequences of 'Japanese' production methods at the Rover Group Longbridge in the first half of the 1990s with widely-held assumptions both then and since, when the plant in question has since suffered a calamitous reversal of fortunes.[17] To complete this process requires some further brief consideration of these assumptions, and in this respect it is useful to commence with Whisler (1999), an addition to the ever-growing list of books on the demise of the British-owned car industry, and one which assesses the Honda–Rover link-up prior to the BMW acquisition in 1995 in a way which brings these assumptions into sharp relief. While it is certainly not suggested that Whisler's study as a whole be judged on this basis (the work is one with a 50 year purview, and one which surveys moreover a number of themes and issues), they are nicely illustrative:

> By the early 1990s there was evidence of considerable improvement in the manu-
> facturing and sales performance of selected Rover model programmes . . . Edwards
> and his successors perceived that recovery was possible by following a course
> outlined by Honda and deliberately sought to direct the firm's institutions and
> strategies towards this path . . . In the early 1990s the professional staff, inundated
> by Honda institutions and methods, shifted towards a new path, leading to enhanced
> performance. (Whisler 1999: 364)

We see here both an assumption that by the 'early 1990s' manufacturing as well as sales performance for the Rover Group had improved, combined with an assertion that this was achieved in a context informed ('inundated') by Honda 'institutions and methods'. On the particular case of the key Rover 200 and 400 series, launched in 1989:

> Honda provided the basic product and process designs as well as specialised manu-
> facturing equipment . . . The car was launched in 1990 as the Rover 200/400 and
> Honda Concerto . . . Both marques were assembled at Longbridge under the
> auspices of Honda manufacturing staff, who were involved to a greater degree than
> in the previous joint production schemes. The Honda personnel provided manufac-
> turing support and implemented a 'just-in-time' component delivery system . . . By
> the end of the second year of production, Rover's supervision of the inventory and
> manufacturing systems had improved considerably. (Whisler 1999: 395)

The above quote gives a fairly good idea of the state of reporting at the time (the principal evidence alluded to in this regard by Whisler are British broad-sheets), and of the view more generally which has taken root in the secondary academic literature. We can note that, like Brady and Lorenz, Whisler takes it as axiomatic that Honda played a major role in the reorganization of the Rover product supply functions: indeed, in this instance, Honda staffs are described as having stood direct watch at Longbridge. More fundamentally, and again like Brady and Lorenz, it is assumed that as a consequence of the introduction of 'Japanese' production methods – here the just-in-time system – manufac-turing performance 'improved considerably'. The point in this regard is not that writers like Brady and Lorenz, or Whisler, are exceptionally uncritical: rather, it is that in this connection they are wholly unexceptional. For exam-ple, another history of the 'British' car industry compiled in the period just prior to the BMW acquisition describes the just-in-time experiment at Rover, and in the context of the 200 and 400 series car line, as representing a 'clear departure' from 'Fordist aspirations', and a move towards greater 'flexibility' (Foreman-Peck et al. 1995: 234); and more generally the Rover Group is lauded for achieving, and in connection with its partnership with Honda, 'spectacular productivity increases' (ibid.: 248). And commentary in this area since has typically also commenced from the outset with the view that the Rover experiments 'worked'.[18]

If we consider the contrast we should commence by acknowledging that by the nature of the assertion it is impossible to disprove the Brady–Lorenz contention that BMW purchased in the Rover Group an indelibly weak and almost exhausted brand: to debate on this terrain obliges one to speculate, since the same series of events cannot be repeated with selected conditions changed to see what becomes of hindsight. By the same token, however, we are also obliged to observe that Brady and Lorenz offer no proof. But their simultaneous assertion that manufacturing strengths from Japan obscured a weakness of the side of market demand – the attractiveness of the Rover brand – can certainly be challenged on grounds that are open to empirical verification and testing. And on this basis it is possible on the basis of the remarks made above to present as an alternative hypothesis for further investigation the following: instead of sound and thoughtfully conceived policies on the side of product supply masking weaknesses on the side of product demand (the no-hope Rover brand), the Rover Group's intended marketing strategy for cars built at its Longbridge facility was undermined prior to the BMW acquisition by the adoption of wholly inappropriate policies *vis-à-vis* production: the attempt to emulate what conventional wisdom at the time decreed was one reason for Japanese success in the industry – reduced parts-inventories – merely served to raise costs and to eliminate the assembly plant flexibilities required by the market strategy.

It could of course be objected that some of the prerequisites for a more 'flexible' outcome were absent in the context wherein Rover implemented its just-in-time programme, on the grounds that success in an organizational venture of this kind would require spatial proximity between component part supply and assembly plant user in order to contain the freight costs of frequent small-scale delivery while easing transport logistics. And on this point no doubt reference could be made to Toyota City, and to the closer proximities between component part suppliers and car assembly plants observed therein. And certainly it looks a foolhardy enough venture to attempt to organize a supply structure with a geographically dispersed manufacturing base for just-in-time assembly. But in accepting this as no doubt true, we must not slip into empirical error. In the first instance, there is no evidence that Toyota or other Japanese car assemblers have ever practiced, or needed to practice, a particularly flexible assembly regime. What one would then be considering is a case of spatial proximity combined with eschewal of a certain type of width in selection, *vis-à-vis* provision of custom-led optional features. We have already argued (in Chapter 2) that this in itself might account for differences in both stock–flow ratios and customer order lead times, even putting to one side other important considerations like demand pressures relative to capacity: spatial proximity would be one additional element to consider when comparing stock levels in production. But it does not follow from this that this has been the secret of Japanese flexibility: the notion is chimerical. Moreover, even the claim that the Japanese *system* is predicated on spatial proximities is suspect, if by this is meant more than a contingently observed phenomenon at a particular point in time in space in the history of the Japanese industry.

What we are concerned with in this chapter, however, is why it should be so confidently supposed that whatever errors BMW made, Japanese production methods had worked well in securing at least a short-term reprieve for the Rover Group; so much so indeed that its German purchaser had been lulled by appearances. Naturally, companies engaging in manufacturing experiments do not publicly report on difficulties: at the point where the present writer was based within the Group, and attending internal meetings which were laying bare the contradictions inherent in the twin policies of reduced stock production and custom-led build-to-order marketing, Rover's public affairs departments were issuing literature boasting of flexible just-in-time manufacture. Such would be neither unexpected nor reprehensible – a choice between indulging in public self-criticism or feeding the beast of public expectation represents no choice at all.

What is perhaps most striking, however, is that Brady and Lorenz, in the course of their interviews not with Rover representatives but with Hans Pischetsrieder, then BMW's chief, seem to have drawn close to the relevant issues. According to Pischetsrieder:

> Rover could never achieve truly premium brand quality and prices unless it got away from what BMW saw as the volume oriented Honda approach . . . The contrast was embodied in the different production systems. Honda's system of making cars in batches, which Rover was still compelled to use because of its dependence on the Japanese company, also conflicted with BMW's marketing objectives for Rover. BMW builds cars to individual customer orders and wanted Rover to do the same.
> (Brady and Lorenz 2001: 43)

If the attribution of the difficulty directly to Honda is put to one side, the contrast drawn here between BMW's hope for a build-to-order programme – one which they doubtless saw reflected in Rover's new product strategy prior to acquisition – and the reality of the types of production system which they found in place, is consistent with the findings of our own contemporary study of the period prior to 1994. The evident failure of Brady and Lorenz not so much to report the view, as to make further progress in digesting it, is reflective perhaps of a more general inability of a generation of business commentators, in Britain as elsewhere, to even countenance serious criticism of 'Japanese' experiments, tending in this instance to something approximating systemic confirmation bias.

3.5 CONCLUSIONS

In the preceding chapter it was suggested that the casting of Japanese car assemblers as harbingers of post-Fordist manufacture is a culturally arresting phenomenon, marked both by a wholesale fictionalization of the history of manufacture and the assertion as obvious truth of empirical propositions at odds with what observation can establish. The case example considered in this chapter – particularly if viewed in connection with the discussion in Chapter 2 of the forms taken by this process of fiction-writing – is an almost ideal case from the viewpoint of propositions evident in much of both the academic and business presses of the past 20 or so years concerning the great transformation in factory potentials purportedly ushered in by Japanese producers. The case entails a product strategy based on 'niche' model positioning and customiza-tion, combined with a policy diktat to factory managers charged with produc-tion to do so just in time, both launched simultaneously at the Rover Group Longbridge site in the years prior to an unexpected acquisition by the German firm BMW, which ended ignominiously. We have suggested that the resulting product supply (production) regime was implemented at just the right time to undermine efforts (within the Rover Group) to build on a rebranded product by repositioning models in 'upstream' price brackets relative to the bulk of industry sales in the relevant market segments, while launching a marketing strategy emphasizing not only product quality but also customizing potentials. The ensuing loss of any vestige of assembly plant flexibility resulting from the new product supply regime, combined with the almost certainly perverse cost trajectories attendant upon the elimination of traditional parts delivery routes from production, served to undermine these efforts right from the onset of production. In terms of operations research – and as an example of mismatched strategies – there is absolutely nothing here which is inconsistent with the terms of our earlier reappraisal of Japanese car assembly in Chapter 2.

Of equal import, however, is the dearth of subsequent critical commentary. Controversy over reasons for the slow demise (if not resuscitated by China) of the Rover Group, in the UK at least, has been intense, as has been interest in critical assessments of the history of the Longbridge car assembly site, our point of focus in this chapter. What is remarkable is that it remains an article of faith that experiments with 'Japanese' production methods within the Group prior to the BMW acquisition 'worked', and worked well. What we wish to suggest is that this points to confirmation biases of a formidable type: local commentary is unable to draw from the parochial context inferences that are inconsistent with globally established 'truths' – or even to conceive of the appropriate questions. We must be concerned to ask therefore whether the same or similar processes to those which have seen the history of a major manufacturing sector fictionalized, with empirical counterfactuals widely asserted and accepted as uncontroversial fact, have also effected a displacement of perspective at other levels, with certain types of question and certain types of inference disappearing from view as a result.

A POSTSCRIPT

One last point is perhaps worth drawing to the reader's attention for consideration. When BMW acquired the Rover Group in 1994, it obtained several production locations in the UK: Longbridge itself, the Land and Range Rover site at Solihull, and the famous Cowley plant in Oxford. A year earlier speculation on the imminent closure of Cowley, operations at which had been heavily downgraded in Rover Group operations, was rife: indeed, a book edited by Teresa Hayter and David Harvey (1993) – *The Factory & The City: The Story of the Cowley Automobile Workers in Oxford* – was published in the year preceding the BMW acquisition and focused on, while campaigning against, what was widely assumed to be the pending closure of Cowley. The decision of the Rover Group to build the 200 and 400 series models at Longbridge rather than Cowley marked a serious set-back for the Oxford plant: 'Cowley and Longbridge effectively compete for Rover investment and models . . . [in] 1989 . . . Cowley lost out to Longbridge' (Greenhalgh and Kilmister 1993: 45). Dan Jones, one of the principal figures then as today associated with the concept of 'lean production' (see later chapters), was contracted by the Oxford authorities to consider the future of the Cowley site and is quoted as offering the following written submission: 'the closure of Cowley makes sound business sense in the context of Rover's future' (Hayter 1993: 178). At this point, therefore, the future of the Longbridge plant looked more assured, while Cowley was deemed to be on the precipice of closure – an assumption both underpinning and undershot by the assumed industrial renaissance at Longbridge widely attributed in commentaries of the early 1990s to the efficacy of 'Japanese' organizational methods in production.

But when BMW five years after making its acquisition decided to break up the Rover Group and dispose of most of the assets, it was Longbridge that failed to find a buyer: on the other hand, BMW also elected to carry on producing at Cowley. In itself the reversal is interesting, and might give pause to a certain type of reflexive judgement almost endemic in public commentary on issues pertaining to plant closures; namely, that it can be assumed as a naturally assured thing that when Company X withdraws its support for future operations at a facility it follows that the facility is beyond redemption. A pause of this kind, however, invariably never comes, and instead precepts are rearranged to accommodate changed circumstances without further ado. In a small way this is evident in the Brady and Lorenz study: while for the main part even-handed and balanced in their assessment of the relative merits of Longbridge and Cowley as production sites with regard to the initial BMW acquisition, they nonetheless veer towards a retrospective judgement that confirms Cowley as the reasonable choice in ways which are exceedingly difficult to reconcile with the actual history of the site. For example, Cowley is described as having possessed advantages over Longbridge from BMW's perspective because it had been 'partly redeveloped' by BAe and was thus 'more compact' – a strange way to describe the *de facto* run-down and looming closure of the Cowley facility prior to BMW's unexpected purchase (see Brady and Lorenz 2001: 68). But in this connection we might picture what more generally might be described as related themes: confirmation bias (Japanese-inspired production methods 'worked'), combined with complex disassociation (the Rover brand was in any event doomed), and a certain elasticity of historical judgement *vis-à-vis* the relative merits of production sites that seems somehow to sway almost ineluctably with commercial decisions of the day:

> Professor Dan Jones . . . said in May 2000 that 'Longbridge is a hell-hole – given the choice you wouldn't start from there' . . . [but] even at the risk of the bottom-line, Pischetsrieder [had been] prepared to take on the burden of Longbridge rather than face the political fall-out that many analysts expected. The result was that, right from the outset, the Longbridge issue was a boil that was festering rather than being lanced. There was only one potentially disastrous challenge, and that was Longbridge. (Brady and Lorenz 2001: 37–8).

NOTES

1. The 'British' car industry shrank alongside the strengthening of the grip of foreign-owned firms over production operations carried out in the UK: in this instance, Jaguar cars went to Ford, the Leyland trucks and van business to DAF. In fact, the UK has long been peculiarly open to overseas manufacturers seeking either to secure a first base of operations in Europe, or to extend their grip in this region: indeed, the Ford facility established at Dagenham (in the London area of the UK) in the latter part of the 1920s, with first production commencing in 1931, was in its day the largest car manufacture and assembly site in Europe, the 'Detroit of Europe' (see Collins and Stratton 1993: 118–24). The decline of the 'British' car and vehicle industry cannot be separated from the emergence of UK-based production as a branch in the regional operations of transnationally-mounted firms (an important subtext in standard histories on this subject, such as, for example, Dunnett (1980) or Church (1994)). It is this context which provides the backdrop to our discussion of incumbent reactions to Japanese encroachments on the British car market in the 1970s, as developed in a later chapter (see Chapter 6). Further historical detail on the 'British' part of the industry prior to 1989 can be found in any one of a number of studies – for example, Willman and Winch (1985), Whipp and Clark (1986) and Williams et al. (1987) – although each naturally has its own preoccupations and its own particular take on issues. A very useful schematic representation of the historical timeline from the formation of British Leyland in 1968 right through to BMW's acquisition and disposal of the Rover Group (as well as the birth and death of MG Rover in its aftermath) is also set out in Holweg and Oliver (2005).

2. That Chinese firms should seek egress to Europe via the UK is perhaps no surprise, since this would be entirely consistent with past patterns of entry from other regions. Nanjing Automobile Corporation, a current owner of MG Rover assets, is rumoured to be considering extending its lease on the Longbridge site. The situation is complicated by the involvement also of Shanghai Automotive Industry Corporation (SAIC), which also claims rights to build Rover cars, and is expected to do so in China: we need not be concerned, however, with the details.

3. The substantive points reported in this section with respect to the organization of just-in-time deliveries to the Rover site at Longbridge are informed by participative field research carried out over a 15-month period from the latter part of 1991 through to the summer of 1992, including time spent working in the logistics unit at the Longbridge site on an almost daily basis, in pre-production planning and control for 200 and 400 series cars, and from subsequent and extended interviews and discussions with middle and senior management working in these areas, as well as interaction with academic engineers and systems simulation experts at the University of Warwick. In subsequent years, a close interest was retained in the progress of the Group (and conversely, first visits were made to the Group as early as April 1990, prior to full access). The material summarized here by no means exhausts the content of research undertaken during, before or after the principal period. All comments expressed can be (and were) supported by reference to relevant bodies of data generated by the constituent parts of Rover Group functions. An original summary of this part of the research was deposited (in 1993) in Warwick's library.

4. To avoid being drawn into what for the purposes of this chapter would be an unnecessary digression on pricing and exchange rates, we focus our examples on the UK domestic market. At the time of the 1989 launch, lower-medium cars accounted for about one third of UK car sales.

5. The differentiated nomenclature adopted by Rover for the 200 and 400 series *vis-à-vis* provision of 3- and 5-door hatchback (200 series) models and 4-door saloon (400 series) models reflected established practice: other car lines selling to the UK lower-medium segment adopted a similar naming convention – GM's Astra/Belmont, Ford's Escort/Orion, VW's imported Golf/Jetta – each with its own spread of model derivatives differentiated by body style, engine capacity and features, and trim-ratings. It is for this reason that niche positioning over volume sales should be interpreted in the first instance in price terms. In the case of the 3-door hatchback, for example, and at the bottom end of the price bracket, cars priced (in 1989) at around the £7150 mark measured the highest aggregate volume by sales in this sub-segment, whereas the cheapest of the Rover models at launch was priced at an 'entry-level' price of just over £8500. Compared with GM or Ford, in every sub-segment Rover 200 and 400 series cars were priced above their nearest matches by body style and engine capacity, this strategy being most evident for the 3-door hatchback and the 4-door saloon, but informing also pricing for 5-door models.

6. The intended vehicle by which to capture 'younger' drivers was the 3-door hatchback: in general, marketing surveys employed by the Rover Group found that new car buyers in this sub-segment tended to be younger, averaging in their early 40s compared to the mid to late 40s found for purchasers of 4-door and 5-door cars, and with one third under the age of 35. By contrast with Ford and GM, with a customer age profile centred in the mid-40s, Rover drivers tended to be older, ranging as new car buyers from the middle to late 50s: by expanding into the 3-door sub-segment and sports-car styling, it was hoped to change this. The entry-level models launched by Rover into this segment were intended as 'feeder' sales, to encourage future purchases from more expensive cars as younger buyer's incomes rose: at the upper end of the price bracket for 3-door cars – aimed at established professionals and executives – the cheapest of the Rover models was priced (in 1989) at just over £11,000, just above the 'volume' mark. It was also hoped that the 3-door car would source some sales from affluent second car buyers.

7. The marketing division's summary documentation prior to launch cited BMW directly: it was intended that the 200 and 400 series cars would be price positioned in a way that might attract some sales from upper-medium competitors, sitting just below the BMW '3 series' range.

8. The resulting model mix was easily the most complex then built by Rover Group. In addition to a range of body styles, the 200 and 400 series was assembled to incorporate derivative specifications from a number of distinct engine families – an aluminium based Rover K series engine (in the sub 1.4 litre range), a larger Honda engine (in the 1.6 litre range), and diesels – in both left-hand-side drive and right-hand-side drive varieties. The overlaps with the Honda Concerto models built on the same assembly line must not be overstated: the Concerto was built in both 4-door and 5-door but not 3-door versions, with a smaller number of models spanning a narrower price-range in each sub-segment, and with a broader mix of Honda engines than assembled in the 200 and 400 series but without the Rover K series model. The overall mix was consequently a varied one, imposing significant logistical demands on the assembly site, a point that would be more evident if space permitted greater detail on componentry. Even 'variety' of the sort that outside commentators are often quick to describe as 'trivial' can add substantially to the part numbers that a plant must manage in tracking components to cars, such as, for example, with 'identity items' of the sort intended to reinforce the visual distinctiveness of models: in this instance, the 200 and 400 series was differentiated from the Concerto in bumpers, lamps, grills, fenders, appliqué and spoilers, rubbing strips, wheel and wheel trim, mirrors, mudflaps, applied graphs, interior steering wheel, facia mats, seat fabrics and finishers – all features in the specification of each car (and before consideration of 'options') intended also to internally differentiate models within series, and in a manner reflecting 'progress' up the price range.

9. It is an interesting question as to *which* texts became popular within Rover Group on the product supply side of the equation as the just-in-time production regime was put together. While an assessment of this issue lies well beyond the intended scope of this chapter, the book which quickly grew in popularity amongst production managers side was Mather (1985) – an approach to manufacturing logistics diametrically opposed to the 'vision' of a BMW-style product.

10. Two years into the just-in-time experiment some 45 percent of numbered parts shipped to this car line from component suppliers came via the timed-sequence route (including Honda-supplied engines) and 30 percent via the consolidated load system at the distribution centre. The remaining 25 percent of parts largely fell into the designated small fit and trim categories, with just 2 percent in a miscellaneous 'conventional category'. These approximations exclude body panels, which had their own delivery route from the Rover Group press-shops in Swindon. The reference here to numbered parts (or part numbers) should be interpreted as follows: a single component type, which in itself may be a potentially complex sub-assembly, can have variants, each of which will be assigned its own part number, as for example variants on a wire harness. Differently numbered varieties of the same component type may or may not come from the same supplier.

11. Steps were certainly taken to restrain operating costs – for example, insofar as this was possible, component part containers were designed to allow easy circulation between assembly plant and suppliers, while dunnage was designed to be easily removed and re-usable. However, in every likely cost category at the level of day-to-day operations the just-in-time routes were deemed by the relevant factory managers in interviews to be most resource-intensive – the more frequent loading and unloading of parts, under strict time limits, for parts handlers, and a significant increase in the managerial 'overhead' being the most obvious costs. It is interesting that at the time of this experiment (and indeed still: see Best 2001) it was something of an article of faith in commentaries on the 'Japanese' car-making system that economies from reduced parts-inventories would accrue first and foremost to cost categories of precisely this type: 'Japanese firms developed the plant flexibility to produce a range of products on the same production lines without driving up indirect labour costs . . . the "just-in-time" . . . system' (Best 1990: 143, see also Abegglen and Stalk 1985: 105–6). But at Longbridge, this did not happen: for example, responsibility for monitoring the movement and correct availability of component parts fell on 'parts analysts' whose job it was to liaise between track and supplier, and all delivery points in between; across all car lines built at the site the number of analysts employed on the timed delivery routes per 'part number' processed were between two and a half to three times higher than for parts taken to the site via non 'just-in-time' supply routes. As with practically every other operating cost, growing car line variety was expected to accentuate cost increments.

12. The difficulties posed for Rover by its commercial relationship with Honda are also noted by Brady and Lorenz: for example, for large cars (built at Cowley) they note that 'Rover paid Honda substantial sums for the car floor-pans and engines . . . plus a royalty on each jointly developed car Rover sold . . . the companies' technology agreement barred Rover from selling Honda-based models in markets Honda wanted to develop for itself' (ibid. 2001: 10). Indeed, the relationship is described as the 'Honda bear-hug', which 'mortgaged any future revival' the struggling Group might have enjoyed against short-term survival (ibid.). This is consistent with views obtained by the present writer when stationed inside the Group, and certainly provides a more realistic cast to the relationship than the rather lachrymose version which was popular at the time, both when BMW beat Honda to acquire the Group, and when it later broke it up.

13. It is worth pausing to consider what the implications of this would be from the viewpoint of the stylized analysis of assembly plant 'flexibilities' set out in Chapter 2, via Figure 2.1. A reduced ability to substitute factory-fit options into the existing production schedule would in this connection be represented by a move from a point like e^0 (say) to a point like e^2, representing an attendant loss of assembly plant flexibility for any expected composition of customer orders. An alternative (but compatible) representation is also considered in Coffey (2005b).

14. The Japanese field-visit took place in the summer of 1992: the author was not in attendance, and our comments in this section are based on the accompanying report and interviews.

15. Note that while the positioning of the 'lock-in' will be reflected in factory order lead times, the two are not synonymous: as is clear in Table 3.1, there are a number of other factors to consider in the determination of the average factory lead, and in any case the lock-in represents the point at which final adjustments are precluded: some model specifications may be locked in before this.

16. In this connection the supposed link between a just-in-time production facility and mixed assembly is frequently emphasized: 'with the just-in-time approach . . . on the same assembly line work might be scheduled in batches of one' (Basu and Wright 1997: 10–11). It is for this reason that a step-by-step delayering is required in any critical apprehension of the literature.

17. Little attempt was made to question these assumptions in successive Parliamentary investigations (on which see in particular: HC (1999–2000a), HC (1999–2000b) and HC (2000–2001)). However, an appraisal of these, as with later official investigations, lies outside the intended scope of this chapter (some of the relevant issues are explored in Coffey and Thornley (2006d); see also Chapter 6, below).

18. One exception to the rule is Christopher (1998: 211), who briefly notes the contrast between a Toyota-like policy of 'limiting the number of options available', and custom-building to order on the basis of a generous factory-fit options list. The same comment touches on the early hopes within Rover that the custom-building approach would provide the basis for their own marketing efforts, but it does not consider the problems which then arose in this instance as a consequence of the just-in-time experiment *vis-à-vis* implementation (although Christopher (2005: 139) touches on related points – production at Rover 'eventually foundered' – that can be readily explained in the terms set out by our observations in this chapter). More generally, however, there is little sense in the relevant literatures of any real appreciation of difficulties. To take another example, a reputable study of Honda, published in the mid-1990s, makes the following observations: 'Honda's North American factories . . . employ thousands of workers to churn out hundreds of thousands of cars per years . . . a limited number of derivatives and very few optional extras . . . going against the idea some people associate with Japan of customizing cars and offering a wide choice of options for the buyer – it is common Honda practice to offer few choices within a model type: few colours even' (see Mair 1994: 184, 237). But at the same time, even while an explicit contrast with Rover Group aspirations for the (then) new 200 and 400 series car line is noted – 'versions . . . to fill a wide range of market niches' – the author's overarching presumption is still one of a positive *synthesis* of methods and goals, leading in the fullness of time to new (and successful) Rover formulation (ibid.: 237, 294–6).

4. Lean production: the dog that did not bark

> ... lean production, as it inevitably spreads beyond the auto industry, will change everything in almost every industry – choices for consumers, the nature of work, the fortune of companies, and, ultimately, the fate of nations ... (Womack et al. 1990: 12)

4.1 INTRODUCTION

It has become so commonplace to see 'lean production' described as a phenomenon which first became obvious in Japan circa the mid-1970s that it is easy to forget that the term itself was only coined in the late 1980s, and in connection with the largest international productivity survey in the history of the car industry. This project was itself largely funded by the survey participants, with sponsors for the survey encompassing most of the major car assemblers in South East Asia and the West. It was carried out (alongside some smaller studies) by researchers working under the auspices of the International Motor Vehicle Programme (IMVP) based at MIT, an association which undoubtedly lent considerable prestige to the venture. And the survey itself was genuinely remarkable, a feature that we must not lose sight of as we proceed to offer some different views on its design and empirical findings. Because it enjoyed unprecedented support, with factory access and funding from the world's car manufacturing industry, the scope of the survey was enormous. The popular account given by Womack et al. (1990) in *The Machine that Changed the World* was based on information obtained from more than 90 car assembly plants distributed around the globe – at the time amounting to what the authors estimated to be about half the world's car manufacturing capacity (ibid.: 76). And a central contention set out in this account, and maintained consistently since, was that it had been conclusively demonstrated that Japanese organizational advantages in production had, for successfully adapting firms, dramatically lowered the hours of assembly plant labour required to build cars at any level of factory automation.

The survey itself was carried out in the latter part of the 1980s, a propitious time from the viewpoint of research aimed at demonstrating the efficacy of production methods in the factories of Japanese car makers, Toyota's in particular. First, Japan's car manufacturers were already at the height of renown as a consequence of their steady and rapid ascension in the world industry; moreover, Japan's domestic car production, driven in part by the boom economy in the home market, was approaching its peak before the onset of the recessions that beset Japan in the 1990s. Second, much of the groundwork was already there for a positive reception of dramatic claims: the preceding decade had seen a rapid consensus achieved amongst opinion formers in the West as to the undisputed truth of other dramatic claims – after all, Toyota *had* swept through the world car industry on the back of an unparalleled flexibility in production and mass customization *was* now the order of the day. The fact that none of this was true was overlooked; easily challenged points passed unchallenged. A little more than five years later, the career progress of lean production was assured, and could be described as such even by a severe critic of its 'flimsy historical underpinnings':

> If historical approaches to the social sciences ever require justification, one need look no further than the flimsy historical underpinnings of modern managerial panaceas. One of the most influential of these in recent years has been 'lean production'. It is probably not exaggerating to suggest that the book about the car industry, *The Machine That Changed the World*, which promoted this concept has already achieved the same following in management ranks internationally that the Hawthorne studies once acquired over a much longer period of time. (Lyddon 1996: 77)

The target of Lyddon's ire here is historical, and we have further developed some of the relevant issues in an earlier chapter. But the assessment is general. And allowing for the complexity of the motives that might conceivably inform management positions within businesses, and business positions in the corporate world – dubious positions can sometimes be held for reasons other than naivety – the point is not overstated: the progress of the 'concept' has itself been a phenomena.

In this chapter we focus on the empirics of the MIT-based International Motor Vehicle Programme (IMVP) world car assembly plant survey, which for brevity will be hereafter referred to as the IMVP survey. The IMVP survey is to be distinguished from the forum in which its findings were most publicly discussed – that is to say, from Womack et al. (1990) – although naturally we are concerned with this as well. One point worth noting at the outset is that the historical framework set out by Womack et al. for the contextualization of the IMVP survey results is the familiar one that contrasts Japanese inspired production methods with Western mass production on the model set down by Henry Ford – 'Henry Ford's mass production drove the auto industry for more than half a century' (ibid.: 30). Taichii Ohno, whom we have previously met as the executive who claimed that Toyota invented mixed assembly in car manufacture and eschewed production schedules, is the 'production genius' hailed as the architect of lean production (ibid.: 30, 49; also ibid.: 17–69). The issues developed in preceding chapters are therefore relevant to any criticism of Womack et al., who certainly play to the gallery on both heads. But the IMVP survey *per se* is something else altogether; it is a major study in its own right, and must be respected as such. Indeed, one of the observations that we will make is that in formal construction and design the terms of the survey owe little to the 'theory' of lean production as expounded by Womack et al. *vis-à-vis* Ohno and Toyota.

The approach taken in this chapter is not to dismiss the IMVP survey, but rather to take it very seriously indeed, because a close scrutiny allows a quite different set of conclusions to be drawn from those which are commonly held. At the same time, this also provides an opportunity to admire the work of J.F. Krafcik, the engineer tasked with developing the IMVP survey methodology. In this regard, the discussion in this chapter touches on a separate point of interest. It is clear that economists are interested in what engineers do when assessing differences in organizational performance in manufacturing industries. Herbert Simon, no less, showed an early interest in the work of the IMVP, and in the Krafcik methodologies (Simon 1991: 37–8), while Chris Freeman and Luc Soete, two economists with a particular interest in historical innovations in industrial production, have made much of the involvement of MIT-based engineers both in this and in related projects (see Freeman and Soete 1997: 151).[1] For this reason alone, the design of the IMVP survey is of methodological interest. The fact that its findings have been widely seen since as the 'undoubted' influence leading to determined efforts in North America and Europe to emulate Japanese production methods – the position held by Freeman and Soete – simply makes this interest more so.

4.2   THE IMVP SURVEY: GENERAL ISSUES OF DESIGN AND INTERPRETATION

It is best to broach the IMVP world productivity survey in steps, and in this section we first highlight some important issues of perspective and basic design, before outlining in a relatively informal way our main line of attack: only after the main issues have been identified and their significance established do we proceed to a more formal assessment of the construction and analysis of the survey variables. The reason for proceeding in successive stages in this way follows not so much from any intrinsic difficulties in the points to be made, but rather from the enormous successes which received interpretations of the IMVP survey findings have since enjoyed. In order to convince that (i) the survey is worth taking seriously, but (ii) that it is open to quite different interpretations from those which are generally accepted, we need to proceed systematically, and with each step in the argument clearly stated. In this section, our points of reference are Womack et al. (1990) and Krafcik (1988a, 1988b, 1989). These latter provide the necessary background details on the construction of the data employed in the IMVP survey to measure the labour input used to build cars in the sampled assembly plants, and comparative levels of plant automation.[2]

4.2.1   General Issues of IMVP Survey Design

An immediate observation is that the IMVP survey deals solely with measurements taken on labour and automation in the later stages of production in the manufacture of a car, in the final assembly plant. In general terms, for a volume car plant this would typically entail: the body shop, where the unpainted body shell, or 'body-in-white' as it is sometimes known in Anglo-American usage, is built up on the framing lines; the paint shop, with pre-treatments and paint work; and the trim and final assembly lines, where the whole car is finally brought together; in addition to the engine assembly line. Supporting sub-assembly lines are likely to be grouped around the main assembly functions, such as, for example, a tailgate sub-assembly station in the body shop, although the degree to which sub-assembly work is undertaken on site will vary from plant to plant, as will the detail of the factory layouts. Womack et al. (1990: 76) justify this selection by highlighting three aspects of work at this stage of production. One is the commonplace realization that while much of the work carried out in the car industry involves assembly – 'because of the large number of parts in a car' – the later stages of production in the final assembly plant are wholly devoted to assembly work, allowing a clear field of view from the viewpoint of comparative study. Another is the particular relevance of the assembly plant to the goals of the IMVP survey: 'we chose the assembly plant for study, because Japanese efforts to spread lean production by building plants in North America and Europe initially involved assembly plants'. The remaining factor identified by Womack et al. is worth spelling out:

> *[A]ssembly plants all over the world do almost exactly the same things, because practically all of today's cars and light trucks are built with very similar fabrication techniques.* In almost every assembly plant, about 300 stamped steel panels are spot-welded into a complete body. Then the body is dipped and sprayed to protect it from corrosion. Next, it is painted. Finally, thousands of mechanical parts, electrical items, and bit of upholstery are installed inside the painted body to produce the complete automobile. Because these tasks are so uniform, we can meaningfully compare a plant in Japan with one in Canada, another in West Germany, and still another in China, even though they are making cars that look very different as they emerge from the factory. (Womack et al. 1990: 76, emphasis added)

In other words, notwithstanding claims of a 'lean' revolution, any radical experiments in intra-plant layout or organization are discounted from the outset when accounting for purported differences in the resources used to build cars in the 1980s: the basic sequence of production activities at the level of work required to be done, and the fabrication techniques employed, are assumed to be properties in common for assembly plants in every region of the world. Nothing is made of this incongruity, although the authors of the IMVP survey do introduce some important qualifications, under the headings of vertical integration, model specification and actual working time per employee. These we now consider.

(i) Vertical integration

The first hinges on the extent to which general production activities are forward integrated into final assembly plants. This will vary depending on the extent to which component parts and sub-assemblies are brought in ready made from outside sites, or built up within the factory itself, and would pose a problem for any productivity comparisons based on a direct calculation of the hours of assembly plant labour employed to build a car. Krafcik (1988a: 3), for example, in explaining the index of labour input used in the IMVP survey, notes that whereas North American and European assemblers were wont to produce their own seats, in Japan this activity was almost always carried out by the assembly plant's suppliers. Thus if all plant employees were included in a survey intended to compare the labour used to build cars in different assembly plants, plants making their own components would employ more labour for reasons unconnected with work (say) on the final assembly line. At any moment in time the number of workers on site is greater than need otherwise be, and 'apples', in the familiar phrase, are not being compared with 'apples'. To overcome this difficulty, the tack adopted in the IMPV survey was to elicit data from assemblers on the number of workers directly employed only in previously identified tasks – 'standard activities' – based on a list of both major assembly and sub-assembly operations deemed representative of those carried out in most plants (see Krafcik 1988a: 3–4; Womack et al. 1990: 80–81).[3] In this way, an attempt was made to establish common bounds for sampled plant activity.

This takes us to the first of several generally overlooked points. In formulating its index of labour input the IMVP survey obtained data on workers directly engaged in the chosen set of 'standard activities', such as, for example, on the number of workers assigned to the car assembly line to apply interior trim. But 'indirect' workers are also employed in assembly plants to support or supervise 'direct' assembly work, such as, for example, in material handling or inspection activities. And to take account of this second category of worker, a pro-rata allowance was made. The way in which this was done is best understood by means of an arithmetic illustration. Suppose on a daily basis a plant hires 2000 direct and 1500 indirect employees, and that half of all workers in the former category are engaged in the 'standard activities'. Following the procedure used in the IMVP survey there would be 1000 relevant direct workers: the pro-rata allowance for indirect workers would be this number times the ratio of all indirect plant workers to all direct plant workers.[4] The relevant total would then be 1000 + (1500/2000)(1000) workers: 1750 in total.

The significance of this is two-fold. The control for vertical integration that was adopted in the IMVP survey is not a watertight one. Consider, for example, the loading of component parts onto a truck at a supplier's site, which is driven to a car assembly plant, where it is unloaded, and the parts moved on. All of these activities could be undertaken by workers hired by the assembly plant, but some or all could also be undertaken by employees of the supplier, or of a third-party contractor: the degree to which indirect activities are forward integrated into a final assembly plant is not functionally tied to the distribution of direct assembly work. The sort of pro-rata allowances made in the IMVP survey methodology for indirect workers would potentially bias the observations in any manufacturing study. But more interesting, perhaps, is that this device does not sit well with the literature on Toyota and other Japanese car assemblers as it had developed up to this point: a great deal was made in the 1980s of the economies a Toyota-like production regime could realize in the area of indirect support activities, notably in materials handling and inspection. Indeed, in their own account of lean production, Womack et al. (1990) emphasize this as a main area of comparative disadvantage for Western 'mass producers'.[5] In this context, the decision to treat indirect plant activity as if a simple reflex to direct assembly work, rather than as a set of separately investigable functions, is incongruous.

(ii)   Model specification
The second qualification is an acknowledgement of the fact that the labour input used to assemble a car is liable to be affected by model specification. In this regard, the relevant dimensions identified for the IMVP survey were the number of welds in a car body, car length, width and height, and differences in the individual equipment loading, reflecting the view that as weld content or size increases, the number of workers, or the time workers take, to undertake assembly will increase, while adding extra equipment to a car creates additional work. To deal with this, the basic estimate of labour input used by the IMVP survey was 'adjusted', by means of weights, in an attempt to control for these differences, on the grounds that 'it would make little sense to compare plants assembling vehicles of grossly different sizes and with differing amount of optional equipment . . . [without] adjusting the amount of effort in each plant as if a standard vehicle of a specified size and option content

were being assembled' (Womack et al. 1990: 81; see also Krafcik 1988a: 10–11). The adjustments in question have given rise to a great deal of controversy, as shown for example in the terms of a critical commentary by Williams et al. (1994) which we consider below. But the basic premise that differences in model specification can account for differences in the labour used to build cars is not controversial, *per se*.

This takes us to a second overlooked point. As we have had occasion to note, what is generally built down an assembly line in a car plant is not a single model specification, but rather a mix of model specifications. And while it is true that the range of specifications of the individual piece or component being assembled into the product may vary substantially at different points in the assembly process, depending on the particular specifications of the car line, it is reasonable to suppose that this type of part variety will have some effect on the labour employed to build a car. But the only aspects of model specification considered in the IMVP survey methodology were those which could be expressed as a *statistical average* over all members of a car line: the average number of body-welds, the average size of the car, the average equipment loading. What were abstracted from was differences in the number of model-specifications assembled – the number of different types of car body, the number of trim ratings, and so forth. This omission might be defensible if all that were being measured was the hours of labour input attributable to workers directly assigned to undertake assembly tasks: for these workers, it could be argued that substituting one set of components for another on a final assembly line (say) as a consequence of mixed assembly does not *significantly* change the assembly task (on which see Krafcik 1988a: 11; also ibid. 1989, who makes precisely this point). But again, however, the inclusion of 'indirect' support staff in the calculation complicates matters: as car line variety increases, the deployment of support staff may grow apace as handling, inspection and monitoring functions become more complex.[6]

(iii) Working time per employee

The last qualification on the uniformity of processes across assembly plants hinges on what Krafcik (1988a: 2) describes as 'social' factors in production. Given the headcount calculated on the basis of standard activities for direct workers, and the pro-rata allowance for indirect workers, a subtraction was made to allow for the effects of plant absenteeism, both scheduled and unscheduled and based on the assemblers' own estimates, on the number of workers retained by the plant. Similarly, the time spent working by operatives in a single standard shift was calculated net of planned relief times (or breaks), allowing for the likelihood of widely differing relief time allowances across surveyed plants. In other words, it was recognized that both absenteeism and relief might be outside the immediate control or jurisdiction of assembly plant managers; and an attempt was made to isolate differences in the labour input used to build cars as a result of different modes of organization in production from these wider influences, by netting out their likely consequences.

We now come to a third overlooked point, and a very important one. No allowance was made in the IMVP survey for work (net of relief times) carried out by individual assembly plant operatives in excess of a *single* standard shift. But the estimates thus arrived at of the hours of labour input forthcoming in the performance of standard activities was then divided though by a *daily* output of cars.

To see why this would be a major issue in any study seeking to compare input–output relationships across a large number of manufacturing sites, let us consider again our previous arithmetic example. Let us suppose as before that 1750 plant employees have been identified as involved in the standard set of assembly tasks, including the pro-rata allowance for 'indirect' activities. Since absenteeism is also accounted for, let us assume that this falls to 1500 available workers. In the first instance, let us assume that there is no overtime and that workers perform a single shift. Suppose that in a single shift 200 cars are finished in this assembly plant, and that the average shift is eight hours after allowing for planned relief times (breaks). If the plant operates for two shifts per day then daily output is 400 cars. On the basis of the sort of calculation described above, and before any 'adjustment' for model specification, the basic measure of the hours of assembly plant labour used to build a car would in this example be calculated as $(8 \times 1500)/400 = 30$ hours per car built.

Suppose as an illustrative thought experiment we now compare the same plant under a quite different arrangement *vis-à-vis* shift work and overtime. Let us assume that there is overtime and all workers currently perform a double shift. This we can assume is reflected in the number of on-site workers retained by the assembler. Suppose for simplicity that as a result this falls by exactly half. This is obviously not a necessary assumption, since all that is required to establish an arithmetic bias in the sort of procedure described above is that employment is lower as a result. With absenteeism running at the same rate, the headcount is now 750 workers. An accurate assessment of the hours of assembly plant labour used to build a car would find no change, since the correct estimate would be $(16 \times 750)/400 = 30$ hours per shift. But if no allowance is made for double-shift working, and we assume that all workers in the headcount only work a single shift, this halves to give $(8 \times 750)/400 = 15$ hours per car built. There is now an undercount, equal to 15 hours for each car built. The possibility that arithmetic biases of this type may be present casts a quite different light on the interpretation of the IMVP survey findings. The detail of our example is obviously less important than the basic issue: we need not suppose that all workers do in fact work double shifts – but the industry is nonetheless one marked both by complex shift patterns and by overtime (paid or unpaid). We will return to this point.

4.2.2 Labour Hours and Automation

Before considering this issue, however, there is a second major problem with the received view involving the interpretation of the relationship uncovered by the IMVP survey between differences in the hours of assembly plant labour used to build cars, and differences in the estimated levels of assembly process automation. We will consider the measure of assembly plant automation that was employed for this purpose in the next section, but the received view on this matter is that (a) differences in levels of assembly plant automation, while not irrelevant, were demonstrated to be of secondary importance when accounting for plant level differences in the number of workers hours used to build cars in sites around the world, and (b) that Japanese car assembly plants as a regional bloc were demonstrated on this basis to be particularly productive, even after allowing for typically high levels of automation. And indeed this is the empirical basis for what Womack et al. (1990: 94) call their 'simple axiom', namely that lean organization is a prerequisite to successful plant automation.

It is instructive to consider this further. When plotted on a graph with the calculated input of labour hours used per car built on the vertical axis, and estimated levels of factory automation on the horizontal, the data obtained by the IMVP survey was suggestive of an overall relationship between the two variables. But at the same time, assembly plants in Japan were clearly very highly automated when compared to plants in other regions covered by the survey: North America, Europe, Australia, and the Newly Industrializing Countries (NICs) – Brazil, Mexico, South Korea and Taiwan. Indeed, even the least automated of the Japanese assembly plants surveyed – the plant in fact selected by Womack et al. as the most 'efficient' plant in the world – still achieved a very high score on automation compared to most car assembly plants elsewhere in the world. In stylized terms, the basic shape of the data could be visualized, following Coffey and Thornley (2006a), in terms of Figure 4.1. While observations as a whole were distributed across a wide area, represented here by W, Japanese observations clustered in the bottom right-hand corner of the scatter, represented here by the region J. Interested readers can compare this with the actual scatter published in Womack et al. (1990: 95, see also Krafcik 1989).

All else being equal, this would evidently suggest that automation played a very important role in accounting for Japan's typically low score on the labour hours index used in the IMVP survey, *vis-à-vis* assembly plants elsewhere in the world. But some elementary statistical analysis, reported in Womack et al. (1990: 94), found that while passing a 'best-fitting' line through the sample of observations did indeed establish a statistically significant relationship of the expected sign, variation in estimated levels of automation seemed to account for only about one-third of the total variation in the hours

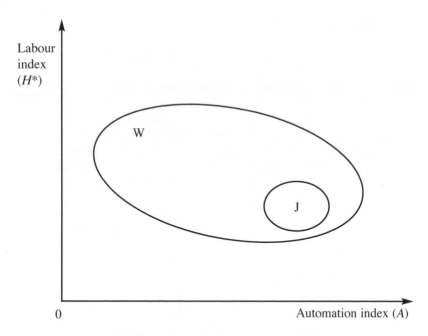

Source: (adapted from Coffey and Thornley (2006a)).

Figure 4.1   A stylized data assessment

of assembly plant labour used to build cars in plants around the world, as measured (one assumes) by the R^2-statistic for the simple regression.

On this basis, automation was downplayed as a major determining factor for the hours of assembly plant labour used to build cars in plants around the world, and the IMVP survey findings were duly interpreted in terms of a simple comparison of output-weighted regional labour input averages. For Japanese-owned plants in Japan, this was 16.8 hours for each car built; for US-owned plants in North America, 24.9 hours; for European plants in Europe, 35.5 hours; for plants in the Newly Industrializing Countries (NICs), 41 hours; and so forth (Womack et al. ibid.: 85). The position of each region in this ranking, and of intra-regional variations in 'productivity', was in turn interpreted as being reflective of the existing dissemination of lean methods.

It would, however, have been possible to draw a quite different inference from the same set of data, even if going no further than visual inspection of the scatter and simple regression, and putting other issues to one side. Because what was immediately evident from this data – even to Womack et al. – was that the highest scores on the labour hours index at each and every level of automation typically fell to car assembly plants located in Europe.

Car assembly plants in Europe with high levels of automation certainly seemed to perform differently from plants with similarly high levels of automation in Japan; but by the same token, they also performed less well than similarly automated sites in North America, Australia, and even, for that matter, in most of the NICs. Judged solely on the basis of the IMVP survey findings, and as even remarked upon by Womack et al. (1990, see ibid.: 86), Europe was clearly distinguished as a region by apparently 'weak' results, as gauged against the scores of assembly plants in this region on the labour input index. But if due account had been taken of this when analysing the data, a much bigger role could clearly have been ascribed to automation when accounting for the relative performance of plants in Japan in the IMVP survey compared with plants elsewhere. The point here can again be captured visually, by reference to Figure 4.2. In order to separate out a possible bias in the analysis of the importance of automation arising from one differently performing region, the observations on the hours of assembly plant labour used to build cars and on automation could have been quite reasonably divided into two sets, one for Europe, and one for the rest of the world (ROW). If a best-fitting line had then

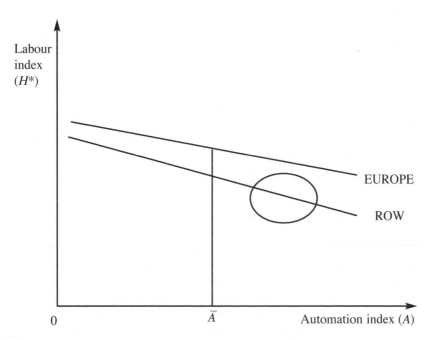

Source: (adapted from Coffey and Thornley (2006a)).

Figure 4.2   A stylized comparison of regions

been passed through each, the result would be as shown: the regression line for Europe would lie above the regression line for sites elsewhere.

But from this perspective, the interpretation of the data would necessarily have to change. Why assembly sites based in Europe should have performed so badly in the MIT survey is obviously an interesting question in its own right, but so far as the rest of the world is concerned, then on the face of things a much higher explanatory value could have been attached to the role of automation than Womack et al. were prepared to do. Indeed, if the data for Europe had been taken separately from that for everywhere else, 'evidence' of a lean revolution would have been much harder to find, because on the face of things assembly plants in Japan would have been distinguished from plants in North America, Australia, and even most of the NICs, first and foremost on the basis of automation. To gauge the likely importance of automation – and again abstracting from other difficulties – after making allowance in this way for the possibly distorting effects of Europe, one might simply look again at the R^2 statistics. On the basis of some experimentation with data similar to the data published in the MIT survey report – as set out in Womack et al. (1990: 94–5) – automation would have looked like a much more important influence in accounting for variation in the hours of labour imputed to the manufacture of cars: it would have accounted for something closer to three-quarters of the sampled variation. Sites located in Europe would have scored somewhere in the region of one-third again as many labour hours per car built than sites else-where, after taking account of regional differences in automation.[7] But so far as car assembly plants in Japan (or Japanese transplants in North America, also identified in the Womack et al. scatter) were concerned, when compared to other plants outside of Europe, evidence of organizational superiority, as opposed to high automation, would have been very hard to come by. On the basis of the unsophisticated but defensible technique of looking at the residuals computed from the exercise in simple regression, it is unclear on what basis Japan would have looked 'organizationally' superior.[8]

4.2.3   Assessment and Interpretation

But it is at this point that the problems noted above must be considered. Of these, the one which looks (on balance) the most important on *a priori* grounds is the systemic bias that would be introduced to any survey that multiplies an employment total by the hours worked in a single non-overtime shift to get an estimate of labour input to production, in an industry where multi-shift working and over-time are common. The question naturally arises as to whether and how this is likely to have impacted on the observations made both at plant level, and also across regions, *vis-à-vis* the likely bias in the estimate made of the hours of stan-dard activities labour used per car. For example, two obvious candidates that spring to mind are: (i) the recent growth trajectory of the facility, and (ii) work-place-specific overtime and shift arrangements. Where a facility has experienced recent growth, it seems likely enough that part of this will be accommodated through higher overtime rates for workers, given the likely preferences of the existing workers, and the costs of hiring and training; conversely, for similarly obvious reasons, where there has been a downturn in demand it is likely that at least part of this will be met through reduced overtime rates. At the same time, workplace-specific overtime and shift arrangements will also count: propensities for workers to work long hours may be more notable in some cases than others.

From the viewpoint of reinterpreting the IMVP survey findings, therefore, there are two different issues. A reasonable case can be made that Japanese car assembly plants looked globally exceptional at the level of site automation, but less so at the level of differences in labour input not ascribable to automation. But in addition, the detail provided by J.F. Krafcik on the design of the survey points to the possibility of a systemic bias in the labour input measure, one which in turn might just as reasonably have been expected to influence results both by plants and by regions. Other factors, including a less than watertight control for vertical integration, might also of course be important for some plants, or groups of plants, but so far as mounting a case for a radical reinter-pretation of results is concerned, the first set of issues are sufficient to point to a quite different reading of the IMVP survey data. We consider this in more detail below, after first confirming some of the details alluded to.

4.3 THE IMVP WORLD PRODUCTIVITY SURVEY: FORMAL STRUCTURES

In this section we consider the formal structure of the indices of assembly plant automation and labour productivity used in the IMVP assembly plant productivity survey in more explicit detail, in support of the preceding commentary. The analysis is as before, but grounded now in a more formal discussion of variables: we reiterate the critique outlined above *vis-à-vis* shifts and work practices in this context. At the same time, we fulfil more generally the commitment given in the introduction to show why some of the remark-able work undertaken in this survey deserves credit. The relevant sources referred to in this section are the same as before, but now with more emphasis on the contribution of J.F. Krafcik. Others are also discussed.

4.3.1 The Krafcik Automation Index

The structure of the automation index referred to in Womack et al. (1990), in their statistical analysis of the IMVP survey data, has been more or less ignored in subsequent discussions, and its form is worth noting briefly. This index is explained in Krafcik (1988b), but while entirely clear the exposition is literary, while our preferred mode of presentation in this section is to be explicit. Without deviating in any way from Krafcik, we might therefore write the index as follows:

$$A = \sum_j w_j X_j \qquad w_j > 0 \text{ for all } j \text{ and } \sum_j w_j = 1 \qquad (4.1)$$

For each sampled plant, a 'total automation index' was constructed using a weighted average of a series of individual measures of automation calculated for the different main stages of the car assembly process. This is represented in (4.1) thus. A is the weighted sum of the individual automation measures. The value of the measure as calculated for each stage j is denoted by X_j: w_j is the corresponding weight applied to each stage, in each case strictly positive and summing up to unity and based on the proportionate distribution of employment in a 'representative' plant (in fact constructed from the average distribution of employment in the survey sample). The individual stages in question were the body shop (welding), paint shop (sealing and surface coating), and trim and final assembly. The individual details on how automation was calculated at each stage are both interesting and ingenious. For example, for installation of trim and final assembly, Krafcik identifies 44 individual process steps, with values assigned to each step of 1 or 0 depending on whether the step was performed via automation (1) or manually (0). The overall level of automation – or total automation – therefore increases with A. One interesting feature of an automation index like that set out in (4.1) is that it supposes that there are no bottlenecks in production that are cleared (or exacerbated) by automation. This follows from the use of given weights: regardless of what is happening in other sections of the plant, the weight attached to any particular section is unaffected. A corollary to this is that automation is assumed only to affect immediately displaced workers. For this reason an index like (4.1) is necessarily an imperfect one.

4.3.2   The Krafcik Labour Input Index

We set this out in order to emphasize that the question of automation, since practically ignored in discussions of lean production, was integral to the original survey. The corresponding index of labour input to assembly can also be succinctly displayed:

$$H_j^* = a_j H_j + b_j \qquad \text{where } a_j > 0 \text{ and } -a_j H_j < b_j < 0 \qquad (4.2a)$$

The constituent terms for the sampled plant j are as follows:

$$H = \left(\frac{l^*}{Q} \right) (h_s - r_s) \tag{4.2b}$$

where:

$$l^* = l_d^{sa}(1 + i/d)(1 - z) \tag{4.2c}$$

$$Q = nQ_s \tag{4.2d}$$

and:

l_d^{sa}	=	direct 'on-roll' workers assigned to standard activities
i/d	=	all 'on-roll' indirect workers to all 'on-roll' direct workers
z	=	absenteeism rate
n	=	number of shifts
Q_s	=	vehicles produced per shift
h_s	=	number of hours in a single shift
r_s	=	relief time in a shift

Using this notation, the structure of this index is most easily understood if we begin with its component parts, before considering its whole. And since we have already described its construction in matching terms, it is possible to be brief. Equation (4.2d) indicates a chosen output measure Q comprised of each plant's daily production of cars at the time of the survey, and equal to the number of cars produced in a shift (Q_s), multiplied by the number of shifts being worked at that time (n). Equation (4.2c) describes the corresponding assembly plant headcount, based on the number of workers retained by the plant ('on-roll', or registered on the plant books as employed by the plant) and directly assigned to the identified set of assembly tasks deemed to be 'standard activities' at most sites, l_d^{sa}. The pro-rata allowance for workers in supporting roles gives a revised headcount l^* equal to l_d^{sa} $(1 + i/d)$ (this is the allowance described in our earlier arithmetic example presented algebraically). A deduction is then made from this headcount based on the site absenteeism rate (z), referring in this context to both scheduled and unscheduled absences. The basic form of the 'unadjusted' Krafcik index of labour input to assembly is then as in (4.2b): the headcount l^* is divided by daily production Q and multiplied by the number of hours worked by each employee in a *single* shift (h_s), minus scheduled breaks (r_s). To fix its final form the basic index for each plant is then 'adjusted' on the basis of formula-constructed weights intended to capture model-specific features, to give (4.2a). One weight multiplies the basic unadjusted index, and an additive term completes the transformation.

Table 4.1 A formal equivalence of notations

The original Krafcik presentation of the IMVP hours formula is set out thus:

(1) $CSAP = (USAP)(WF)(PSF)(SAHE/SAE) + (USAP)(WF)(PSF)(SASE/SAE) - ECA$

where: $SAE = SAHE + SASE$

and SAE = standard activities employees
$SAHE$ = standard activities hourly employees
$SASE$ = standard activities salaried employees

Some elementary high-school algebra gives:

(2) $CSAP = (USAP)(WF)(PSF) - ECA$

where: $USAP = (SAE \times h)/(s \times v)$

and h = number of hours in a single shift minus relief time
s = number of shifts worked in a single day
v = number of cars made in a single shift
WF = weld factor
PSF = product size factor
ECA = equipment content adjustment
$USAP$ = uncorrected standard activities productivity
$CSAP$ = corrected standard activities productivity.

This can be rewritten using our alternative notation adopted in the main text:

(3) $H^* = a[l^* \times (h_s - r_s)]/Q + b$

where: a = $(WF)(PSF)$
b = $-ECA$
l^* = SAE
Q = $(s \times v)$
H^* = $CSAP$

This is the notational form employed in (4.2): it is formally identical to (1). The productivity measure is positive because restrictions are observed on a and b.

4.3.3 Notation

The minority of readers who have consulted the original explanation of this index in Krafcik (1988a) may object that it looks nothing like this. To establish that all that has been changed is notation, the one-to-one correspondence of terms is shown in Table 4.1. The reason for our rewriting the Krafcik formula is that the original explanation is rather opaque; a consequence perhaps of a desire to avoid an overly 'formal' presentation, with acronyms used to represent variables. We need not spend time spelling these out, but line (1) in Table 4.1 reproduces the Krafcik notation exactly: following through to line (3) sets out the corresponding terms using our own notation. A comparison of line (1) with the *formally identical* line (3) – line (3) is the same formula as spelled out above in (4.2a)–(4.2d) – establishes our simpler presentation, achievable in part via the expedient of collecting similar terms to simplify the algebra. Reading from top to bottom in Table 4.1 cumulatively defines all terms, and shows how these equate with the notations employed in (4.2a)–(4.2d), above. What is perhaps of most interest, when the formula for the labour input index is rewritten, is that the considerable *elegance* of its construction becomes far more obvious. The fact that the 'weights' applied to the unadjusted data (in Table 4.1 these take the form of two multipliers denoted by WF and PSF, and an additive term, ECA) effect a linear transformation is almost totally obscured in the original notation. The elegance of the construction, when brought out cleanly, vitiates any suspicion of carelessness.

4.3.4 Shift Work and Hours

It is therefore all the more surprising that no apparent consideration is given to the dangers of bias that could be introduced by a decision to divide a survey headcount through by data on a daily factory output, while weighting each worker only by the net hours worked in a *single* shift, given the prevalence of complex shift patterns and overtime work – both paid and unpaid – in the car industry.
Define:

$$x = h_s (1 + \theta) \text{ such that } \theta = \frac{x - h_s}{h_s} \tag{4.3}$$

where:

x = shift of average length net relief time plus proportionate extra work

This gives the actual hours worked by an assembly plant employee if it is allowed that workers may exceed a single shift in a day, whether this work is paid or unpaid. If workers work in excess of (or less than) a single shift, this will introduce a bias to the labour input measure used in the IMVP survey. The variable θ captures this: it is positive when workers work in excess of a single shift, zero if they work only a single shift, and negative if they are on short rations. If we use the word 'overtime' to capture all work beyond a single shift, then θ rises with overtime.

Define what we will refer to as the *bias factor* as follows:

$$B = \frac{l^*h_s - l^*h_s(1+\theta)}{Q} = -\frac{l^*}{Q}h_s\theta \qquad \text{where } B < 0 \text{ when } \theta > 0 \quad (4.4)$$

This gives the difference between the Krafcik measure of labour input to car assembly and the actual labour input, if account is taken of work in excess of a single shift, after allowing for scheduled relief times. B has a negative sign, so that it will take the opposite sign to θ, when this is not equal to zero. This means that if there is positive overtime, the Krafcik measure will be an *underestimate* of the hours of assembly plant labour used to build a car, and in the case of short rations, where there is not enough work to make up a full shift, it will be an *overestimate*. Only when θ is just zero will there be no bias in the measure. It is for this reason that we can think of B as the bias factor in the Krafcik labour input measure, and hence in the IMVP survey. Its effect would be consistent with the arithmetic example given in the preceding section.

4.3.5   Growth and Work Practices

In the preceding section we speculated that the most likely determinants of the size of this bias factor would be the immediate growth trajectory (positive or negative) of the assembly plant in question, and its existing work practices. We can express the same idea here, by making θ a function of these variables:

$$\theta = f\left(\frac{\dot{Q}}{Q}, C\right) \qquad \text{with } \theta \text{ increasing in } \frac{\dot{Q}}{Q} \text{ given } C \qquad (4.5a)$$

and hence:

$$B = -\frac{l^*}{Q}h_s f\left(\frac{\dot{Q}}{Q}, C\right) \qquad \text{with } B \text{ decreasing in } \frac{\dot{Q}}{Q} \text{ given } C \qquad (4.5b)$$

where $\dot{Q}/Q$ denotes the proportionate rate of change in Q for the relevant site, and C a vector of relevant workplace characteristics that impinge on overtime.

One other comment seems merited here. Other studies have proposed that changes in capacity utilization, as measured by proportionate rates of change in output, exert a statistically significant, and quite large, effect on the relationships between measured inputs and measured outputs in the car industry: in particular, even after taking account of corresponding changes in capital–output ratios, a higher rate of capacity utilization typically generates more output per worker hour. This proposition, to be quite clear on the point, is one which has been raised in the more general context of the larger literature on the car manufacture and assembly sector: the explanation given by the authors of the most sophisticated econometric studies takes the view that labour is a quasi-fixed factor, the services of which are more fully employed as plant and equipment gets utilized at higher levels, given prior investments.[9] It is important to note, however, that the bias factor expressed in (4.4) and (4.5) deals with something else entirely, and these quite different issues must not be confused. It is essential to be clear that if a higher rate of capacity utilization indicates more output per worker hour as measured via the Krafcik index as a consequence of a change in B, this will be because of an increase in the absolute size of the *measurement error*, not because of any 'real' change. The index would record a change because of a bias that is sensitive to changes in overtime and shift work *even if* the hours of labour actually used to perform the standard tasks were insensitive to changes in capacity utilization.

4.3.6   The IMVP Survey Questionnaire

Our assessment of these details of the IMVP study naturally relies on the accuracy of the originally published descriptions of each index employed in the analysis. The possibility, however, that J.F. Krafcik should have slipped at some point in his published accounts for the world industry (and a generation of commentators) without subsequent correction appears vanishingly small, and is not to be countenanced: the sheer elegance of the formulations as formal constructs vitiates the idea. Nonetheless, we might add in this connection, and at this juncture, that in the course of field research undertaken in the UK-based car industry near the time when the IMVP world assembly plant survey questionnaires were being distributed and filled, we were able both to inspect copies and to discuss responses with plant managers. While naturally not intending to go beyond what is in Krafcik's published explanations, we can testify both to the accuracy and the formidable preciseness of the latter: there is *no* doubt. In particular, the data obtained on plant employment would not permit an assessment of the size of the bias factor as set out in equations

(4.3)–(4.5) above: unless supplementary information were sought (of which we are unaware), then the effects of this potentially significant measurement error were not allowed for.

4.3.7   The Krafcik Methodology: Appreciation and Criticism

It is difficult not to admire the ingenuity shown in the Krafcik methodology, both from the viewpoint of its elegant formal structure, and of the manifestly impressive display of knowledge-in-depth of car assembly processes. To devise a survey questionnaire that would command respect from the world's car assemblers is difficult enough; but the procedure employed by Krafcik using the data thus obtained to effect a linear transformation in a basic labour input index for each plant using its own data on product characteristics in order to 'adjust' for model-specific features shows an almost extraordinary boldness of conception. At the same time, we have already observed that the formal structure of the Krafcik survey design owes little to the eminence awarded production concepts associated with Toyota MC, notwithstanding the weight given such concepts in Womack et al. (1990). Rather, it sits within a particular tradition in car assembly sector research, where there is a long history of studies that compared calculated labour inputs to assembly via formulae that try and 'adjust' for the industry's many complicating considerations.[10] In this connection, we wish to praise Caesar, rather than bury him.

In this chapter we are of course intent not only in admiring Krafcik's work, but in vigorously contesting received interpretations of the results thereby obtained. It seems likely, however, that one reason why this contest has not been hitherto vigorous is that critics have been side-lined by the complexities of the Krafcik methodology, and in particular by the attempts to adjust within for model-specific features. We might think of this as the 'red herring' effect: the 'adjustments' made in the Krafcik survey methodology for differences in weld-contents, car size and car equipment loadings – the difference between (4.2a) and (4.2b) above – attracted immediate and vociferous criticism, but some of the larger issues were perhaps lost sight of. It might be too that the somewhat complex notations employed by Krafcik did not help (for this reason we have elected not to dwell on the 'adjustments' controversy, and have taken care to reconsider the relevant formulae in easy stages so as to better allow discussion). But the most likely reason for the extraordinary success of the IMVP survey findings, as interpreted for a wider public by Womack et al. (1990), is that the claim that definitive evidence had been found of a manufacturing revolution in Japan accorded so well at the time with the expectations of the audience. The door was open.

4.4 LEAN PRODUCTION: CRITICAL ISSUES AND INFERENCES

In the introduction it was observed that it comes as a surprise to recall that the words 'lean production' were first coined in connection with an international survey of the car assembly sector, carried out in the closing part of the 1980s. In fact, the phrase was actually coined by J.F. Krafcik, to describe what was perceived to have been the findings of the IMVP survey (see Womack et al. 1990: 13). Our intent in this chapter is to argue that this received interpretation of the survey is awry. But it is perhaps worth pausing to note that even if our contra-interpretation were accepted in its entirety, it is likely that many of the academics and business commentators who are happy to use the words 'lean production' would still be prepared to deny that this in any way amounts to an effective rebuttal of the concept: indeed, it is not hard to predict that disassociations between the IMVP survey and lean production would be sought and asserted, in blank denial of the parentage of the latter. This in itself would not be without sociological interest, and the prediction is consistent with the wider themes of our own study: there is a great deal more to the reception accorded to a concept like lean production than can be explained solely by reference to what evidence will actually support when discussing developments in the car industry. And this is a point to which we will certainly return again, in later chapters. But be that as it may, lean production as a production concept has always lacked solid material support in the industry for which the phrase was coined – quite recently, and in the explicit context of the findings of the IMVP survey.

Nonetheless, there have been a number of commentaries on the IMVP survey by writers who are certainly fully aware of its significance in the short history of lean production as a production concept. An obvious question, therefore, is what shape formal assessment and criticism has taken, most particularly when avowedly critical in content and purpose: or, to put the same point differently, how do the propositions set out in the preceding sectors differ from existing critiques. To some extent what seems to have happened is that writers disposed to accept the IMVP survey findings on the basis of the estimation offered by the survey architects have done so; writers not so disposed have issued some voluble attacks, invigorating as polemic, but so sweeping in their dismissal that the survey's considerable merits have passed unnoticed, alongside possibilities for a positive reappraisal of findings.

Consider, for example, Williams et al. (1994: 206–15, 223–6), an influential critique which upon inspection does not really deal with the IMVP world survey, but rather a pilot case study (of the General Motors Framingham assembly plant and Toyota Takaoka; see ibid.: 211–14; also Womack et al. 1990: 80–82) for the survey, necessarily an incomplete basis upon which to arrive at a judgement. This is by no means to disregard the points Williams et al. make, and they score palpable hits: for example, Womack et al. are properly chastised (see Williams et al. ibid.: 223) for asserting rather than testing their hypothesis. But the IMVP world survey itself is summarily dismissed, as 'blooming, buzzing confusion' (ibid.: 210), without much in the way of mediating assessment; indeed, Williams et al. seem averse to the notion *per se* of a survey methodology applied on a large scale.[11] Their conclusions as a result of this particular orientation do not go as far as they might when assessing what could reasonably be inferred from the IMVP data. And more must be said.

Turning to salient points, perhaps the first to note is the non-correspondence noted in the introduction to this chapter between the formal construction of the resource measures used in the IMVP survey, and the 'theory' of lean production, as expounded both in Womack et al. (1990), and in a hundred books and articles since. What we have in mind here pertains to the treatment of 'indirect plant labour'. We can summarize the points made under this heading if we simply note that in the IMVP survey, as designed by Krafcik, indirect plant labour is not accorded any privileged status in the investigation of labour inputs to production, and the likely effects of component part variety on these particular workers is ignored. This would not preclude the possibility that a Toyota-like production regime (and Toyota is the relevant company from the viewpoint of the 'theory' of lean production) helps economize on indirect support workers, regardless of variety. However, the question was not deemed of sufficient interest to be isolated in the IMVP survey methodology – rather, a simple *ex post* accounting device was used to 'add' indirect support staff to a plant measure clearly focused on workers *directly* employed in car assembly. As a consequence, the control adopted in the survey for vertical integration was by no means watertight, while relevant types of automation were only partly measured.

So far as the general question of investment is concerned, Coates (2000: 26) points to a number of careful studies (including Thurow 1992 and Baumol 1994) which establish a marked difference in rates of investment in plant and equipment through the 1970s and 1980s between rapidly growing regions like Japan – where investment was notably high – and more slowly growing regions of the industrial world. A number of economists, looking at Japan as a whole, have indeed argued that this is partly what makes Japan distinctive from the viewpoint of economic theory:

> Neoclassical economists, both in Japan and elsewhere, had urged post-war Japan to specialize in labour intensive industries and to eschew capital intensive industries like automobiles. However, G.C. Allen, one of the first European economists . . . to study Japan intensively, pointed out that the advice of MITI prevailed within the Japanese governments, rather than that given by the Bank of Japan: 'Some of the advisors were engineers who had been drawn by the war into the management of

public affairs. They were the last people to be guided by the half-light of economic theory. Their instinct was to find a solution for Japan's post-war difficulties on the supply side, in enhanced technical efficiency and innovations in production. They thought in dynamic terms. Their policies were designed to furnish the drive and to raise the finance for an economy that might be created rather than simply to make the best use of the resources it then possessed.' (Freeman and Soete 1999: 154 citing Allen 1981: 74)

In this context, it is not surprising that the IMVP assembly plant survey discovered that Japanese sites were very highly automated as a bloc. Gronning (1995: 411–12), for instance, summarizing work carried out by Japanese researchers for the car industry, observes that Toyota's investments in plant and equipment was relatively large compared to other car assemblers in the 1980s; a spending pattern which accelerated in the later 1980s, as also for other Japanese assemblers. While investment in plant and equipment can mean many things, the IMVP discovery that assembly process automation was particularly advanced in Japan is a consistent finding.

But at the same time, it is also clear that 'automation' has not emerged as the 'big' story when the IMVP survey results were published. Freeman and Soete (1999), for example, in a preamble to the above passage, suggest that lean production, like high rates of investment more generally, reflects a predisposition in Japan to focus on labour saving innovations in production as a policy imperative. In a manner analogous to the role awarded engineers in advisory capacities at state level in accounting for high overall rates of Japanese investment (and indeed for the initial decision to invest in a capital-intensive industry like the car industry), Freeman and Soete attribute the 'intense effort' to save labour in Toyota factories to the involvement of engineers in the workplace: 'the close involvement of engineers with production workers facilitated numerous small innovations' (ibid.: 154). Since Freeman and Soete have no particular axe to grind on this issue, we can take this inference as nicely illustrative of how successful the received account has been. Our own view, by contrast, is that lean production is a chimera: even on a 'face-value' reading of the data, the data collated in the IMVP survey points to displacement via aggressive automation, rather than via a new style of management and plant organization, as the basis for the expulsion of manual labour from Japanese car assembly.

But this, of course, is not the end of it, and a 'face-value' reading will not do. Here we must invoke what we have called the bias factor in the IMVP survey. Suppose in this regard one were to ask the following question: of all the assembly plants in the world, which would be most likely to have benefited, in the late 1980s, from a biased count of labour hours to assembly, if the size of this bias were a function of growth rates and working practices? Given the likely direction of the influence of these latter, one might reasonably answer – car assembly plants in Japan.

So far as prior growth rates are concerned, the late 1980s saw 'abnormally high growth' in the domestic Japanese market for cars, with an 'explosion' in sales between 1987 and 1991. From a steady rate of expansion, of between 2 and 3 percent per annum, sales accelerated to rates which generated an average yearly increase in the region of 500,000 units – the peak year coming in fact in 1990, with over 7.7 million domestic sales; and in the same year, domestic car production, with buoyant overseas sales, also hit a peak, at around 13.8 million units. This pertains to Japan as a whole, but in the particular case of Toyota, for example, the pattern through this period was broadly similar: a steep escalation in domestic sales, albeit with a less exaggerated movement in domestic production, rising by just over half a million units between 1982 and 1990, to 4.21 million units (see Kawahara 1998: 237). This was also a period of positive growth in Japanese sales overseas. And so far as working practices are concerned, Japanese overtime was proverbial:

> Long work hours are a defining feature of Japanese manufacturing. In Japan, manufacturing workers average 2,088 working hours per year compared to 1,989 in Britain, 1,957 in the United States, 1,646 in France, and 1,638 in Germany. Japanese workers take an average of 7.9 holidays per year compared to 9.2 in the United States, 25 in Britain, 29 in France and 27.9 in Germany. Working hours are even longer for Japanese automobile workers who average more than 2,100 hours annually, hundreds of hours more than their counterparts in the United States and Europe but less than Korea where manufacturing workers average 2,400 plus hours per year. This represents on-the-job hours only and does not include the large number of hours devoted to after-work socializing. In addition, overtime is mandatory in Japan. A 1986 survey by the All Toyota Union found that approximately 124,000 of its total members suffer from chronic fatigue. (Kenney and Florida 1993: 264)

The materials drawn upon for this passage are sourced to the years just before and just after the IMVP survey. In reporting on field-work carried out amongst Japanese managers in the manufacturing sectors, Kenney and Florida emphasize what is referred to elliptically above – 'massive amounts of overtime' (ibid.: 330). Even higher estimates of average hours working in Japan – the difference may in part be ascribed to what is and is not included in the Kenney and Florida figures – are presented in Coates (2000: 131), who asks: 'in what other advanced capitalist economy could a government survey (in 1992) report that one in six male manufacturing employees then worked more than 3,100 hours annually, and add that to work more than 3,000 hours (or 60 hours a week) was potentially lethal?'. The point need not be further laboured: Japanese workers work long hours, and they work long hours both in manufacture as a whole, and in car assembly. Upon visiting Toyota at Takaoka in 1988, Williams et al. (1994: 211) found a plant working, like much of Japanese industry, 'well above notional full capacity thanks to bottleneck breaking and long hours of overtime'. This was near the time of the IMVP survey, and on this basis it would be hard to conclude other than that the bias factor – arising from a decision to weight each plant worker by a single non-overtime shift, while dividing through the resultant product by the total daily output of cars – would have been liable to underscore Japanese labour inputs to assembly, compared with other sites.

This naturally points to a very fundamental re-evaluation. As we have argued in the preceding sections, taking the IMVP world survey data on its own estimation indicates that assembly plants based in Europe employed more labour hours to perform a set of selected assembly plant activities than plants in the rest of the world, at the time of survey in the late 1980s. The same data does not, however, give any confidence in claims of Japanese organizational exceptionalism: after allowing for very high levels of assembly plant automation, Japanese car assemblers included in the survey – including plants managed by Toyota – do not seem to have differed systematically in their employment of labour from (non-Japanese) plants in North America, Australia, or, for that matter, most of the NICs. But if one also considers in this light the bias factor identified above (in (4.4) and (4.5)), it is possible to go one step further on this point. If Japanese sites were in any case 'privileged' because of a measurement bias in the IMVP survey, did the data collected actually point to an unexpected issue: were Japanese car assembly sites, by the latter part of the 1980s, and nearing the peak of the boom, struggling to convert hours of scheduled work into completed assembly tasks? In other words, did the IMVP survey, rather than uncover evidence of 'lean' production, as a matter of fact actually stumble across something quite different, to wit, plant level difficulties of a type that would have been otherwise masked – in the absence of world survey data of this kind – to the outside world by (i) high levels of automation, and (ii) long working hours.

It is tempting, naturally, to consider the converse in accounting for Europe as a differently performing region at the point when the IMVP survey was made. In observing long working hours, Coates (2000: 131) quotes Tabb (1995: 144) on data which shows a more than ten hour difference in the average working week in Japan versus Europe; considering this issue in reverse, then, could this help reconcile the IMVP survey findings with what appear otherwise to be striking anomalies? For example, French manufacture is currently held in high repute for its productivity measured against the conversion of hours spent at work into finished goods: at the same time, workers are observed to benefit from a *shorter* working year. This is true, and there is no real dispute here, whether one compares France against Japan or against North America (and indeed against neighbours like Great Britain). But in this case, why in the particular case of the IMVP world assembly plant survey should French sites – included, one imagines in the survey sample[12] – appear to have fared badly, at least on the received interpretation? Wherein lies the explanation?

4.5   CONCLUSIONS

The principal goal of this chapter has been to address the main empirical plank underpinning the concept of 'lean production' as popularized in Womack et al. (1990), and taken up subsequently in an enormous body of literature. The plank in question pertains to the notion that Japanese car assemblers as a bloc were shown in a major international survey, carried out in the late 1980s, to be so far ahead of the rest of the world in terms of their ability to make cars with fewer resources as to provide compelling evidence of a fundamental manufacturing revolution. Taking the evidence collated seriously, and giving due credit to the survey architects, we have argued that a quite contrary set of conclusions might have been drawn. First we dispute that evidence was ever presented to indicate that Japanese car assemblers possessed a discernible organizational advantage over Western competitors once due allowance was made for differences in measured levels of assembly plant automation. Second, we show that the data in question was biased in a way that could have been expected to benefit assembly plants that had recently experienced high rates of growth: on this basis, we suggest a prima facie case for considering whether correcting for this bias would in fact suggest that Japanese assemblers were at this point struggling to convert worker effort into finished cars, *vis-à-vis* Western competitors. We note that this would not preclude cost advantages accruing for a range of other reasons pertaining to assembly plant employment but, insofar as the ability of an assembler to convert hours of effort into finished goods is concerned, Womack et al. (ibid.) may have given an account inadvertently at odds with a more plausible interpretation, a point which is further developed in the next chapter on the reorganization of work at Toyota.

NOTES

1.   Simon cites Krafcik and Womack (1987) on a Californian joint venture between Toyota and General Motors – in fact the NUMMI venture commencing in 1984 – to highlight the productivity gains that might be had from a change in managerial organization for given levels of automation and with similar workers, and within a national context. But Simon's overall concern in this paper is with the comparative analysis of organizations and markets in economics, and not with the car assembly sector *per se*. Freeman and Soete, however, are concerned with transformations in this sector, and their chapter on this topic – others look at industrial innovations in electricity and steel, oil and chemicals, synthetic materials, and electronics and computers – is nicely illustrative of the influence of Womack et al. We have already encountered Freeman and Soete, in the introductory chapter to our own book.

2.   One oddity in Womack et al. (1990), which has been noted by other writers, is that while the summary findings of the IMVP survey are presented, *vis-à-vis* estimates made both of the hours of labour used to build cars and on levels of factory automation, there is no accompanying detail on how these estimates were constructed, or at least not in a way that facilitates precise assessment: for this, the Krafcik papers must be consulted.

3. For the main assembly stages this list included: welding the main body panels; cleaning the body, sealing its joints, and providing a primer and topcoat for painting after electrolytic treatment; dressing the engine, fitting wheel and tyre assemblies, installing basic equipment, seats and glass, and applying interior and exterior trim. For sub-assemblies it included the manufacture of components like bumpers, struts, wheel and tyre assemblies, and clutch and brake-pedal arrangements. Other activities – for example, assembling body harnesses – were netted out as non-standard activities. A good account is given in Krafcik's overviews.

4. In identifying the relevant types of 'indirect' workers Krafcik (1988: 3–4) chose to exclude all commercial workers, product engineers, purchasers, and 'residual' non-production related personnel like security guards, amenities personnel, 'customs' officers, or fire and safety officers. The relevant categories of indirect workers would then be principally constituted in materials handling, inspection and supervisory functions.

5. For example: 'indirect workers became ever more prominent in Fordist, mass-production factories as the introduction of automation over the years gradually reduced the need for assemblers' (see Womack et al. 1990: 32); 'a classic mass-production environment with its many dysfunctions . . . the aisles next to the assembly line . . . were crammed with what we term indirect workers – workers on their way to relieve a fellow employee, machine repairers en route to troubleshoot a problem, housekeepers, inventory runners' (ibid.: 78); and so forth.

6. At one point the present writer saw in these points the most fundamental basis for criticism of the IMVP survey results. In an early comment (see Coffey 1995) the point was illustrated as follows. Data for two separately assembled car lines was obtained which generated the following observations. In one factory, 84 bodies and 68 engines were incorporated into the car line, and on the other 5 bodies and 9 engines (the details of the construction here are less important than the general points – but the definitions employed for 'bodies' and 'engines' in this exercise were fairly broad, although not exhaustive). Both car lines comprised units of a similar size, and weld contents were also similar: the average number of welds per car body in the first instance was 4480, while in the second it was 4420. The more complex car line, however, made a more extensive provision for factory-fit options. But given the similarities in two of the three model-specification indicators, the IMVP survey methodology would have tended to treat both car lines as not hugely different at the level of model specifications, notwithstanding that one line was much more varied than the other. The more varied car line was also built in a more automated facility, so that a comparison of labour content (the data was for hours of direct assembly work per car, but gross of relief times) found that the simpler set of products were built with 10 percent more direct assembly labour; however, when a pro-rata allowance was made for 'indirect' support work, the ranking was reversed, and the low-tech simple car line was built with 5 percent less assembly plant labour. This the author attributed, at the time, to the effects of model variety on support staff numbers. As will be clear, however, the position now taken is that while an important consideration that might make a series difference in some plant-by-plant comparisons, there are other issues that vitiate the received interpretation of the IMVP survey findings even if is disregarded.

7. The sort of decomposition in mind here would be as follows. If $\bar{H}^*$ and $\bar{A}$ denote the average values taken by each variable for a sample of observations, and α and β are the estimated intercept and coefficient terms from an exercise in simple regression, two separate regressions (one on Europe-based plants and one on the rest of the world) could be employed to construct a simple decomposition of differences in $\bar{H}$ as follows:

$$\bar{H}^*_R - \bar{H}^*_E = (\alpha_R - \alpha_E) + (\beta_R - \beta_E)\,\bar{A}_E + (\bar{A}_R - \bar{A}_E)\,\beta_R \qquad (*)$$

Subscripts distinguish Europe-based plants ('E') and rest of world plants ('R'). In this particular instance, since the difference between the overall average levels of automation for Europe based and rest-of-world based plants does not seem large, the last term can be ignored. The remainder decomposes differences in the average labour input used in assembly (that is to say, the difference between $\bar{H}^*_R$ and $\bar{H}^*_E$) into a difference between estimated intercepts ($\alpha_R - \alpha_E$) and a difference between estimated coefficients ($\beta_R - \beta_E$) (weighted by A_E). Data similar to that displayed in the Womack et al. (1990: 95) scatter of observations for the IMVP survey findings suggests that final assembly plants located in the European region built cars with around one third as much again labour input as in the rest of the world, after allowing for differences in average levels of plant automation: about half of this, taking the approach set out in this note, would be attributable to a difference in intercepts, and about half to a lower 'return' to automation, if this is how one interprets $\beta_R < \beta_E$.

8.   We have in mind here an unsophisticated but defensible technique of looking at the sign and size of the residuals computed from an exercise in simple regression. An observation on the regression line (with a residual exactly equal to zero) would imply that the corresponding assembly plant is using just the expected hours of labour to build a car, if it differed from other plants in the sample only in its level of factory automation: an observation lying above the line (with a positive residual) would indicate that more labour was being used than expected, and conversely for an observation lying below the line. Too much should not be made of this given the problems we go on to raise about the manner in which shift work was handled in the IMVP survey, but using similar data and excluding the observations corresponding to Europe failed to provide any indications that Japanese assembly plants as a group differed from plants elsewhere: some used more labour than expected, others less, given their typically high levels of automation (see Coffey 2003: 50–51). The point is not to recommend this method (but see Barrow and Wagstaff 1995; see also Krafcik 1989), as much as to note that the assertions made in Womack et al. (1990) are manifestly leading ones.

9.   A leading example here is given by the results reported in Fuss and Waverman (1992), a sophisticated econometric study of comparative productivity growth rates in the North American, Japanese and Western European car industries in the 1970s and 1980s. Allowing for differential rates of capacity utilization (assumed proportionate to year on year rates of change in the total numbers of units built), Fuss and Waverman were able to re-estimate differences in comparative rates of productivity growth in a way which established that capacity utilization plays a significant role in international comparisons. Not surprising, they found that Japanese assemblers maintained higher rates of utilization throughout: their estimated difference in productivity levels after allowing for this effect still showed an advantage to Japanese assemblers, but smaller than generally suspected. One possible criticism that might be levelled at the Fuss–Waverman methodology, in common with Krafcik's, is that no attempt is made here either to consider car line complexity issues.

10. A good starting example here for other studies in this lineage would be the earlier projects of W.J. Abernathy and collaborators (see Abernathy et al. 1981, 1983), which attempt to make 'adjustments' for factors like vehicle size and vertical integration: a review of some of the problems with this type of study is given in Fuss and Waverman (1992, op. cit.).

11. The points Williams et al. (1994) make also include the following: 'Krafcik's results are difficult to interpret because . . . [they] do not clearly and separately focus on individual plants, companies or sectors . . . [but] present results for bundles of plants grouped by region of operation and by region of origin of the company which owns this plant. Krafcik thus compares American-owned plants in America with Japanese-owned plants in America, but does not identify or compare individual plants, companies or sectors' (ibid.: 210). But while companies were certainly rendered anonymous, the survey in question was clearly a plant-level survey, carried out for the car assembly sector, while the reference to 'bundling' ignores the publication of scatters for most of the data. And in the rush to dismiss, the finer details of the Krafcik methodology are missed: for example, the 'adjustments' to the data to allow for differences in plant-level model specification are described as based on 'cumulative subtraction' (ibid.: 209), when in fact the procedure was one of linear transformation. But more important is that some of the important issues raised by Williams et al. are not developed to their best advantage – 'long hours of overtime' in the Japanese car industry being one.

12. If one considers the composition of the 'Europe'-based part of the IMVP survey sample we might note one further possibility that can be thrown into the pot *vis-à-vis* difficulties with the received interpretation of the findings: some of these 'poorly' performing sites – at least

if one takes the findings on the estimation set out in Womack et al. (1990) – may in fact have been Japanese transplants to Europe. Womack et al. (1990: 85) claim that data was collected in the IMVP survey on 22 separate sites in Europe, of which 13 were 'European', and 9 North American or Japanese transplants to Europe: only 18 of these are displayed in the accompanying scatter of observations also provided and 4 are 'missing' (see ibid.: 94–5). No explanation is given, but as a matter of arithmetic this means that an appreciable subset of the Europe-based sample was in fact comprised of transplants from regions with ostensibly 'better performing' sites: that is, between 5 and 9 of the 18 Europe-based sites were either North American or Japanese. If the 4 'missing' sites do not include all of the Japanese transplants surveyed, then some of the (ostensibly) 'badly performing' sites must have been Japanese owned. This in itself would be very damaging to credibility: it is notable that in the scatter no attempt is made to differentiate the Europe-based sites by region of origin (whereas by contrast for the North American observations transplants are clearly indicated).

5. Back to the future: the reorganization of work at Toyota

Whilst Toyota Motor's economic performance is widely regarded as superior, its employees are also believed to be operating under high pressure. As at virtually all assembly lines, the physical working conditions are tough. Assembly workers operate under a tight time schedule on which they have no influence, and perform repetitive tasks at a high pace. (Benders and Morita 2004:435)

Toyota has developed an approach to boost morale in an assembly plant by (1) redesigning the assembly plant into many split-lines and (2) improving working conditions by introducing ergonomic measures to alleviate fatigue.
   Toyota promotes these improvements to forestall labour shortages in its plants. (Monden 1998:xvi)

5.1   INTRODUCTION

It is hardly a secret that when reference is made to flexible manufacture or lean production in the Japanese car industry, the company at the forefront of the commentator's mind is most likely to be Toyota MC, a point that we have had occasion to note more than once when disputing the considerable literature which lays claim to the view that Japan has been at the epicentre of a revolution in the basic organizing principles of manufacture in this industry. At the same time, the company itself remains nonetheless a significant international manufacturer with a global impact and presence, and its internal evolution as a producer is for this reason of considerable intrinsic interest, even if claims of a major comparative advantage in process 'flexibility' and resource (labour) 'productivity' have not been shown – as the preceding chapters contend – to be well-founded. Moreover, it is by no means a static organization, and by the 1990s it had become evident that some important changes were underway in the design and management of work, in the latter stages of production at least, in Toyota's car assembly plants. We are interested, in this chapter, in these changes, and most particularly in the introduction to a Toyota car assembly plant of a 'segmented' assembly line, in which a conventional line is replaced by a larger number of 'mini-lines' connected by intra-process buffers. Since Toyota's first experiments in this regard it has been evident that the persistent characterization of the company as one which treats all deposits of semi-processed parts or products as the visible symptoms of 'waste', and planned reliance on buffers and stocks as demonstrated inefficiency, is at odds with revealed facts on the assembly line: it is now apparent that Toyota has attempted to navigate problems affecting its capacity to produce effectively by experimenting with intra-process buffers. The context informing the onset of these experiments is an important one: at the height of the Japanese economic boom, Toyota experienced problems with its workers.

On these issues a controversy has duly arisen as to whether this means that the 'just-in-time' production principle popularly associated with Toyota has been wholly abandoned, locally revised, or maintained fully intact. Further to this, the explanation advanced by Toyota for this reorganization of the car assembly process – namely difficulties in recruiting and retaining workers for its car assembly plants – has heightened speculation about the limits of a Toyota-like system, from the viewpoint of worker tolerance: for example, in Sandberg (1995) an entire section is devoted to the phenomenon of Toyota's changing work regime, despite a principal focus on alternative work regimes of the sort experimented with by Volvo. While the majority of commentaries on the Toyota segmented assembly line appear to accept a departure from hitherto revered production principles at Toyota, albeit frequently with the proviso that the departure pertains to *one* aspect only of operations, a leading authority on the company, Yasuhiro Monden (1998), has set out a contra-proposition that *none* of the changes in the organization of production operations at Toyota is inconsistent as such with a just-in-time imperative. After a brief hiatus, following this first flurry of commentary, Benders and Morita (2004) have returned to the topic of the reorganization of operations at Toyota, with a valuable update on developments that raises anew the question of what one makes of the introduction of segmented assembly lines connected by intra-process buffers at Toyota.

We now review the terms of this controversy in order to show that it is possible to place the whole matter on an entirely different footing, while accepting the empirical facts of the case *vis-à-vis* changes to the assembly line. In this respect our intent in some ways parallels that in our earlier case example chapter (Chapter 3), but whereas there we encountered a situation where external observers seem locked in a state of denial as to the possibility of a damaging experience with just-in-time production, in this chapter we are concerned to show how quite different inferences and conclusions can be drawn from agreed empirical data once initial premises change.

In this vein we propose:

(a) that the reorganization of the assembly process at Toyota is best viewed as a possible disclosure of hitherto undisclosed problems with line-stoppages;

(b)   that this is an issue which is separable from preoccupations with just-in-time production, although one that is entirely consistent with a 'crisis of work'; and

(c)   that much might be gained from a comparison of Toyota's experiments with antecedent experiments in the West, as a basis for providing a properly constructed historical framework within which to better consider these issues.

It will be recognized that the first of these propositions offer a consistent perspective within which to locate the reinterpretation of global data in Chapter 4, a point to which we will naturally return, while with regards to the last we offer some generally relevant comments on 'team' versus 'task' work; but we commence in this chapter and in the first instance with some issues of operations management.

5.2   THE REORGANIZATION OF ASSEMBLY AT TOYOTA: OPERATIONS

From the point of view of initially establishing a description of the segmented car assembly line as introduced at Toyota, a newcomer to the topic could do worse that to commence with Monden's (1998) account, an expansively illustrated depiction and analysis by a writer with first-rate access to the company.[1] Monden describes the organization of the segmented line at the Toyota Kyushu plant, which commenced operations in December 1992, as comprising for the latter stages of production – after the painted body leaves the paint-shop – 11 functionally divided 'mini-lines', each 100 yards or so in length (over 90 metres): three trim-lines for electrical parts, two chassis lines, five 'further' assembly lines and an inspection line, each separated by an intra-process buffer. More recent descriptions concur with this, so the detail as such is not a point of controversy. A car undergoing assembly would pass progressively through each of these mini-lines, while spending time in between, in a successively more finished state, in the mediating buffers. The location of this particular experiment at Kyushu is perhaps worth noting, since the facility in question is frequently described as the Toyota 'laboratory' site. The plant is located in a different part of Japan from Toyota's traditional home-base.[2]

According to Monden (1998) Toyota's experiments with line segmentation are intendedly organized around fine groupings of functionally similar parts. For example, electrical parts might be grouped into three sub-categories – wire-related, instrument panel-related and pipe-related – each with its own mini-line. The hoped for outcome is that this will facilitate the job while enabling workers to 'better identify' with the process as a whole, thereby improving morale on each section, a step change supported by a series of ergonomic measures in the factory (ibid.: 350–52). The number of workers assigned to a mini-line for main operations are said in this account to range from between 12 and 20, while averaging around 15: these groups ('kumi') have a group manager or foreman, and are in addition split internally into two or three smaller team units with their own team leaders ('Hancho'). Each of the line segments therefore has its own group hierarchy. Adjacent to the mini-lines, which are laid out in parallel in the factory, there are also sub-assembly lines for front and rear doors, instrument panels, front and rear suspensions, and of course engine assembly, all of which feed onto car assembly (ibid.). In general terms, the number of segments in the line is held by Monden to reflect considerations which also include estimates of the number of cars to be built, the time to be allotted to production, and the degree of variety allowed in the car line. In this sense, the considerations are similar to those that would impinge on the length of a conventional line.

In their update on the Toyota experiments, Benders and Morita (2004) provide an account of the reorganization of work at Kyushu that is consistent with Monden, with a matching description of segmented assembly lines and intra-process buffers. But in addition to developments at Kyushu – the 'laboratory green-field' – they also describe experiments at Toyota Takaoka, and the Toyota Daihatsu subsidiary plant at Ikeda. And from a purely descriptive viewpoint, Benders and Morita give some additional flavour of the width of recent and ongoing experiments at Toyota: one obtains a clear sense of a mixed set of policy initiatives – experiments not only with segmented assembly lines, buffers and ergonomics, but also with extended mechanization and task automation, less pressured work environments and supporting personnel policies. As a complementary overview of initiatives this is extremely useful. One issue which they do not touch on, but which Monden does emphasize, is the introduction of women workers to Toyota's car assembly lines, with a place (or places) allotted to women on each line segment at Kyushu: 'each split line also has at least one female worker . . . not surprising in the Western world, it is rare for a woman to work in the final assembly line of a Japanese automobile company' (Monden 1998: 352). In both accounts the initial impetus for these changes is ascribed to Toyota's crisis in recruiting workers in the Japanese boom years of the early 1990s.

But the variety of Toyota's experiments notwithstanding, the focal point in both accounts is provided by the fact of line segmentation at Kyushu, and the introduction of intra-process buffers to Toyota car assembly plant. The reason for this is easily guessed: 15 years of previous literature on the 'Toyota Production System' had expounded on a distinctive system of manufacture in which all stocks and buffers are deemed to be 'waste' – or 'muda' – so that when Toyota first began to experiment with line segmentation and intra-process buffers the immediate response to this development was a rush of speculation as to whether this spelled the end of an era at Toyota's car assembly plants. Benders and Morita (2004) convey well the sense of initial shock caused by the Kyushu experiment: the introduction of intra-process buffers was widely viewed at the time as a 'breach' with the just-in-time manufacturing principle, held to be integral to Toyota's production system – 'a major break' with the past (ibid.: 434, 442–3). Their own contribution is located within this literature, and focuses on Toyota's subsequent momentum. But a quite different interpretation is advanced by Monden: here the argument advanced is that the reorganization of the assembly process at Kyushu is far from being a departure from the traditions of the Toyota and is instead a rigorous application of the famous just-in-time production principle. Let us consider this further.

The Monden defence hinges in part on prior definition. If just-in-time production were simply defined as a production system in which all intra-process buffers are axiomatically regarded as 'waste', then the replacement of a conventional assembly line by a series of mini-lines connected by intra-process buffers would by necessity be a step-change that entails abandoning the just-in-time principle. But an alternative tack is to measure the *time* it takes to assemble a car once production begins, and on this basis Monden argues as follows: if the reorganization of operations at the Toyota Kyushu site has helped Toyota maintain a downwards pressure on total throughput times in production when the factory is actively running, then regardless of the introduction of intra-process buffers it is an initiative which is *ipso facto* compatible with just-in-time production (Monden 1998: 357–62).[3] In the first instance, therefore, dimensions are specified so as not to make just-in-time production axiomatically dependent on the elimination of all stocks and buffers.

But it also depends on empirics. In an unbuffered conventional assembly line, an unplanned stoppage at any single point on the line will stop the entire line, thereby increasing the throughput time for all the cars on that line; the more frequently the line stops, the bigger the increase. Monden's contention, in abstract terms, is that because a conventional assembly line is subject to temporary unplanned stoppages, there is scope for line segmentation to successfully lower the average length of time it would take an assembly process to make a car, provided that mediating intra-process buffers can absorb the temporary effects of problems on one mini-line without causing the factory process as a whole to stop. In other words, problems with stoppages can be tackled by means of line segmentation with buffers. If work stops on one section, the remaining sections can continue undisturbed, so long as the problem section makes good the depleted buffer before a problem repeats. In concrete terms, this is what Monden argues has proved to be the case at Toyota.

To better understand this, some elementary process analysis is helpful. We can follow Monden (1998: 357) in defining *total throughput time* for a car undergoing assembly as the time it takes for the product to flow from the beginning to the end of the assembly process, when the factory is operating. For purposes of exposition, but without loss of generality *vis-à-vis* the essential point, we can also follow Monden (ibid.) in making some simplifying assumptions. Let us therefore assume that actual processing time – the time it takes for operatives to fit parts to the car under assembly under normal working conditions – is approximately the same regardless of whether the line is conventional or segmented. If this is the same in each case we can net it out of the comparison, allowing us to focus on what will definitely be different, namely stoppage times and buffer times. Let us also suppose, again for simplicity of exposition (although without affecting main points) that when the line is segmented and buffers introduced factory stoppage time is held at zero.[4] The question is then whether stoppage times under a conventional system would exceed the addition to throughput times accruing to the buffer zones in a segmented system.

At this point it is helpful to be explicit. In a conventional assembly line a stoppage at any single point must cause the entire line to come to a halt. The total stoppage time for units built can be calculated from knowledge of the frequency with which the line is stopped on average before a unit is finished, and of the average stoppage duration, provided of course that we refer to stoppages when the factory is operating:

$$T_s = \text{frequency of line stop per product} \times \text{average duration of line stop}$$

For a non-conventional segmented assembly line with intra-process buffers, total buffer time is measured simply by the number of units held as stock between segments of the assembly line, under normal conditions and in the absence of section stoppages, multiplied by the corresponding production cycle for the factory. This is the same thing as multiplying the number of buffers by their average capacity:

$$T_b = \text{number of buffers} \times \text{average buffer capacity}$$

We can write these definitions more formally if we denote constituent terms thus:

f = stoppage frequency per product on a conventional line
t_d = average duration of stoppage on a conventional line
m = number of buffers in a segmented line
c = average buffer capacity

Following Coffey and Thornley (2006b) we then obtain as expressions:

$$T_s = ft_d \tag{5.1}$$

$$T_b = mc \tag{5.2}$$

Suppose now that total stoppage time under a conventional arrangement would indeed be greater than or equal to total buffer time when the line is segmented. This would mean that the expression in (5.1) is greater than or equal to (5.2). If this were true, then by rearranging terms the following inequality would be observed:

$$f \geq mc \, \frac{t_c}{t_d} \, (\Rightarrow T_b \leq T_s) \tag{5.3}$$

Again following Coffey and Thornley (ibid.), we can use this inequality to better assess Monden's argument *vis-à-vis* his defence of the just-in-time principle.

What Monden is in fact implicitly arguing is that stoppage frequencies (f) under conventional arrangements at Toyota have been such that the Kyushu experiment with segmentation has achieved an overall reduction in total throughput times. To take a hypothetical example, suppose there are ten intra-process buffers, corresponding, as at Kyushu, to 11 line segments, and that the buffer capacity in each case is five units. In this example, we can deduce from this data that $m \times c$ is equal to 50 – the number of buffers (m) is in this instance 10, while the average capacity (c) is 5. Now suppose that the intended production cycle for the factory (t_c) is one car completed every minute. If all of these numbers were slotted into inequality (5.3) then line segmentation could be said to have reduced total throughput times if $f \geq (50)(1)/t_d$. Here we would have to interpret f as pertaining to what the stoppage frequency per product would be in the absence of intra-process buffers, with t_d the average stoppage duration. Suppose, for example, that the average duration of a stoppage would be two minutes. Substituting this into our expression, we would obtain $f \geq (50)(1)/2 = 25$. We could interpret this to mean that the incorporation of intra-process buffers into the assembly process succeeds in maintaining a downwards pressure on total throughput times if in their absence factory managers would expect the average car built to be subjected to 25 or more unscheduled in-assembly stoppages before completion (see also Coffey and Thornley ibid.).

The argument can also be presented diagrammatically. Figure 5.1 displays total throughput time (T) on the vertical axis, and stoppage frequency (f) for a conventional assembly line on the horizontal. If the assembly line arrangement is indeed conventional (no intra-process buffers) we obtain a curve like X relating stoppage frequencies to total throughput times: for any given average

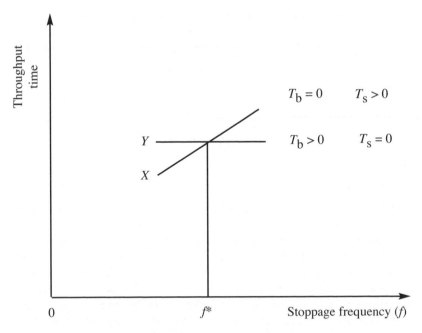

Figure 5.1   Factory stoppages and throughput times

stoppage duration, total throughput time will rise as the stoppage frequencies increase. But suppose that the line could be segmented and intra-process buffers installed; then if, as we assume, the temporary effects of a stoppage on any segment is fully absorbed by means of the mediating buffers, total throughput time will be unaffected. In such a case the stoppage frequency on a conventional line is irrelevant, but we can superimpose the given value – represented by curve *Y* – of the throughput time. Now if the stoppage frequency under a conventional arrangement were *f** there would be nothing to choose between this and a segmented line *vis-à-vis* throughput times. In this case, and by reference to (4.3), *f** is just equal to $m \times c \times (t_c/t_d)$. What Monden in effect proposes is that at Toyota *f* would typically exceed *f**.[5]

If Monden is correct then stoppage frequencies under conventional arrangements at the point where Toyota embarked on its Kyushu experiment were such that a fall could be envisaged in total throughput times for the car assembly process by means of the introduction of intra-process buffers. This can presumably be interpreted to mean that stoppages frequencies were proving generally problematic for Toyota at this time, with segmentation one solution. But if we consider this thesis for Kyushu itself the results are quite striking. The figures used in the hypothetical example above for the number of buffers (*m*) and the average buffer capacity (*c*) are in fact the appropriate data,

Table 5.1   Imputed stoppage frequencies at Toyota Kyushu (examples)

(i) Stoppage duration	(ii) Imputed minimum stoppage frequency
5 minutes	$f \geq mc \dfrac{t_c}{t_d} = 10 \times 5 \times \dfrac{1.7}{5} = 17$
1 minute	$f \geq mc \dfrac{t_c}{t_d} = 10 \times 5 \times \dfrac{1.7}{1} = 85$

given the available details for Kyushu (see Monden 1998: 353; Benders and Morita 2004: 436): $m \times c$ is reasonably estimated at about 50. So far as factory production cycles are concerned, Monden states that in the first years of operation Kyushu worked with a cycle of 1.7 minutes; at the same time, the duration of a typical stoppage – the effects of which are absorbed by the buffers – is indicated to have sat typically in the range of between one and five minutes (see Monden 1988: 360–61). Using this data, and substituting in (5.3), allows us to obtain the sort of expected stoppage frequencies that would justify incorporating intra-process buffers at Kyushu in its first years of operation, if a premium were placed on maintaining downwards pressure on total throughput times in assembly. The results are shown in Table 5.1. These show that if Kyushu was only able to maintain throughput times at existing levels because of intra-process buffers, stoppages must otherwise have been expected to run from at least 17 stops per product to 85 stops per product, upwards.

Monden is, of course, concerned to maintain that what Toyota has done is consistent with a general adherence to just-in-time manufacture. And it is fair to say that this entire debate has remained within the walls set by a particular assumption, namely that what counts is the compatibility of a segmented assembly line system and intra-process buffers with a received understanding of the Japanese assembler. But suppose now that we step outside of the walls confining that particular debate.

The most obvious inference is one which is consistent with the argument and analysis in the previous chapter. It will be recalled that we have challenged the standard interpretation of the MIT-based IMVP world survey of the hours of assembly plant labour used to build cars in the late 1980s. According to Womack et al. (1990), for most readers the source of their understanding of the IMVP survey, the gulf revealed in this survey between average resource requirements in Japan and elsewhere was proof positive of what they called a 'lean' revolution: the difference in resource requirements, at least in the global survey, was inferred from the claim that at any level of assembly plant automation factories in Japan required on average fewer workers hours to build a car *vis-à-vis* a core set of (standard) activities. Without reprising the whole of our previous interpretation of the IMVP survey structure and results, we identified in the course of our reassessment that there was a discernible bias factor in the calculation of the number of worker hours employed: in particular, hours worked in excess of a single standard shift (net of relief times) were omitted from the formula used and therefore ignored at the point of survey construction, so that the total of worker hours might be badly undercounted in some plants. In this connection, we observed that Japanese assembly plants were notorious at the time when the survey was conducted for the long hours imposed on workers. If this bias were eliminated, we inferred that the global comparisons might have looked quite different to the received interpretation of its findings broadcast at the time.

If in this context we consider the implications of a high stoppage frequency, then the most obvious is simply that it takes more worker hours to finish a car. If stoppage frequencies were indeed becoming problematic for Toyota in the late 1980s – the clear implication of Monden's own dimension analysis – so much so that a reorganization of assembly-line structures was thereby made necessary, then this is potentially corroborative evidence; completing production schedules in these circumstances would be consistent with an extension in the length of the working day, provided of course that workers in each shift were obliged to work beyond it. This would be consistent with problems in converting unit effort into outputs, and with a more extended working day – issues not tackled effectively in the IMVP survey.

5.3   THE REORGANIZATION OF OPERATIONS AT TOYOTA: A WINDOW

Anyone who has ever tracked the trends of fashion regarding best practice in any manufacturing sector over a sufficiently long interval of time will be familiar with the following syndrome. A way of doing things is hailed as the 'best' way of doing things and a standard for others to emulate, if not disabled by incompetence or a peculiarly thick-headed take on the world; at some point a leading practitioner of the said best practice does things differently, at which stage problems hitherto concealed or denied are pushed centre stage. The problems may of course be exaggerated in the initial rush to justify or explain, and with the passage of time details may blur; but provided more is not inferred than the data will plausibly allow, it may nonetheless be possible in the interim to peer through a window opened. This, it might reasonably be ventured, is as true of Toyota as of any other manufacturer. While a general point of interest, in this section we pause to consider what can be seen, and how this relates to our criticism of the concept of lean production. It will be convenient in this regard to refer once more to the original well-spring, because Womack et al. (1990) in fact have much to say about the question of line-stoppages at Toyota.

Womack et al.'s view on this issue hinges on an appraisal, as they see it, of one of the achievements of the redoubtable Taichii Ohno, the late Vice President of Toyota MC also previously encountered in the earlier chapters of our own book. In their view, and in this they are not alone, Ohno was inspired to realize that keeping an assembly line running regardless of errors would cause errors to 'multiply endlessly'. Rather than allow a situation to persist in which each worker let errors go, to be caught 'at the end of the line' because of a fear that a stoppage at their own section might result in a reprimand or disciplinary action, Ohno believed in taking the opposite tack:

> So in striking contrast to the mass production plant, where stopping the line was the responsibility of the senior line manager, Ohno placed a cord above every work station and instructed workers to stop the whole assembly line immediately if a problem emerged that they couldn't fix. Then the whole team would come over to work on the problem . . . Not surprisingly, as Ohno began to experiment . . . his production line stopped all the time, and the workers easily became discouraged. However, as the work teams gained experience identifying and tracing problems to their ultimate cause, the number of errors began to drop dramatically. Today, in Toyota plants, where every worker can stop the line, yields approach 100 percent. That is, the line practically never stops!' (Womack et al. 1990: 56–7)

If we take these points in order, the gist of this passage is that Ohno broke with Western production practices by encouraging workers to stop the line when problems arose. As a consequence, and here we should note that Womack et al. are writing in the present tense, so that 'today' must refer to the later 1980s, Toyota achieved an outcome where work flowed unceasingly: 'the line practically never stops'. But while this view was recorded just before Toyota's experiments in segmented assembly lines commenced, if Monden – a sober and formally precise writer, with a close association with Toyota and an unparalleled degree of factory access – is correct, this is not how the situation was at all; instead, the prognosis would have to be that unplanned line stoppages at Toyota were reaching such a level that Kyushu was assigned to embark on an experiment with intra-process buffers to control the problem.

Other contrasts are equally apparent. For example, on Toyota's philosophy about the amount of plant space required for production, Womack et al. (1990: 79) say: 'Toyota believes in having as little space as possible so that face-to-face communication among workers is easier, and there is no room to store inventories'. But in Monden's account of the problems then besetting the Japanese firm, issues of confinement to ageing brownfield sites loom large. At the Toyota Motomachi plant, for example, bulky engines and transmissions components, in the absence of adequate space, are said by Monden to have blocked the factory walkways, forcing managers to relocate the inspection line to the centre of the plant. Owing to extant layout, this meant even more difficult working as a consequence of the resulting gas, water and noise pollution: 'exhaust gas is emitted, water flows, noises are made, and the workplace itself is narrow' (Monden 1998: 350–51). The problems Monden describes with respect to *frequent* line stoppages – 'they stop the line quite often' – is attributed to poor working conditions of this type, where workers struggled with difficult material access and handling conditions; the problems for all concerned are described as having been compounded at this site by the fact that the noise from the relocated inspection line drowned out the buzzers which signalled a line stop, requiring the installation of an even louder alarm (see ibid.). In this example, the Toyota 'philosophy' of little space, to encourage communication, metamorphoses into a cramped, wet, fume-ridden and frustrating workplace suffering incessant din.

We must certainly allow for exaggeration on both sides. But the attendant details supplied in this instance are sufficiently precise as to undermine glibness. Moreover, other details supplied also convince. It has long been argued in the literature pertaining to Toyota that the assembler's just-in-time manufacturing systems facilitate product variety by economizing on space. But according to Monden a steady expansion in the number of 'parts and parts functions', driven in part by technical innovations and more stringent safety parameters, but also by a rise in the overall complexity of car lines compared to the very simple ranges Toyota commenced with, also meant growing problems with space congestion, even when parts were brought to plant in carefully scheduled sequences (see ibid. 1998: 350). Without belabouring the point, the reality of factories, designed at a time when Toyota offered very simple car lines, struggling with space as car line variety increases, even with careful production sequencing, is hardly consistent with the vision of the lean revolution.[6]

Again, exaggeration must be allowed on both sides. But the contrasts are striking not least because Monden is justifying, not criticizing, Toyota. If what he claims is even approximately accurate, then it falsifies much in Womack et al. In terms of the intended theme of our own study, we have been concerned to establish the points at which what has been claimed on behalf of Japanese production methods in the car industry departs from what can be shown. We have progressively set about deconstructing untenable claims which have acquired the status of truth, and are for this reason of some intrinsic interest. We have argued that what a firm like Toyota does at the interface between customer and factory might best be understood in manufacturing terms that are prosaic rather than radical, and we have rejected any suggestion that 'flexible' assembly is the provenance of the Japanese industry; similarly, we reject the empirical plank that might justify talk of a lean revolution. For these and other

reasons, we might eschew approaches that look at the issue of the reorganization of work at Toyota in terms set down by the forms of the existing literature
(even while admiring the diligence with which details of the reorganization
have been recorded). Looked at from the viewpoint of an emerged problem
with line stoppages that coincides with difficulties in recruitment and retention
to factories run at a hard pace, there is much that is still profoundly interesting.

5.4   BACK TO THE FUTURE

This is especially so if due regard is given to comparative historical contexts.
So much is written about Toyota as if it were necessarily in the vanguard of
global developments in the world's car industry that it is perhaps worth noting
that even its experiments with line segmentation and buffers have antecedents
in the industry. The best place to begin, and our comments are necessarily
brief, is probably with the wave of organizational experiments that swept car
assembly plants in mainland Europe in the early 1970s, since in form they hold
out the promise for a fruitful study of parallels and differences in some more
extended future study: a précis of some of the issues will also allow us to say
something about team-work in the car industry. This period is interesting in
part because the initial impetus to experimentation was also given by tight
labour markets, and a shortage of suitably motivated workers.

A good contemporary overview of developments in Western Europe in the
earlier part of the 1970s, and a sense of then extant debates within the car
industry more generally, can be obtained from Hartley (1977), a pithy survey
article written for a non-academic industry-based audience, with one eye on
British prospects. 'After a decade or so of virtual stagnation', this piece
begins, 'car manufacturing methods seem about to change dramatically' (ibid.:
14). The reason for this, according to the survey, was problems on the employment side of the factory equation. In Britain disruptions to production were
unacceptable, as were high rates of absenteeism in the rest of Europe; as a
result, change was needed: 'try as they may to make fundamental improvements in manufacture, engineers and managers are wasting their time unless
they can gain the complete co-operation of the workforce . . . any new method
of production must improve the working conditions or job satisfaction' (ibid.)
The article provides a short summary of initiatives of this type amongst car
assemblers around the world, contrasting the preference shown in North
America at this time for fast mechanically-paced assembly lines with a
number of experimental forms of organization aimed at easing 'tensions' on
the shop floor in Europe.

In a longer review it would be interesting to compare Hartley's descriptions
of a plethora of initiatives in Europe at this time with Benders and Morita's

later account of the range of experiments currently in progress at Toyota. Hartley describes a trend towards greater mechanization and automation in areas hitherto characterized by the assignation of workers to heavy or repetitive or unpleasant tasks: for example, the introduction of transfer machines and linked lines supported by mechanized loading and unloading operations to reduce heavy work, in-process gauging to eliminate scrap and task repetition in the machine shop and improved shielding for noise in foundry work.[7] Ergonomics is also highlighted by Hartley as a key area of research. But the main focus of Hartley's article quickly turns to the reorganization of work in areas with limited scope for automation, given then existing technologies, and with particular regard to assembly methods for engines, transmissions, bodies and trim.

Some instances display the variety of routes taken in different plants. In engine assembly, for example, experimentation at Renault included dividing workers into teams of three, two of whom were assigned to building engines individually and a third to testing, with an overall production rate of just under five engines an hour; at Saab-Scania, workers were again assigned to teams of three, to collectively assemble engines at the slightly higher rate of six engines per hour; at Volvo, a mix of teams and individually assigned workers were employed in the manufacture of engine parts, while the engine itself was built up progressively by several groups working in sequence. Experiments with hybrid systems included the Francaise de Mechanique factory in the north of France, which employed a mix of automated assembly, mechanically paced assembly and unpaced assembly steps on each of two production lines supplying engines to Renault, Peugot and Volvo. Similarly, Fiat was experimenting with job enlargement at Termoli, with workers standing in loops around the main assembly line and spending around ten minutes each working on each engine: evidently, this proved to be unpopular, and was replaced by a conventional track (see Hartley 1977: 15–16).[8] Experiments with group assignments – following an initial but aborted attempt to enlarge individual jobs – are also reported at another Renault facility (Le Mans) in the manufacture of suspensions, with teams of four working in pairs to build left- and right-hand suspension assemblies.

For the specific case of car assembly – the area which permits most easily of direct comparison with the Toyota experiment at Kyushu – initiatives extended to include direct experiments with segmented assembly lines. For example, at the Renault plant at Douai, a single standard assembly line was replaced by four shorter lines (a similar move to a larger number of shorter assembly lines is also reported for Fiat at Cassino); each was 200 metres long and subdivided into three sections by intra-process storage buffers, allowing limited autonomy in each section (Hartley 1977: 17). Hartley also discusses a study by Ingersol Management Consultants (IMC) which, investigating the failure of the Fiat Termoli experiment, recommended an alternative form of work reorganization based on a move away from mechanical pacing of manual work, with a series of individual group-based 'lines' instead working in parallel for the manual component of engine assembly, and with intra-process buffers used to separate these sections from mechanized sections (ibid.: 19). What is perhaps most resonant from the viewpoint of later experiments with segmented assembly lines is that Hartley, writing in the mid-1970s, concluded that this was also the most likely way ahead for car manufacture in Britain – team-based line segmentation with buffers: 'some form of assembly in which lines are divided into sections by buffer stores seems preferable' (ibid.).

There is nothing *per se* surprising in any of these observations. In basic form and function a mechanically paced assembly line appears potentially absolutist in its implications for the loss of individual freedoms in the ordinary course of work, and the subjugation of the rhythms and arrangements of manual tasks. Criticism is proverbial, both in the car assembly sector and in other manufacturing sectors, because a system organized in this way seems to conform in every relevant way to a production regime characterized by what Edwards (1979) calls 'technical control', wherein workers' actions are directly coerced by the physical structure of the working environment. It is no surprise therefore to find that in a period of tight labour markets – and in the case of Western Europe in the early 1970s growing worker militancy – experiments will be undertaken by employers into different ways of doing things. What should be clear, however, is that if line segmentation is not original to Toyota, neither are attempts to organize assembly plant workers into groups or teams. The particular association that makes group or team work synonymous with Japan, and a new 'cultural' practice introduced by this route into the Western car industry, is as historically ungrounded as the frequently accompanying assertion that Fordist mass production reigned supreme until Toyota 'invented' mixed-assembly and wide selection. The history of the car industry is in one sense a history of debates over how to (and whether to) organize workers into groups or teams, how best to offset resistance to paced assembly.[9] Nor is the now common contrast between 'team work' and 'task work' a sensible one: teams can be organized around individually set tasks on conventional lines; teams can be organized around enlarged jobs on conventional lines; jobs can be enlarged without teams on conventional lines; more radical experiments with and without teams, with and without job enlargement, are possible – but not always sustained. And in the latter stages of car assembly the conventional paced assembly line remains (globally) a dominant form of organization.

The ebb and flow of experimentation in relation to changes both in the wider economic context and in the self-organization of workers is obviously an important question. Michel Freyssenet (1995), in a valuable paper organized in the form of a short history, describes the 'crisis of work' that beset the French car industry in the 1960s. Dating this from 1967, just prior to the wave of social and industrial unrest that swept the country the following year, Freyssenet describes the crisis as a combination of 'often spectacular' conflicts, problems with growing absenteeism, problems with turnover, and an increase in the volume of work requiring rectification. The initial response from Renault, the subject of the study, and consistent with the company's practices from the 1950s, was first to attempt to deal with these problems via improved wages for workers, and second to pursue a more general initiative involving a nationally-agreed reduction in working time and provision of further training ('continuous training') for workers (ibid.: 294). But the third response was to experiment with the organization of work – rotating operatives between positions, 'walking' products down the line to facilitate a more complete assembly input from individuals, and adopting longer work cycles. These experiments inevitably also included various types of team-work initiative, with teams defined and organized in contexts set by component, mechanism, or sub-assembly, and with unit leaders in each instance a first element in the hierarchical chain. All of this is consistent with Hartley's earlier survey, where Renault is prominent: Freyssenet, for example, gives a matching account of experiments at Le Mans, and the installation of four shorter assembly lines rather than one long line at Douai (ibid.: 295). But Freyssenet also notes that the 'crisis of work' at Renault ended with the slowdown in economic growth and the rise in unemployment in the late 1970s: 'There was a close correlation between the reduction of manpower at Renault, beginning in 1978, and a steady fall in absenteeism and turn-over' (ibid.: 296).

In this connection it is interesting that the experiments at Toyota have continued past the point where Japan's economic downturn is likely to have vitiated the initial problems experienced by the assembler in recruiting and retaining workers. This downturn, combined with aggressive overseas production, has almost certainly meant that difficulties with recruitment as such are over (in Japan) at present. Indeed the question which Benders and Morita (2004: 434) initially set out to answer was whether Toyota had persevered with its experiments after the 'bursting of the bubble' in the Japanese domestic economy (on which see also Chapter 6). It would be interesting to know if there is a contrast here with Western experience: clearly the revolution anticipated by Hartley in the organization of work in the British car industry did not materialize, while reviewing developments more generally certainly suggests a petering out for employer enthusiasm for radical experimentation. To identify contrasting experiences in this sense – Freyssenet (1995), for example, is clear that continuities in team-working are important in the French industry, and that to identify team-work simply with Japanese practices is a mistake – both country by country, and employer and employer, would reveal much. To know more about what became of past European experiments with line segmentation would be valuable.

Moreover, even a casual reading of the contemporary literature in the 1970s suggests a possible regional divergence outside of Japan towards issues of organization. For example, Hartley identifies radical experiments with Europe: America is identified as the abiding home of conventional assembly, with short production cycles (in other words assembly involving a fine division of tasks and 'fast' lines, see Hartley 1977: 19). It may be that this perception reflects a bias in the literature of the period resulting from particular instances of industrial unrest in North America at this time, such as, for example, with the almost iconic case of the GM plant at Lordstown. This General Motors car assembly plant in Ohio experienced widely reported industrial unrest that was also widely associated by contemporaries with problems of work on a 'fast' track.[10] But Hartley also seems to have in mind American transplants in Britain, an observation that is consistent with other studies of the period. In Ford Motor Company, for example, workers in the 1970s wrested some degree of control over some production lines from their employer, but only in the teeth of resistance.[11]

It is obviously important, however, to avoid naivety on content when considering an experimental work-form in any manufacturing process. The history of experimentation in manufacture *vis-à-vis* work-forms has been characterized by a healthy scepticism and suspicion regarding substance and content, and in assessing a change like a buffered assembly line split into segments it is important to be clear that it has the potential for intensifying the experience of work.[12] If a conventional line stops because of a problem, everyone has a 'breather' while the problem is handled. If temporary stoppages on a segmented line are 'absorbed' by buffers, then nobody gets a breather. Moreover, workers on the problem section have to make up the buffer by working more rapidly once the problem is handled – since otherwise a repetition of the problem will then have knock-on consequences for the whole system. The whole package needs consideration: more intense work in a given period might come with less extended work as measured by the overall length of the working day. But it is worth remembering that 'line stops' are multidimensional: a cynical hypothesis that would require serious consideration alongside other hypotheses is that having experienced line-stop problems during a boom time characterized by problems with recruiting sufficiently well-motivated workers, Toyota is intent on devising work-forms that will keep their workers' consciences clean in the future.[13]

5.5   CONCLUSIONS

The aim in this chapter has been to consider how carefully collected evidence pertaining to the reorganization of assembly work at Toyota and published in the extant secondary literature on the company might be interpreted in light of the overall themes of this book. The perspective adopted is that a sudden change in a manufacturing practice that seems to be a departure from previous 'best' practice offers a window by which to see problems hitherto concealed. In this context, we show that the data published by leading Toyota observers is consistent with an hypothesis that the company was suffering from significant problems with assembly process stoppages just at the point where it was being hailed in the wider world as the luminary of 'lean production', a chimerical if now culturally embedded construct.

NOTES

1. As noted in the introduction to this book, there is little room for detailed exegesis of even prominent texts in the canon of literature pertaining to its chosen themes. But a few words in this instance are merited: Monden is the author of a series of progressively updated books on factory organization at Toyota, produced with an unsurpassed access to the company. He is also a singularly scrupulous writer, and favours a more formal mode of exposition than has been typical more generally: as such, while we depart somewhat from his interpretations here and elsewhere, we would be inclined to take his *empirical* views on process dimensions very seriously. If every point in our own book were accepted, Monden should still be studied.
2. Benders and Morita (2004) provide a useful historical précis. Toyota Kyushu was established as an independent operating company of Toyota Motors at Miyata on the Southern Island of Kyushu, chosen as a greenfield site 'far from Toyota's traditional homebase in the Aichi Prefecture', and intended to act as a 'laboratory' for new ideas on operations and personnel management (ibid.: 438). Benders and Morita also note that the move was in part to recruit from a more rural workforce, in light of problems elsewhere.
3. The strength of the point arises because work-in-progress is more than just an inventory of parts and semi-completed products held *in situ* between processes; it includes in-process time. In particular, even on a conventional assembly line with no buffers the car assembly process will still take time, even if worked at a continuous rate, because of the semi-finished cars, at various stages of completion, distributed down the line. For an introduction more generally to throughput times as a measure of work-in-progress, see Groover (1987: 62–6).
4. It is important to be clear that assumptions of this type can be made because they simplify presentation and allow easy first approximations on relevant orders of empirical magnitude, but without sacrificing anything essential from the viewpoint of the analysis. If these assumptions were relaxed (data permitting) our key points of analysis would be the same.
5. A somewhat more complex diagrammatic analysis is also provided by Monden, involving total throughput times on the vertical axis (as in Figure 5.1) and what is referred to as the 'trouble ratio' on the horizontal, defined as 'the number of problems occurring within a certain time span' (see Monden 1998: 357–8). The two presentations are compatible.
6. There is an element of *déjà vu* here. L.J. White, in discussing the developing complexity of car lines in North America throughout the post-World War II period, notes the pressures space constraints could thereby put on line speeds: 'an increasingly complex product has been requiring more space, both on the line and for inventories' (White 1971: 28). If we confine comment to space on the line, the issue is not dissimilar to that Monden notes in the later case of Toyota. White's example pertains to the GM plant at Framingham: built in 1948 and designed for 45 cars an hour, with growing complexity this had fallen sharply – 'the same floor space now supports an optimum flow of only 30–35 cars an hour' (ibid.: 28). In their account Benders and Morita (2004) provide corroboration of space problems at Toyota by noting that limited space at the Toyota Daihatsu subsidiary at Ikeda made line

segmentation with intra-process buffers difficult; more generally, they identify trade-offs between the desire to automate (space-using), and to introduce buffers (likewise space-using).

7. As previously noted, Benders and Morita (2004) give a very full sense of the range of Toyota's responses to problems with recruitment and retention, including steps to lower labour demand *per se* via automation, and to target particularly heavy or unpopular tasks (ibid.: 435). A similar dichotomization of strategies aimed at workers retained in manual components of a job, and strategies aimed at eliminating these workers, is also employed by Hartley in his own survey – the similarities in this respect are rather striking.

8. Further detail (not supplied by Hartley) on the reasons for this, both in this and in similar cases, would be interesting from the viewpoint of informing current debates on work-forms. Debate on different work systems by the nature of the subject matter remains intense: see, for example, Appelbaum et al.'s (2000) survey and study for the US, which takes a circumspect view of 'lean' thinking, and which has generated a considerable secondary literature.

9. There is in this sense again little that is new under the sun. In the case of France, for example, Ernest Mandel (1968: 138–9) cites Friedmann (1953: 64–5) on two forms of work organization in the car industry. The Berliet factory in Lyons employed a 'simplified version of the Taylor method of rationalising labour', with 'norms' for task performance times set by 'ace' workers, and then presented as reasonable: this was 'supervision in the technical sphere', supported by 'disciplinary supervision'. Citreon in Paris, however, employed more 'subtle methods' with induced rivalries between teams supported by foremen and supervisors. Nonetheless, the outcomes were the same. In the first case, pressure was placed on the individual workers treated as an isolated unit and subjected to obvious and direct controls; in the second, pressure on each individual was generated by suitably orchestrated group activities – but still 'they expect you to show an unheard-of-quickness in your movements, as in a speeded-up motion picture'.

10. The Lordstown case is much cited in the radical literature of the 1970s, including both the canonical Edwards (1979) and Braverman (1974). Unrest at this site was precipitated, at least in part, by an attempt by GM management to operate the line at very high speeds: 'Assembly fits the worker to the pace of the machine . . . For example, within a minute on the line, a worker in the trim department had to walk about 20 feet to a conveyor belt transporting parts back to the line, pick up a seat weighing 30 pounds, carry it back to his workstation, place the seat on the chassis, and put in four bolts to fasten it down by first hand-starting the bolts and then using an air gun to tighten them according to standard. It was steady work when the line moved at 60 cars an hour. When it increased to more than 100 cars an hour, the number of operations on this job were not reduced and the pace became almost maddening. In 36 seconds, the worker had to perform at least eight different operations, including walking, lifting, hauling, lifting the carpet, bending to fasten the bolts by hand, fastening them by air gun, replacing the carpet, and putting a sticker on the hood' (Arnowitz 1973: 22–3). As this passage makes clear – 'the number of operations on this job were not reduced' – the increased pace of the line came with an intensification of the pace of work for the operative. This same passage is cited by Edwards (1979: 20), and to this effect, to illustrate the essential antagonism between employee and employer-driven work discipline. The pressures of pace and intensity aside, for Braverman (1974: 33–4) the industrial unrest at Lordstown also laid bare the underlying tensions in an erstwhile model plant occasioned by the sheer tedium of employment in a 'boring' and 'repetitive' job. The Lordstown case also figures prominently in studies of job satisfaction in North America in this period (see, for example, the collection in Rosow 1974 devoted to this topic, in particular: Strauss 1974: 73, Salpukas 1974: 105–6, and Henle 1974: 143). Its impact, however, is perhaps best signalled by the fact that in 1970s editions of his best-selling *Principles* the economist Paul Samuelson (no less) devoted space to informing his students of the abiding (if diminishing) relevance of class antagonisms in the North American workplace, by describing the detail of the 'slowdown strike by young GM workers in Lordstown, Ohio, protesting speed-up on the monotonous Chevrolet conveyor-belt assembly line' (Samuelson 1976: 43–4). On the continental side, Pierre Dubois, a French sociologist quite befittingly interested in the phenomenon of sabotage in industry, chose to highlight other aspects of the

Lordstown unrest: the disruption of workshops to stall the pace of work, the abuse of fire hoses to transform workshops into 'giant swimming pools' and the explosion of engines (Dubois 1976, 1979: 67–8). Dubois, drawing on North American accounts of the Lordstown case, including Brecher (1972) and Rosow (1974), contrasts this with French experience. Unlike most North American commentators, however, Dubois emphasized the positive aims of the Lordstown saboteurs, including rest, fun and a quality protest against shoddy goods.

11. For example, Beynon (1973), a classic study of work relations at the Ford Motor Company assembly plant at Halewood, in the UK, describes something akin at this time to a state of guerrilla warfare – abuse of the safety wire to halt the line, workers holding the key to a line to prevent managers 'speeding up', and workers assigned to count throughput to check on cheating by managers on other lines (ibid.: 139), and empowered to 'stop the line'.

12. It is perhaps worth noting that even the Swedish experiments in work redesign have met with cynical responses. For example, Andrew Zimbalist (1979: xx), describing the Volvo plant at Kalmar, in Sweden, felt moved to add to a pithy summary of the key improvements a some-what sourer note: 'And just in case workers are less than delighted with the new arrange-ments, management has constructed the hexagonal Kalmer plant so that each work team has its own entrance, locker room, cafeteria, and work area. This, of course, precludes commu-nications between work teams during the course of the day.' More recent assessments of Swedish work experiments in the car industry in light of preoccupations with Japanese manufacturing methods (and vice versa) are given in Berggren (1992, see also Berggren 1993), as well as in Sandberg (1995).

13. The possibility that Japanese workers might 'abuse' the stop-cord to control work pace is one scarcely countenanced in the literature: 'the workforce only uses this power to bring production to a halt in the interest of the firm, rather than to alleviate the backbreaking pace of work' (see Kaplinsky 1988: 464). This seems (to the present writer) unlikely, and it is interesting to speculate in this vein on high stoppage rates at Toyota in the late 1980s.

6. Rivalrous asymmetries and the Japanese myth

> FDI can create externalities, spin-offs or spillovers that confer benefits on the host economy over and above the strictly economic benefits of trade . . . It is frequently pointed out, for example, that the American and British economies have greatly benefited from the high levels of Japanese investment in their economies; this FDI has encouraged firms in both countries to adopt Japanese 'lean production techniques' and to increase product quality. (Gilpin 2000:175)

6.1 INTRODUCTION

In this chapter we consider some global issues. Instead of explaining the fact of successful Japanese entry into Western car markets by reference to revolutionary breakthroughs in the organization of manufacturing activities, it is reasonable, in light of the propositions set out in earlier chapters, to ask if the processes of myth making about Japanese prowess in the car and other sectors might in part be explicable by reference to the stresses of 'globalization' – or better, to the stresses of asymmetric market encroachments by major new players in world industry. We consider too the shifting nuances in the relevant body of Western literature as the initial sense of crisis occasioned, in North America at least, by Japanese import penetration has receded, and as the comparative strength of Japan's domestic economy has waned.

No pretence is made of an exhaustive treatment, but in brief order, and with a view to raising and framing some of the relevant issues, we proceed as follows. First we consider the mounting tide of reaction through the 1970s against Japanese inroads into markets hitherto dominated by Western car assemblers, broached from the viewpoint more generally of what one would expect when a newly emerged world power starts to penetrate existing markets dominated by powerful incumbent interests. The form of this reaction is best broached in the first instance if due consideration is given to the emergence of asymmetric opportunities for profit making in a highly rivalrous industry, with significant features of oligopoly, that has been unsettled by the changing balance of the international political economy. This provides a context in which to gauge not only the initial lobbying for state supported sanctions in the West against Japanese imports, but also the accommodations of the 1980s:

the joint ventures, collaborative arrangements and transplantation of facilities. In connection with this process of accommodation we reassess too the so-called 'world car' controversy, a rather particular topic but of considerable illustrative value. From here, however, we progress to the bigger picture: to properly understand the reaction to Japanese economic encroachments in the 1970s and beyond requires an explanation of the wider political context that permitted Japan, defeated by its principal rival in World War II, both to develop its manufacturing industries and to access Western markets shielded more definitively from other entrants, while at the same time jealously guarding the frontiers of its own domestic economy against competition.

If these provide likely contexts within which to locate the formation of a myth about Japanese manufacturing prowess, this chapter is also concerned with the durability and plasticity of its terms as international relations evolved through the 1980s and the growth engine in Japan stalled and spluttered in the 1990s. What is of particular note here is that while Japan's malaise has otherwise seen a wholesale slaughtering within Western literature of any number of sacred cows *vis-à-vis* the potency of Japanese culture and institutions as a competitive force in a global economy, assuredness about a manufacturing revolution – a 'lean' revolution – seems unperturbed; yet at the same time, and in a trend that seems to have become more pronounced as Japan's travail's continued, the tables have been turned in a subtle way. What was only a few years earlier hailed as the basis for Japan's competitive 'success' is now cited as an explanation for its subsequent 'failure', and in a manner which seems to affirm in every important respect the primacy of a Western or (more specifically) an Anglo-Saxon 'model' of a 'free' economy as an appropriate vision for modernity.

It is also the intent of this chapter to develop an observation made in passing in earlier discussions – one which might seem so obvious as to merit no further consideration, but which nonetheless sometimes seems frowned upon as an improper topic. The acceptance of a set of palpably counterfactual claims about Japanese manufacturing methods might be at least partly explicable not only by reference to the cultural stresses occasioned by changes in a global economic order, but also by the policy imperatives of some of the principal parties affected. To develop this point is simply to acknowledge that for some corporate bodies and state agencies there may be considerable political utility in sustaining the idea of a defining shift towards a more 'productive' – and 'consumer-led' – type of manufacturing organization, quite apart from what is actually supported by empirical evidence. This is certainly not to attempt to reduce the phenomenon which is the subject matter of this book to the level of a deliberate plot by a select group of interested parties, but equally it seems naïve to deny any practical advantages to knowing contrivance or assertion. We ask accordingly if the wheels of accommodation between old interests and new interests in an industry like the car industry might not in the event be oiled more effectively if defended by reference to a 'lean' revolution demanding collaboration; we ask too if a commitment on the part of state bodies to inward investment might not similarly discourage a too close interrogation of even the most unlikely claims.

6.2   RIVALROUS ASYMMETRIES IN THE WORLD'S CAR INDUSTRY

The world's car industry, as Garel Rhys (2005) notes, is characterized by competitive features that point to a particular kind of arena: highly rivalrous oligopolistic groupings, market shares that can be observed to shift over time on both national and regional measures, spectacular exits (failures) and major entries. This is witnessed by the rapid ascendancy of Japan's car assemblers, first as exporters to, and then as direct producers in, major overseas territories (see ibid.): the industry is lacking neither in large powerful firms with supporting state interests, nor in drama. Our main aim in this section is one of orientation: we wish to emphasize the importance of the emergence of a significant asymmetry within the network of global and regional rivalries in the world industry in accounting for the extent of the alarm caused by the steady growth of Japanese car exports to the West through the 1970s, before accommodations with incumbent interests could be sought and reached.

To make headway in considering the rising tide of the reaction to Japanese advances in world markets through the 1970s and into the 1980s it is in fact probably best to stand back initially from North America, which was then under the most obvious pressure from Japan. Our first point might indeed be best made by considering 'foreign' car sales to a Western European country particularly notable for its openness more generally to import penetration over this period: the UK. For this purpose we might do worse than to consider Cowling's (1982) analysis of the co-existence of intensely rivalrous behaviour with collusive dispositions in industries dominated by what are essentially oligopolistic groupings of firms, including the car industry. In industries of this kind, periods of ostensible co-existence can intersperse with periods where 'normal' relations between rivals appear to break down completely. Cowling emphasizes in this regard the *destabilizing* consequences of any asymmetries in the views that might be taken towards potential rivals by participants in the game. A firm which perceives that it has less to fear from its rivals' retaliation than it has to gain from a more aggressive posture *vis-à-vis* their markets will act accordingly. And in a generalization to the sphere of international trade, the unsettling effects of emergent asymmetries – of the sort that might 'normally arise due to processes of unequal development as between national economies'

– are duly stressed: 'circumstances will change as the balance of international power changes . . . as asymmetries occur which render it profitable for new participants to enter the fray or old participants to take on a more aggressive stance' (ibid.: 130). Thus for the world's car industries:

> The emergence of the Japanese car industry as a dominant element in the international trade in cars is a case in point. With the growing strength of the Japanese economy, and substantial protection in their home market, Japanese car firms had a very asymmetric view of rivalry and could see substantial profit opportunities in taking an aggressive stance over market shares. It is interesting to note that when the British car industry talks about the threat of imports and the question of protection it talks not about imports in general, but about Japanese . . . imports in particular, despite the fact that the most buoyant growth in imports is from other countries. (Cowling 1982: 130–31)

In Cowling's view, the processes of 'unequal development' had seen Japanese car assemblers emerge not only as new players on the world stage, but as players inclined to adopt an aggressive posture *vis-à-vis* their rivals' markets. Thus while the Japanese share of imports to the UK market was by no means the largest or the most rapidly growing, the ability of Japanese firms to encroach asymmetrically on rivals' sales to that market guaranteed a united and particularly hostile response from existing corporate interests, encompassing both British and non-British firms:

> When the Society for Motor Manufacturers and Traders or Sir Michael Edwardes (Chairman of British Leyland) talk about the threat of imports, they talk specifically about Japanese . . . imports, and yet the record is clear. Between 1975 and 1979 the share of imports went up from 33 per cent to 50 per cent, but over the same period the share of Japanese cars went up by less than two percentage points (from 9.04 per cent to 10.78 per cent), whereas the share of EEC cars went up almost eighteen percentage points (from 20.34 per cent to 38.20 per cent). In fact the SMMT has taken direct action, with state support, to limit sales of Japanese cars in the UK and yet has at the same time sought to argue against protectionism in general. The answer is clear, the 'British' car industry has an EEC base . . . and is not interested in any restrictions on trade and/or investment flows within this theatre of operations. In contrast, Japanese . . . producers are seen as an external threat, against whom Western European and American producers have formed a common front. (Cowling 1982: 143)

The superficially lopsided concern shown by corporate lobbyists in the UK in the 1970s about the threat of Japanese entry is explicable in these terms. As a result of strategically placed North American transnational producers already operating across the EEC, and the terms of treaty within the EEC, any case that might have been made to 'protect' the British market against imports as such would by this time have been something of a busted flush, but a united front by all players in the UK market could, nonetheless, be held against the newcomers from Japan. Thus while the British-owned car industry had, by the latter part of the 1970s, suffered badly as a consequence of imports from the EEC to the UK home market – and not least by Ford, which doubled in the 1970s both as a major UK-based producer and as a major importer of cars from its transplant operations elsewhere in the EEC (see Cowling ibid.) – lobbying for import controls within Britain, via the Society of Motor Manufacturers and Traders (or SMMT), and even British Leyland (the 'home' producer), was targeted instead at Japan, although still a relatively minor player in terms of units sold. This is not surprising. In the first phases of encroachment by entrants upon corporate territories hitherto dominated by a different set of nationally- or regionally-based firms, one would naturally expect to see a heightened sensitivity to this fact amongst the spokespersons for the adversely affected incumbents, their employees and, where relevant, the government bodies which become subject to the lobbying effort. This is to be expected, and this might be sufficient to engender some sense of 'crisis' even if the entrants were of a common or garden variety type *vis-à-vis* their production capabilities. It is worth stressing this last point: in this earlier period little was made of how Japanese assemblers actually built cars, even though import penetration was clearly an issue.[1] But faced with encroachments on their territories, the affected 'Western' firms operating in the EEC – or, more specifically, the incumbent firms – initially responded via a concerted effort to lobby to impede further advances.

For Cowling, this would prove to be the response only in the shorter-term:

> We can in fact expect two responses to this sort of asymmetry and the competitive behaviour it leads to. In the short and medium term established, domestic monopolies and oligopolies will seek the help of the state in securing protection, subsidy or restructuring. Again the UK car industry is a case in point, with the state-supported restriction on Japanese imports, the state's direct involvement with British Leyland and its subsidisation of investment and production by foreign car companies in the UK. In the longer term we can expect a further accommodation by US and European car producers to the emergence of the Japanese car industry and the restoration of a more stable collusive arrangement. The recent agreement between Leyland and Honda is indicative of such accommodation . . . An increasing accommodation between European and American producers and Japanese producers can be expected in the immediate future. (Cowling 1982: 131, 143)

So far as relationships between the major car producers selling to Europe are concerned, this proved an accurate prediction. That accommodations were quickly sought can hardly be doubted: the 1980s saw a series of collaborative arrangements between Japanese and Western producers, a process facilitated in no small measure by the move on the part of Japanese assemblers to establish overseas sites in the regions liable otherwise to impede market entry. And there is no compelling evidence since that Japanese car sales have come at the expense of a major or sustained assault on existing industry price–cost margins: while certainly offering price-competitive products – the prices listed for each model specification – price–cost margins in what is now the EC appear, for example, to have been maintained even after restrictions on the sales of Japanese cars were lifted, allowing of course for the inherent complexity of the evidence and the discriminating pricing policies that assemblers pursue as a matter of course when selling to different markets (see Rhys 2005). This does not mean that there have been no gainers or losers, but equally Japanese car assemblers have not swept their competitors away – indeed, while Toyota and Honda remain very significant players in the world industry, subsequent developments, as with the acquisition of Nissan by Renault, have testified both to the complexity of the changing patterns of global ownership, and the limits of 'Japanese' dominance, in the EC as elsewhere.[2] In this regard, and provided that one does not exaggerate the sense of stability, the initial shock of Japanese entry has passed, and following a complex of political and collaborative responses by incumbent firms, 'less fraught' relations have been restored, albeit in a global context still characterized by conditions of intensely rivalrous oligopoly. The UK, dominated by North American transnationals and large European producers in the 1970s, is now a shared dominion which recognizes the 'permanence' of transplant-supported Japanese car assemblers.

What for the UK in the late 1970s was a heightened sensitivity to Japanese import penetration in the car industry was in the case of North America a reaction closer to panic, given the much larger export thrust from Japan in this direction. By 1980, Japan was exporting twice as many units to the smaller North American region as to Western Europe, and whereas Europe still enjoyed a net trade surplus in cars with the rest of the world, North America (and the US) was in overall trading deficit.[3] And while the sale of cars built by European firms to North American markets had also grown sharply over the course of the 1970s, the interests of the big US producers were represented in Europe (via transplant operations) in a way that was clearly not the case when countenancing the one-way trade flows from Japan. In this context, and again not surprisingly, it was principally against Japan that lobbying was aimed: in this theatre of operations, as much as in Western Europe, the strength and form of the reaction by incumbent interests can be better understood if the asymmetries in the pattern of market encroachments are emphasized. Even a cursory sampling of the literature of this period impresses the point, as for example in colloquia of the sort called by the University of Michigan to discuss the future of the American car industry in the light of Japanese entry: notwithstanding that European imports had also made substantial egress into North American markets, speaker after speaker, invited from government, the corporate sector and labour, lined up to discuss the problems posed for the US by Japan (see Cole 1981). And while Japan was congratulated for its 'highly developed industrial sector', it was also criticized for shielding its own markets, via 'a costly and often a seemingly impenetrable distribution system that effectively limits imports' (McCracken 1981: 6–7, in Cole ibid.) (this speaker also criticized 'an undervalued yen', a recurrent theme right up to the mid-1980s, when the yen began to appreciate against the dollar). The asymmetry in the trading relationship was here very much to the fore of debate. And in this context, no less than in Europe, the ensuing progress in the 1980s of joint ventures and Japanese direct investment in facilities based in the US was again predictable.[4] It can be observed, too, in North America as in Europe, that the long-predicted assault on industry price–cost margins by Japanese assemblers has never materialized – the contest, while real, has remained consistent with different forms of engagement.

It is interesting in this connection to see that following the groundswell of opinion to the contrary in the 1980s – to the view that industry was indeed being transformed – the evolving structures of ownership, collaboration and procurement in this and other world industries are sometimes discussed as if everything were being driven by 'improvements' following on from Japanese production principles. This view has been neatly summarized by Professor Robert Gilpin, an eminent authority on international economic relations, in the following pithy terms:

> The American era of horizontal FDI was based on what some scholars call 'Fordism' – the manufacturing system of mass production of standardized products, strict division of labour, and single-site manufacturing – but this system of industrial production has become less competitive. The continuing shift from mass production to 'lean and flexible' manufacturing means that a firm must incorporate technological sophistication, maximum flexibility, customized products, and extensive networks of suppliers if it is to compete internationally. And consequently, corporations more and more frequently interact on a global scale through a wide range of external corporate alliances, for example, joint ventures, subcontracting, licensing, and interfirm agreements. Multinational firms have gone beyond exporting and building foreign facilities through FDI to establishing intricate international alliances and networks of research, production and marketing. (Gilpin 2000: 167–8)

We reject as untenable – although not uninteresting – the view summarized in the first half of this passage, for reasons that will be inferred from the propositions set out in the other parts of this book. As a corollary, we similarly reject as unconvincing any attempt to account for the (further) development of global structures and alliances in the world's car industry as if these were functional outgrowths of the appearance of 'lean and flexible' production systems, evolved in Japan. The empirical facts concerning the initial patterns of entry and subsequent patterns of corporate accommodation in the world car industry continue to unfold, and to this extent investigation of the patterns of Japan's encroachments continue to make headway, and in ways that can be divorced moreover from any immediate controversy over the role of innovations in manufacturing methods *per se*.[5] What is remarkable, however, is that the transition from 'Fordism' is – as Gilpin (ibid.) notes – now posited as a driver of the forms taken by the 'internationalization of business'. While hardly acceptable as a thesis, it is an association that highlights the question that provides a point of departure for this chapter: can myth-making about an industry be better understood if due attention is given the global contexts in which fictions about production – Japan's 'lean and flexible systems' – take root and grow?

6.3 RISE AND DECLINE OF THE WORLD CAR CONTROVERSY

Since we are concerned with raising and framing some of the relevant issues, it is important that some sensitivity be shown to the nuances of changing opinion. The importance of so doing can be illustrated via assessment of some emerged paradoxes in the evolving body of literature that deals with Japanese manufacture. For the first of these we evoke the changing contours of the debate on so-called 'world car' strategies. Preoccupations with a 'world car' design – in this context a consolidated design to be marketed globally, and in most accounts to be built transnationally – might seem a mere reflex to some of the manifest pressures in the world industry that are conducive to consolidation of designs across regions and the establishment of global production and marketing networks. But on closer acquaintance, debates organized around this theme have evolved in an interesting way.

In the North American context of the later 1970s and early 1980s, for example, the debate took a rather particular form. The essence of the 'world car' strategy as publicly discussed in this period is surveyed in Sinclair (1983), a useful contemporary study that gives a sense of the speculation at this time. A leading example widely discussed at this juncture was a car line (the 'J-car') introduced by GM in 1980 and produced across eight regions to be sold in markets encompassing North America, Europe, Australasia, Japan and Brazil, on the basis of 'global' appeal: attendant publicity no doubt partly accounts for the attention this drew at the time, both from academics and other commentators (see ibid.: 5, 72–4).[6] But more generally, the sense that one would obtain from much of the associated commentary is that in response to unit cost differentials perceived to favour Japanese exporters the inevitable response would be a major shakeout, achieved via the pooling of production facilities and a reduction in the number of basic model designs, with global supply chains taking advantage of low (wage) cost regions. This is, more or less, how Sinclair framed the influence of Japan (ibid.: 24–7, 75), as did others at the time. Lee Iacocca, a then prominent figure in the American industry, is quoted to illustrate what the pending 'shakeout' would entail: 'the goals of all auto companies will be the same . . . to find the right combination of manufacturing plants and dealer–distribution networks worldwide that will produce the lowest costs and highest profit . . . it will be a global shakeout equal in scope to the consolidation of the US auto industry after world war one' (see ibid.: 55).[7] Those companies too small to participate in such a strategy could embark on joint ventures, be acquired or merge, or risk disappearing from the scene altogether. In other words, commentary frequently took a form – not least from industry spokespersons – which both built upon and added to a sense of imminent crisis, particularly in North America. A similar preoccupation with Japan with respect to the world car can certainly also be found at Europe at this time, although levied through with other preoccupations that perhaps reflect the lesser extent of Japanese import penetration compared with North America. But in general terms the 'world car' project quickly became identified with responses to Japanese encroachments, an unsurprising association in the circumstances.[8] And not surprisingly, as panic has subsided and accommodations have been reached, debates on the world car (in the West) have cooled.

But what is striking is that the memory of the form of this debate has been taken up as an embellishment in the narrative on Japanese production methods. Moreover, it is one which has practically inverted the account given of the impact of Japan's emergence as a global player in the world's car industry, because whereas an earlier brand of commentary depicted the world car strategy as a response to Japan, Japanese manufacturing methods are now more typically said to have undermined a separately emerging world car strategy. In particular, and on the production side, it is now commonly stated that 'flexible' assembly is inimical to the world car strategy, on grounds that the sort of complex global supply logistics which may have worked in the age of 'Fordism' – or 'global Fordism', following Kaplinsky (1988: 451) – are less viable in the age of Toyota: 'flexibility in production . . . is just not possible within the context of the "world car" concept and . . . few of the US and European car firms are thinking in these terms any longer' (ibid.: 456). And indeed, this is a proposition which has now entered the standard texts: Dicken (2003) opposes the world car concept, as practiced by Ford and GM in the 1970s and 1980s, with the requirements of a modern assembly plant required (following Japan) to tailor each car built to individual 'variations in customer demand' (ibid.: 381).

Judged from the perspectives developed in Chapter 2, it hardly needs saying that this is an unconvincing hypothesis. Wide selection practices were already decades-established realities for producers like Ford and GM at the point when world car debates became entangled with fear of the Japanese menace; moreover, from an operations perspective, the supposition that 'flexibility' in production, or the incorporation of variations in the final product assembly, should be somehow incompatible with global supply chains is unconvincing.[9] Moreover, Japanese car assemblers are players in the world industry who have typically eschewed precisely the sort of width in selection now being (wrongly) identified as a new element in competition that has significantly altered the appeal and feasibility of transnational production and distribution networks for the industry's global firms.

But the upshot is that a debate about an imminent global 'shakeout' driven by the aggressive entry of Japan's car assemblers in an earlier decade has somehow transformed itself into a reassuring scenario in which a new type of production – and one moreover that is predicated on an ascendant consumer – is argued to constitute a mitigating factor *vis-à-vis* the potentially disturbing consequences of the globalizing propensities in production of large corporations in a global industry, even at the level of disallowing or at least penalizing global sourcing in component parts.

Viewed as a reassuring scenario it is interesting to contrast this with the narrative reviewed by Professor Gilpin, above: this actively acknowledges the global ambitions of giant corporations but justifies the attendant patterns of collaboration and ownership by reference to the imperatives of a new kind of production, one based on factories which are more flexible and thus better able to meet the diverse needs of consumers, and resource requirements which are leaner. The abatement of the world car controversy also marks (on the Western side, at least) the emergence of an account that reassures *vis-à-vis* the medium-term impact of Japanese entry onto the world stage, and to some extent the two views are complementary.[10] We could pursue questions of contrast further, however, because whereas Gilpin describes a narrative that does at least admit to a globalizing propensity in the world economy, the emerged wisdom on the world car treats 'new' production methods in a way which emphasizes instead a dissipating influence on the reality of global structures in industry. We might explore the inconsistencies between these visions further, but to pursue the question in this way would be to ignore the several 500lb elephants wrestling for space in the middle of the room: each vision, each with a message of reassurance, possibly inconsistent but possibly complementary, is founded on myth.

6.4 LEAN PRODUCTION AND THE JAPANESE CRISIS

Another interesting shift in the nuances of opinion is evident in the context of the still ongoing debate about the difficulties that beset the Japanese economy in the 1990s, following the dramatic and steady successes of the preceding decades. Because some of those same writers who have ascribed Japanese encroachments on markets previously dominated by leading Western firms to significant advances in the organisation of manufacture have since shown themselves willing to transfer the same boot to the other foot, Japan is now said to be suffering precisely because much of its past gains in trade in manufactures were predicated on production methods that could first be learned and then successfully emulated by competitor firms in the West.

Consider, for example, Porter et al. (2000). In this recent prospectus, Michael Porter, in collaboration with co-authors Hirotaka Takeuchi and Mariko Sakakibara, portrays both the Japanese model of government, and of proactive state industrial policy, as abiding sources of microeconomic distortion that have served to stymie rather than encourage growth and effective industrial development. To some extent there is little in this account of Japan's malaise which is entirely new; there has always been a critical viewpoint on the role of the Japanese state in underwriting its past successes, and one has grown more voluble since the recessions of the 1990s. In this example, care is taken to place the collapse of the 'bubble economy', with its overvalued equities and real estate, in a context of 'over-regulation' and 'over-protection' by 'meddlesome government', of an 'over-bureaucratized', 'over-taxed' and 'overly export dependent' economy, all a consequence of state interference (see ibid.: 1–2). And in this context, again a not entirely unfamiliar stance, Porter et al. adopt a 'two Japans perspective', in which much is made of the fact that industrial and sectoral productivity gains in Japan over the relevant periods have been unevenly distributed.[11]

What is of interest, however, is where Porter et al. next lead the argument. While the relative 'backwardness' of sectors like (the interpretation is Porter et al.'s) retail, wholesale and energy, and the relatively weak trading positions of industries like agriculture, chemicals and medical products, are attributed to the long-term consequences of state interference and protectionism, the successes enjoyed in key consumer goods industries like cars and electronics are attributed to gains achieved by means of innovative practices in production. These practices, purportedly adopted in a range of Japanese industries, are summarized by Porter et al. under the rubric of the words 'lean production', referring to a system pioneered at Toyota:

> The lean production system played a central role in the Japanese corporate model. Pioneered by Toyota, lean production treats product development, production and purchasing as a total system. By optimizing this system, Toyota achieves high levels of quality, productivity, timely delivery and flexibility simultaneously. (Porter et al. 2000: 70)

This provides the basis for their explanation of the sharp advances made by the Japanese economy *vis-à-vis* international competitors in the post World War II era. The successes enjoyed by some segments at least of the Japanese economy, are sought, to a considerable extent, in the *transient* gains achieved by means of the set of innovative *operational* practices in manufacture:

> In the 1970s and 1980s, the Japanese set the world standard for operational effectiveness – that is, for improving quality and lowering cost in ways that were widely applicable to many fields. Japanese companies taught the world an array of approaches . . . that improve productivity in nearly ever company in every industry. (Ibid.: 78)

But on grounds that there are very finite limits to the competitive advantages to be had from improved operational methods in production, because emulation will first close and then eliminate the 'efficiency' gap, Porter et al. next explain the relative decline in the fortunes of Japan – given the deficiencies attributable to state interference that they believe to be a feature of the Japanese economy at large – as the inevitable consequence of a process of 'competitive convergence'. They argue that the gap in operational effectiveness between Japanese and Western companies began to narrow from about the mid-to-late 1980s, and that subsequently Japan's competitors have begun to forge ahead on the back of another type of revolution: 'having successfully emulated Japanese operational practices, US companies in particular began to push the productivity frontier outwards themselves, especially through the use of information technology' (see Porter et al. 2000: 79). In a nutshell, the thesis therefore advanced is this: 'lean production', employed here as a shorthand for practices affecting dimensions of production like manufacturing flexibility and resource productivity, gave only *temporary* advantages to the adopting Japanese corporations, advantages which have dissipated with the passage of time. This in turn is made the basis for a second tranche of criticism *vis-à-vis* Japan:

> The most generic operational improvements – that is, those involving widely applicable management techniques, process technologies, and input improvements – diffuse the fastest. There is a deeper problem with the Japanese approach to competing, however. Relentless and single-minded efforts to achieve best practice tend to lead to *competitive convergence*, which means that all the competitors in an industry compete on the same dimensions . . . Because Japanese companies think of competition only in terms of operational effectiveness – improving quality and cost simultaneously – they have made it almost impossible to be enduringly successful . . . Having lost their decisive lead in operational effectiveness, slower growth and competitive convergence have become a painful combination for Japanese companies . . . By competing on organizational effectiveness alone, then, many Japanese companies have been caught in a trap of their own making. (ibid.: 81)

While this point is expanded upon by Porter et al. at greater length, the gist is clear. Japanese corporations are roundly criticized for failing to innovate in areas where emulation by competitors would have proved more difficult, for failing to undertake steps to combine *operational* effectiveness, 'concerned with performing the same or similar activities better than competitors' (ibid.: 89), with *market strategies* that would also set them apart from competitors' profiles and products, making emulation more difficult and their own brands more distinctive. Porter et al. argue that while both operational effectiveness and strategic effectiveness are necessary for success, a distinctive market strategy – 'harder to imitate' (ibid.: 91) – is essential to longevity.

The argument is here very clearly put. But Porter et al. are not alone in this; rather, they provide a particularly clear expression of an emergent view. In a subsequent study to that already cited (in section 6.2) Professor Gilpin observes that while it is widely held that 'various techniques associated with lean production . . . highly efficient techniques, pioneered at Toyota and associated with the technological and organizational revolution, diffused rapidly throughout Japanese industry', it is also believed that 'the overwhelming Japanese advantage decreased' as these techniques diffused also to other countries; and if this accounted for the initial advantages enjoyed by Japan's export industries, 'America's corporations . . . regained much of the competitiveness they had lost in the 1980s' (Gilpin 2001: 136–7). At the same time, and in a way which mirrors Porter et al.'s argument, it is maintained that 'superiority in manufacturing processes *rather* than in product innovation has been the key to Japan's outstanding export success' (ibid., emphasis added). The inferences are not drawn as starkly, but the implication is there: a production-based advantage, not product–led distinctiveness, has accounted for Japan's past successes, but the source of this advantage has dissipated with overseas emulation.

Judged against the positions developed in our own study this is not an adequate basis by which to account for Japan's previous successes: Porter et al. rely on the reality of a manufacturing revolution, an idea which (we maintain) is chimerical. But equally it is clear that in the prospectus set out by Porter et al. a very considerable burden of weight indeed is placed on what for summary purposes they call lean production: this provides the fulcrum upon which much else is made to turn. Moreover, and this deserves emphasis, what Porter et al. maintain is not only that the Japanese model of government has been deleterious to its economy, but also that transient advantages in production have obscured serious weaknesses in the Japanese management model, *even in* those corporations in the vanguard of hitherto leading sectors. Here lean production has become a suitable point from which to deliver not only Japan's state institutions with a good kicking, but also Japanese competition.

One last observation seems germane here. If the changing positions taken around the import of Japan's 'contribution' to the world of manufacturing activity are interpreted as ciphers by which to read underlying attitudes in the West, it is possible to see here the potential for a reawakening of a disposition that was marked in popular discourse in the 1960s and 1970s, before the extent of Japan's market encroachments became fully evident. We might broadly summarize this as a grudging acceptance of Japanese talent in mimicking products conceived of in the West, and manufacturing them effectively, but qualified by a denial that any real innovative flair was involved – this latter being retained as the historic and inherited provenance of Western industrial cultures. We must not be clumsy or unfair: we do not ascribe such a view to Porter et al., but wish rather to note the potential for a clumsy and unfair reading. The view that Japanese corporations have in a sense achieved success in one dimension only – in the sphere of imitable 'operational improvements' rather than in *strategic* innovation – and this as a consequence of deficiencies in a Japanese corporate mentality evolved, one imagines, in a context of prior imitations of Western achievements, seems to carry with it a particular charge that could lend itself to easy (mis)interpretation.

6.5   MYTH MAKING AS PRODUCTION POLITICS

We commenced this chapter with the question of asymmetries of the sort that might emerge as a consequence of 'unequal development' as between national economies, because it is here, we suggest, that it is best to begin if one is to understand both the mounting reaction against Japanese imports in Western business circles through the 1970s and into the 1980s, in the car and other consumer goods industries, and the subsequent patterns of accommodation sought and reached with affected incumbent interests. In this regard, we emphasized too that the car industry is both highly rivalrous and characterized by significant features of oligopoly. Neither the rising tide of reaction to Japanese imports in the 1970s – strongest in the US but striking even in regions less obviously affected than North America – nor the subsequent patterns of collaboration, joint ventures and transplantation, are surprising *per se*; and neither requires that Toyota be invoked as a harbinger of post-Fordist manufacture. At the same time, and as the initial shock of Japanese entry recedes, it is obviously of some interest to consider how this latter narrative has evolved in the West in light of the subsequent travails of Japan in the 1990s, allowing of course for the pertinence of distinguishing between positions that might be said to be reflective of broader streams of written opinion and commentary, and those which are more selective.

It is important to be aware of the possibilities of self-interested myth-making in a global industry, as viewed from the perspective (say) of large corporate players. For example, one does not have to give over wholly to cynicism to see possible advantages in the notion of a Japanese-inspired lean revolution in the manufacture and assembly of cars, from the viewpoint of Western assemblers, quite apart from any issues actually arising from the material evidence, coldly assessed. If, for example, the medium-term response by incumbent interests in North America and Western Europe to the fact of Japanese entry has been one of accommodation (the contingent restoration of a 'less fraught' engagement between highly rivalrous firms), it has doubtless been easier to defend the resulting joint ventures and collaborative deals as a consequence of presenting these as corollaries to a process by which the consumer will be enriched, via newly learned production techniques that will deliver a more flexible and custom-driven manufacture as well as resource economies; moreover, in this particular narrative, collaboration becomes a competitive necessity. The success of this posture, in its own way quite extra-ordinary, has already been illustrated: when Professor Gilpin, whom we cited in a passage above, observes the view that global interactions demand 'a wide range of external corporate alliances' as the necessary counterpart to the purported shift towards the 'lean and flexible', he writes not as a representa-tive of one of the contending university branches from which one might draw up a list of likely suspects – sociology, industrial relations, political economy, business management, or even for that matter, engineering – but rather as the Eisenhower Professor of Public and International Affairs Emeritus at Princeton, describing an emerged strand of thinking on international economic relations. In much the same way, it might be (and doubtless is) easier for corporations seeking to sell changes involving the derogation of previous agreements with labour unions if these can be presented as ineluctable coun-terparts to a newer and 'necessary' system. This will naturally still be true even if claims are empirically well-founded; but even when they are not, there may be other no less tangible benefits to 'adopting' firms.

The same, of course, applies to governments concerned to shore up domes-tic or regional interests against encroaching rivals. As already indicated, national governments in the mature industrial economies have played an important role in facilitating the processes of corporate accommodation in the car industry, for reasons that no doubt include concerns about maintaining domestic production and employment as well as more narrowly defined and motivated responses to corporate lobbying. At the same time, and as again observed by Professor Gilpin in the passage cited at the outset as an epigraph to this chapter, great credit has been given governments in both the US and UK for introducing lean production techniques to their domestic industries via the expedient of Japanese FDI, said to have encouraged the uptake of 'lean production techniques' and improved product quality. Consider, in this light, the following statement from a UK government department:

> The advent of Japanese vehicle manufacturing transplants in the UK, starting with
> the arrival of Nissan in 1986, had an important impact on the UK component sector

and has provided the opportunity for a whole generation of UK managers to understand the principles and practices of lean manufacture. A number of UK component
companies are now acknowledged best practitioners in lean techniques and continuous improvement . . . Indeed the UK is recognised, after the US, as the leading
practitioner of lean manufacturing in automotive (sic).

Despite the improvements in productivity made in recent years by vehicle manufacturers and by many component suppliers, the UK's overall productivity
(measured by Gross Value Added per person) is lower than that of our main
competitors in the EU. This is a situation similar to that in some other sectors of
manufacturing. The reasons are complex but include issues such as the macroeco-
nomic instability of the past, which discouraged long-term planning and investment
(including in training); the relative value of the products manufactured; capital
intensity; and labour productivity. (HC 2000–2001: 95–6)

From the first passage we learn that the UK-based automotive industry as a
whole, including both vehicle assemblers and component part suppliers, and
extending to encompass its foreign-owned firms, is the 'leading practitioner'
of lean production outside of the US: by implication, it is the leader amongst
European countries. This is an achievement directly attributed to the impact of
Japanese investment. Reading the second passage, however, we are confronted
with a qualification: 'despite the improvements', and note that the passage is
still referring here to the automotive industry – in 'a situation similar to that in
some other sectors of manufacturing' – and the sector as a whole still suffers
from *low* productivity *vis-à-vis* the EU, as well as other problems which
include the 'relative value' of products manufactured. On the basis of the
memorandum from which these passages are excerpted, Britain is thus doubly
distinguished when set against its main European partners and rivals, contriving somehow to have both the leanest producers and also the least productive.

The memorandum itself is a significant one, issued by the UK's
Department of Trade and Industry (DTI) in response to a House of Commons
Trade and Industry Committee investigation into the state of the UK-based car
industry, following a series of decisions by overseas producers to dispose of,
or cease, operations at long-established car manufacture and assembly sites
located in Britain.[12] With respect to provenance, it could hardly be a more
'official' assessment of a state of play. For sheer contrariness it would also be
hard to beat, and as such it makes an ideal exhibit by which to illustrate the
sense of our more general point. UK government, or at least the relevant
departments of government dealing with trade and industry, as indeed in North
America, has reaped credit for inculcating lean production via inwards FDI, so
much as to merit mention by distinguished professors of international affairs
seeking to outline for readers the shape of current issues in the global economy. But at the same time, while prepared to *actively* lay claim to this credit
as due recognition of the advantages of a policy skewed towards attracting
foreign investors, no bones are made about abiding weaknesses in UK-based

manufacture. It might of course be the case that the senior civil servants
responsible for drafting departmental responses to investigating Parliamentary
Committees can in all conscience cleave to two exclusive propositions simultaneously, so that being a world leader in lean production can entail lower
labour inputs for each good produced *and* lower labour productivity:

> 'When I use a word', Humpty Dumpty said, in rather a scornful tone, 'It means just
> what I choose it to mean – neither more nor less.'
>   'The question is', said Alice, 'whether you can make words mean so many
> different things.'
>   'The question is', said Humpty Dumpty, 'which is to be master – that's all.'
> Carroll (1998: 186)

But a contrariness of this kind points also to other things.

In this regard the UK has a particular value as an example by which to illustrate the potential political utilities of a lean revolution in manufacture,
evidence aside. It is sad that the UK should be distinguished in this way, but
one might struggle to find a comparable North American document in which
the announcement of world leadership in lean production techniques is qualified in such a contrary way.[13] However, the point would be the same: if those
countries which have gone furthest in attracting Japanese FDI in the automotive industry are routinely cited as the principal beneficiaries of an attendant
manufacturing revolution, it must also be remembered that state bodies in
these countries have little to gain from challenging this. Study after study finds
that manufacture based in Britain is not more 'efficient' when compared to
comparator sectors in countries like France or Germany, so much so that
announcements of world leadership in production techniques delivered by the
relevant government department will sadly acknowledge as much on the same
page. But difficult questions that might then be asked are not liable to be
asked, and if in the UK the more obviously enfeebled state of the manufacturing base occasionally generates absurd documents, occasionally critical
comments are easy to live with. As with corporations, the production politics
of industrial accommodation matter.

But what must still be explained is how and why a situation would be
permitted to arise that permitted Japan to develop the strategy capacity to
penetrate North American and Western European markets in the first place,
and why it was allowed to do so in a context where its own domestic markets
were simultaneously protected.

On this point what is certainly required is that an answer be sought within,
and a position taken on, the global political economy and on international relations in the post-World War II era. Here we have sympathy for the view
discussed and summarized in Coates (2000): after the cessation of overt hostil-
ities at the end of World War II the US, then an occupying power, was initially

disposed to undertake policies aimed at 'de-industrializing' Japan, 'removing heavy machinery as part of reparations and repositioning Japan as an under-developed economy dominated by agriculture and small business'; but the course of foreign policy changed shortly thereafter, with the US deciding (from 1947) that Japan had better be rebuilt instead as a 'bulwark against communism', and as a consequence assistance was given to an active policy of rapid industrial development (ibid.: 215). Coates cites a telling phrase which sums the point neatly: Japan became 'a US invited guest in the exclu-sive club of the rich and powerful nations of the West . . . in a perfect exam-ple of what Immanuel Wallerstein has called *development by invitation*', followed, as Coates observes, by American finance (Arrighi 1994: 340, cited in Coates ibid.: 216). Japan's economic infrastructure was re-established in the 1950s, and by 1955 ways were being sought to break free from 'excessive dependence' on the US. By the mid-1960s attention was moving on from 'industrial catch-up' to encompass trade, with a shift in Japanese state priori-ties towards export promotion focused initially on consumer durables like cars and consumer electronics (Coates ibid.: 216–18). Dispensation thus came first for state-led industrial development in Japan, along with US financial assis-tance: access to Western markets (and Europe) followed, even as Japan asserted its industrial independence, and for similar reasons of geo-political interests. The asymmetries entailed in Japan's encroachments on Western markets can be placed in this context, as also the initially muted and then more overtly active responses to these encroachments *vis-à-vis* accommodations with affected incumbent interests.

It is in this context too that one should consider the evolving literature on the manufacturing revolution as this pertains to Toyota and other Japanese firms. Its evolution must be judged not only in the context of America's resur-gence as an industrial power in the 1990s, and Japan's comparative difficul-ties, but also in a context where Japan's geo-political significance has changed. In a more recent and elegant essay on the 'rise and fall' of Japan as a model of 'progressive capitalism', Coates (2006) highlights the view that the US has adopted a progressively tougher stance with respect to Japan as Cold War tensions have eased: Japan became a frontline state in the Cold War when Beijing fell to Mao; US state policy became more responsive domestically to corporate lobbying with the ending of the war in Vietnam and rapprochement with China; and as the Cold War drew to its close US pressure for re-evalua-tion of the yen intensified (with concessions from Japan in the Plaza Agreement of 1985), as did pressure on Japan to open its domestic markets to American corporations. If judged from a Western perspective, stories of trans-formation and change predicated (first) on 'flexible' and (then) 'lean' factories took root over a period stretching from the early-to-mid 1980s through to the earlier part of the 1990s; the same period in which Japan's car manufacturers were engaged in making their major investments in North American facilities, and in a typically collaborative fashion with respect to incumbent US interests. But the international context in which this story is told was changing throughout both the 1980s, with growing pressures from America on Japan for policy 'reform', and the 1990s, with Japan's domestic economy beginning to struggle, and it is of obvious interest to consider developments in the narrative *vis-à-vis* the changing global polity.

What is notable, and here again we consider Western perspectives, is that the problems experienced by Japan's domestic economy, and reflecting no doubt the diminished status of Japan as an ally in the Cold War, has at one level seen a wholesale assault on recently established wisdoms. In a more recent essay on the rise and fall of Japan as a model of 'progressive' capitalism, Coates (2006) describes the emergence of a very large body of Western academic and policy literature extolling the merits of Japanese economic institutions as a model. While earlier treatments written in the post-World War II period were posed mainly in terms of the orthodox economic treatments of the day, with perhaps something of a bias towards the market economy as the basis of growth, contributions came increasingly from writers schooled in the wider social sciences. From the 1970s and on through the 1980s a series of leading scholars (including luminaries like Ronald Dore) began to explore questions of what made Japan distinctive – in its corporate practices, in its state practices, and in its employment relations. This generated, in the broader sense of the word, a 'vision' of Japan as an 'alternative' model of capitalism. Questions as to the cultural specificity of Japanese economic success (the role, for example, of a Japanese Confucian as opposed, say, to an Anglo-Saxon protestant heritage) began to make their mark, as did speculation on transferable difference on the shop floor. In particular, critics of neo-liberalism in the 1980s, and of the economic and social policies of Thatcher and Reagan, developed these latter themes (see Coates ibid.). But with the onset of Japan's difficulties in the 1990s, and with American confidence resurgent, attempts to construct Japan as the basis for an alternative to unrestrained market capitalism have without exception come under considerable pressure.[14]

At the same time the one element from the 1980s that pertains to Japanese exceptionalism that still seems secured in its place in the firmament is the one which in our own study we argue is easily shown to be evidence-inconsistent. Indeed, in the hands of writers like Michael Porter the circle is completely squared: lean production methods, hitherto the provenance of Japanese corporations, are now part and parcel of the artillery brought to bear by better organized and more adventurous US corporations on the state-encumbered domestic economy of the Japanese foe. In this way the purported manufacturing revolution – a chimera – has proved not only remarkably resilient but also versatile in the hands of gifted interpreters. What is of particular note in this recently emerged strand of commentary is that an abiding belief in the appearance of a new way of organizing manufacturing operations, as a consequence of innovations in the factories of firms like Toyota and other Japanese producers, *coexists* with an otherwise wholesale dismissal of Japanese institutions.

There is something in all of this (in the view of the present writer, at least) that reminds one of Jules Henry's (1968) comments on social and psychological preparations for war. In a stimulating essay on this topic, Henry, an anthropologist and sociologist, broached the thorny question of 'defining the enemy' in a way which seems oddly apt. Whereas in simpler (or at least, earlier) types of social formation, the enemy is an entity which stands outside the social system as it exists for its inhabitants, in the 'modern' world the enemy must by necessity be both a part and not a part of that system. In all likelihood connected by chains of diplomacy, cultural ties, and trade, war between parties necessarily occurs within the social system, but at the same time requires that the enemy be clearly defined as standing outside it: 'relations must be broken'. In this context, the use of 'former enemies' against 'former friends' becomes inevitable, and here Henry chooses as one case in point 'America's use of Japan . . . as a staging area and source of supply for the war in Vietnam' (ibid.: 51). As a result, defeat and occupation by the US became a victory for Japan, allowed to reindustrialize and to compete with American capital around the world.[15] But at the same time Japan, now a conditional friend of the US, was nonetheless still a past and potential future enemy, and Henry was of the view that this as much as the war against communism was pertinent to US regional strategy: 'business and technological know-how combined with low wages have given Japan such economic power that U.S. involvement in South-East Asia is aimed as much at monopolizing that market against Japanese penetration as against Chinese. The Vietnam war is indirectly a war against Japan, who is part of our social system, and whom, at the same time, the U.S. is using in order to further her ends in Asia' (ibid.: 52).

It is interesting that Henry saw the renaissance of Japan from an American viewpoint in such layered terms, given the more recent and singular emphasis on the declining threat of communism as the basis for a tougher US policy. But more generally the pertinent points here are first of all an interdependent world political economy with enough conflicts of interest to make potential enemies of all, combined with what is depicted in Henry's essay as the 'evolutionary achievement' of modern times – a psychological disposition to accept other nations as inimical as and when required to be defined as such, a readiness to accept invention (Henry 1968: 52–53). And while specifically concerned with the social and psychological preparedness for war, by construction this preparedness encompassed a general state of mind: an inculcated sense of vulnerability and threat, a proneness to shifting sentiments and a permanent state of confusion as to the changing status of friends and enemies. The comment that seems particularly relevant is offered by Henry (ibid.: 67–8) as a corollary, 'a condition of contemporary perception' that extended to the 'academic world', namely the 'withholding of commitment to any view of the world', a plasticity of thought. The modern world, in Henry's view, is the enemy of 'intrinsic definition'.

If this line of argument, or rather this perspective, is to be developed further, research must naturally turn also to consider Japanese writing for Japanese readers. It can hardly be supposed that opinion in the West be shared in Japan, nor can it even be supposed that simple comparisons are either possible or desirable. On the very specific point of the 'lean and flexible', for example, even if Toyota's claims to have revolutionized worldwide manufacturing practice as are as widely accepted in Japan as they currently are in the West – a surmize only – the historical and cultural contexts within which this myth has taken root are nonetheless not Western contexts, and the sort of thesis developed by Porter et al. no doubt plays very differently there. And if we adopt a broader purview by which to understand myths about production, one rooted (for example) in our understanding of the changing international economic and political context, a Japanese-centred study must again cast different light.

We will pause to venture one speculative observation. It has been proposed, and in clear contradiction to the thesis expounded by Porter et al. (2000), that the difficulties faced by Japan's domestic economy owe less to the international dissemination of best-practice methods of production that have removed a transient advantage than to the processes by which Japanese capital has been 'liberated' from national boundaries: globalization is invoked, but in a quite different way. What we have in mind here is the simultaneously advanced position of Cowling and Tomlinson (2000), who identify globalization with the 'hollowing out' of Japan's industrial base, as Japanese firms – including car assemblers like Toyota – have relocated overseas. Whereas Porter et al. criticize the Japanese state for too much domestic interference, Cowling and Tomlinson subject it to critique for lacking perseverance in regulation. Fuelled by a desire to avoid domination by US-led transnational corporations, foreign direct investment (FDI) was for a time restricted by Japanese domestic policy-makers, both in the sense of inward FDI and in the sense of Japanese investments abroad. But the Ministry of International Trade and Policy (MITI) practices of selective targeting of industries, of promoting corporate groups and of cartelization programmes aimed at encouraging mergers to absorb failing firms, backfired (according to Cowling and Tomlinson) over the long run. The creation of 'national champions' meant the formation of powerful corporate groupings dominated by giant firms, which in turn came progressively to disassociate commercial from domestic interest: aggressive lobbying in turn led to a relaxation of restrictions on Japanese outward investment, to facilitate transnational production networks and outsourcing via overseas affiliates. It is this which is held to be responsible for a significant diversion of investment away from Japan's domestic industrial regions in the 1990s, an increasingly isolated small firm sector with depressed orders and profits, and a concomitant rise in business failures, bankruptcy rates and domestic unemployment (see ibid.: F373–9). The travails of Japan are in this way accounted for not (as per Porter et al.) by too much state regulation, but rather by the *capture* of the state apparatus by giant firms (for further discussion and examples, see also Cowling and Tomlinson 2003): from this viewpoint, the problem has been one of insufficiently stringent regulation.[16] The problem is attributed squarely to globalization in production and supply.

As a contra-thesis to the one established by Porter et al. this is a view that still needs broader contextualization, because account must also be taken in understanding the rationale for Japan's relaxation on its strictures against overseas investment of the changing international context, as described above, but it is undoubtedly true that the travails of Japan's economy in the 1990s have coincided with a period in which the relocation of production overseas in the car and other industries has been marked.[17] In the car industry Japan's domestic car production fell by almost 3 million units in the aggregate between 1990 and 1993, almost twice the drop recorded for car sales, which fell by less than 1.5 million units in the same period (Kawahara 1998: 237): this reflected in part the consequences of an appreciating currency and a drop in exports from Japan, but also the increased scale of production operations overseas. Sales and production for Toyota have displayed (broadly) similar trajectories. It is interesting therefore to note that if Toyota's claim to have reinvigorated worldwide manufacture seems untouched (at least superficially) by the misfortunes of the Japanese domestic economy, we might observe that as a profit-seeking organization it has over the same period become progressively detached from that sphere *vis-à-vis* the location of production and employment in a globalizing world.

Accordingly, we close with our observation, which is perhaps best framed as a question: does the disassociation envisaged by Porter et al. between lean and flexible corporations on the one hand, and Japan on the other, also reflect in some subtle way the reality of the growing disassociation between Japan and its producers?[18]

6.6 CONCLUSIONS

Rather than account for the transformation in post-war international economic relations between North America and Western Europe on the one side, and Japan on the other, by reference to a revolution in manufacturing production potentials, in this chapter we have sought to set out some issues relevant to a different sort of approach. The question framing this approach is whether a transformation in international economic relations driven by other considerations might not in turn provide a context by which to better explain a sustained fiction about a manufacturing revolution. In this regard, however, what is almost as noteworthy as the weight given to a narrative account of a shift from mass production to lean and flexible factories is that the nuances attached by commentators, on the Western side at least, appear to be shifting in discernible ways as national and regional fortunes have waxed and waned. It is of particular interest that while it remains a publicly agreed 'fact' that Japanese manufacturers, led by the flagship car assembler Toyota, spawned a 'lean' revolution in production, the terms of the debate on Japanese economic success can turn in a way which tacitly serves to dismiss in every other regard the potency of Japanese economic institutions *vis-à-vis* a Western or (more specifically) an Anglo-Saxon model: the 'lean' revolution is being progressively distanced from Japan.

In its most fundamental aspects this chapter explores the associated themes of durability and plasticity. It is not difficult, on a number of levels, to interpret the rise of the 'lean and flexible' Japanese factory as reflecting in part on anxieties and responses to pressures of globalization, at least on the Western side. It is unlikely, however, that this constitutes the whole story: if the emergence of a new industrial power (Japan) should occasion a sense of engendered crisis in the West, an explanation is still needed of the forms taken up by the associated fictions – and of the ease with which histories can be revised, rewritten and accepted to match. It does not seem unlikely that the durability of the lean and flexible resides in its identification with the corporate side of a capitalist economy: Japanese corporations can detach themselves from the Japanese economy as transnational producers; Western corporations can 'learn' the methods and rise once more to ascendancy. At the same time, this seems only a starting point for a proper understanding of the great transformation in production potentials falsely identified by a generation of observers, and made the basis for a veritable sociology of industry: in this connection, plasticity – of memory, of perception, of loyalties – seems an oddly germane metaphor, as does a purview which commences with the possibility that social(–global) tensions can be (and are) mediated by acts of collective (and unconscious) invention.

NOTES

1. Later commentaries on Japanese import penetration are sometimes written as if the concerns expressed by Western incumbent firms at this time can be cited retrospectively as *de facto* evidence of a watershed in manufacturing organization and technique. The dangers of so

doing can perhaps be best illustrated by considering another 'menace' of the time. Here we can again cite Cowling (1982: 131, 143), who observes (parenthetically) that after Japan the second source of anxiety for the dominant EEC-based car producers was the prospect of loss of markets to imports from East Europe. The example should be enough to underline the obvious point that anxiety about import penetration, when expressed by the representatives of an incumbent national or regional interest, need not imply that there is some belief that the 'threat' in question is possessed of some proven advantage in manufacturing know-how. Thus while there was no suggestion from the 'troubled' Western quarter that East European car plants possessed (in the 1970s) any technical (as opposed to cost) advantages in production, there were nonetheless occasional expressions of concern about an imminent problem. In fact, there is much that is potentially salutary about responses to the Eastern bloc. Alec Nove, writing twenty years before Cowling, in the revised second edition of his standard work on the Soviet economy, was cautioning against industrial fear-mongering: 'Dr Balogh, for example, is apt to warn us of the likelihood of very intense Soviet competition on world markets, while less serious writers make our flesh creep' (Nove 1965: 316). The cold-war propaganda of the time (produced by flesh-creeping writers) was certainly awash with lurid images of a new type of machine economy, ruthless in its efficiency and alternately serviced by either crushed or Stakanovite workers – not entirely dissimilar as literary archetypes to the factory operatives that inhabit any number of the works about Japanese factories produced by North American and Western European writers in the 1980s. It is interesting to speculate what further turns this earlier strand of commentary would have taken had the threat concretized and socialist-bloc firms made serious headway with exports to Western markets.

2. Thus Tony Woodley, now General Secretary of the Transport and General Workers Union (TGWU), giving evidence five years ago before a British Parliamentary Trade and Industry Committee investigation of the car industry: 'There is no disputing the fact . . . that if anyone had said to us that we would have seen in relative terms a small company like Renault taking over Nissan, or we were to see Daimler taking over one of the American big three in Chrysler, if someone had told us that some years ago I think we would have really questioned their sanity. The reality of it is that we have an industry that literally is awash now with mega-mergers, takeovers and joint ventures' (Woodley 2000: 34).

3. According to the data presented in the first MIT world survey, for example, by 1980 Japan was exporting a total of 2.0 million units to North America, compared to 1.0 million units to Western Europe, but domestic production in Western Europe at this time was 10.4 million units compared to just 7.2 million units in North America (see Altshuler et al. 1984: 28), while the regional balance of trade for Western Europe was in surplus at this time. If one adds to this the considerable heterogeneity of experiences within Western Europe – trade between countries *within* this bloc accounted for the export (import) of 3.7 million units – it is not surprising that the concerns caused by the rise in Japanese exports to each region occasioned a panic in the US and Canada that was of a palpably different order to that in Europe, even though Japan's car exports to Western Europe were by no means negligible (and in fact growing at about twice the rate as those to North America through the 1970s).

4. A summary of Japanese transplant production facilities and collaborative ventures as things stood by the end of the 1980s in both North America and Western Europe is given in Womack et al. (1990: 202–3). A more extended overview is provided in Tomlinson (2005).

5. The very recent and quite comprehensive study by Tomlinson (2005), for example, looking at the time sequencing of decisions by Japanese car assemblers to acquire production capabilities overseas – in North America, South America, Asia, Europe and Oceania – shows the relevance for industry analysis of an empirical framework that explicitly recognizes the importance of rivalrous behaviour *between* the different Japanese assemblers in accounting for their overseas investment decisions, as well with their Western competitors. Examining the worldwide overseas acquisitions of Toyota, Nissan, Honda and Mitsubishi over a 40-year period stretching from 1960 to 2000, Tomlinson finds evidence of a distinct 'bunching' pattern in the overseas movements of each firm region by region: thus as one of these assemblers made its move to a strategically important region – North America, say – the others quickly followed suit. Evidence of this type adds depth to our understanding. Each

assembler, encroaching on markets overseas, would have been under pressure – at least from North America and Western Europe – to establish production facilities in the regions in question, but both here and elsewhere the moves were bunched, consistent with an impetus that also reflected in part mutual rivalries – the fear of being left behind.

6. A good summary account of the GM J-car and of Ford's parallel efforts in the 'Erika' programme (producing the Ford Escort) is also given in Jurgens et al. (1993: 53–8). They see the world car strategy as entailing 'simultaneous introduction of a new type of car with a basic standard design at all of the world "production centres"' (ibid.: 53), involving similarly specified car lines for different regions, differing perhaps in exterior finish and options but with major components designed to be produced at consolidated points around the world, with perhaps multiple sourcing to mitigate the risks of exchange rate fluctuation.

7. The quote itself is taken by Sinclair from *The Washington Post*, 5/4/81.

8. For example, Wilks (1984: 69, 247–8), writing a review drawing on European materials, gives weight to other factors like the 'multi-nationalization' of component part manufacture by firms like Lucas and GKN, substantial manufacturing concerns in their own right. But for perhaps a majority of writers at this time, the issues involved in world car projects quickly became inseparable from the question of Japanese encroachments: for instance, writing only a few years later, and just at the point where the now familiar contrast between 'Fordist mass production' and Japanese manufacturing propensities was taking firm root in the social science literatures, Tolliday and Zeitlin (1986) broach the GM world car strategy as one possible response to Japan's emergence on the world scene, aimed at reaping further economies of scale via international standardization on a 'Fordist' model: in keeping with our next point, then they propose that this strategy was eclipsed by the 'achievements' of Japanese assemblers in 'product diversity' and 'productive flexibility' (see ibid.: 16–17).

9. As we have noted in an earlier work (see Coffey and Tomlinson 2003: 122–3), the stance taken on this issue appears for Kaplinsky (and for others) to stem directly from an ostensible critique of the logic of forecast-driven manufacture, in which it is maintained that global sourcing of inputs to production is viable only when the overall quantity of units demanded is large relative to the number of alternate model specifications, since otherwise accurate delivery schedules for the component parts to be supplied to assembly plants cannot be drawn up in advance of production with sufficient accuracy. Presumably it is supposed that as the overall 'width of selection' grows, global sourcing in production becomes a less meaningful strategy. This is a proposition which might even be argued via an appeal to the law of large numbers, since if the total specification count is large relative to the total number of units that will actually be built, even a perfect knowledge of an underlying probability distribution of orders will cease to provide any sort of guide to an assembly plant with respect to the actual frequencies with which orders will be placed. But this would be to confuse the number of alternate model specifications for finished car assemblies with the number of varieties of individual component parts: the further back upstream one travels, the fewer will be the number of varieties against which to forecast demand – even if for the final product the number of alternate model specifications can be counted in the billions.

10. The disappearance of controversy over the 'world car' should not be confused with the different question as to whether and to what extent the global giants of the industry have in fact pursued this type of endeavour. So far as GM is concerned, for example, the middle part of the 1990s saw some re-emergence of public discussion of this type of policy, and in the particular context of expansion into emerging markets: the goal of designing common vehicle platforms to be sold globally (with local streaming) was again publicly debated – the 1998 Cadillac Seville and the 1998 Opel Astra being amongst the examples cited – alongside the advantages of abandoning a tradition of overseas expansion via acquisition by turning instead to new facsimile replicas of a 'model' factory (see, in this connection, the commentaries in Blumenstein 1997; Simonian 1997; Howes 1998; we are grateful to Dr Martin Carter for drawing our attention both to these articles and these examples). What is perhaps ironic is that in this more recent round of commentary the Japanese giants Toyota and Honda have started to emerge not as 'antithetical' examples to, but rather as leading practitioners of, 'world car' strategies; however, this view has yet to make headway in the wider literature, and it is still commonplace to find published commentaries contrasting a

'debunked' Western 'world car' strategy, based on Fordist principles, with a more 'flexible' Japanese alternative.

11. This is not in itself a new point: a number of writers have contrasted what they perceive as differential performance across sectors as a means of criticizing, or at least qualifying, Japanese economic success (an approach which seems to understate the complexities of inter-sectoral arrangements in an industrialization process, although this is an issue that lies outside the intended scope of our book). The point is raised, in one way, in El-Agraa (1997: 1508–14), and in another in Krugman (1994), and a long list could be drawn up representing every shade of opinion in between. The point is also made in Eberts and Eberts (1995: 270–72), a work distinguished by a careful, and ultimately quite compelling, critical dissection of the evidence on the comparative 'quality' of Japanese cars: since this is not an issue that we tackle directly in our own study, it is recommended to the reader. This last work is also of some particular interest because it is a distinctly 'patriotic' study aimed at a US audience, but one which seems to have elicited a smaller following than might have been expected given the cogency with which it musters evidence on product 'quality' issues in the US car market: it may be that this respect its findings challenge expectations in too blunt a manner.

12. In itself it is remarkable that this was the best the DTI could do as a response to public anxiety occasioned by the successive decisions by transnational operators to cease operations at long-established manufacturing sites in the UK (one of these was in fact the BMW decision to divest itself of Rover Group and to cease operations at Longbridge: see Chapter 3). A fuller assessment of this response, and of the rather sanguine acceptance of assurances by the Parliamentary Trade and Industry Committee self-tasked with investigation, is given in Coffey and Thornley (2006d, see also Coffey and Thornley 2006c; Coffey 2003: 51–8), which also investigates in detail the circumstances surrounding the decision of Ford MC to withdraw from car assembly operations at Dagenham: this separate case study is germane to the themes in our book, but raises a distinct set of issues *vis-à-vis* manufacturing practices. A broader account more generally of the issues raised by recent UK industrial and labour market policy and performance can be found in Coffey and Thornley (2003).

13. It would be wrong to think that British government structures alone within Europe have made claim to the benefits of lean production (for an EU level exercise, see Keegan 1998), but it has been widely noted that 'British governments in particular have made clear their faith in the ideal of lean production' (Bradley et al. 2000: 32). The lack of any publicly expressed doubts *vis-à-vis* the abiding 'productivity gap' is for this reason all the more striking.

14. It is of course also possible to construct an explanation of Japan's recent economic difficulties in a way which gives pride of place to Japanese culture and institutions without in so doing ascribing to a hostile view of either (see, for example, Katzner 1999, 2006). Such approaches must be carefully distinguished from Anglo-Saxon institutional imperialism.

15. 'Nowadays Japanese capital competes with American almost everywhere in the world, Japan is almost as deeply involved as the United States in Canada, and Japan has heavy investments in Alaska. Indeed, Japan's economic fate is so closely linked to that of the United States that on 9 February 1967, when rumours of peace in Vietnam broke out . . . stocks on the Tokyo market dropped' (Henry 1968: 52). This paper was published in a still interesting collection from a conference organized by the Congress on the Dialectics of Liberation held in London in 1967, which included a great deal of reflection on the Vietnam war. The overall view taken by Henry was that as a consequence of developments prior to World War II the US economy was best regarded as an economy on a permanent war footing. Henry (ibid.: 62–3) takes stock of relationships between the military and industries including the US car industry: Robert McNamara, former President of the Ford Motor Company, was then Secretary of Defense, while Charles Wilson, a former Secretary of Defense, was then President of General Motors. In Chapter 8 we will coincidentally touch upon the recent enthusiasm shown by the US government for 'lean thinking' in military procurements.

16. Cowling and Tomlinson are broadly sympathetic to the past role of the Ministry of International Trade and Industry (MITI) in nurturing Japan's industrial economy, adopting a view more or less in line with Chalmers Johnson's (1982) model of the 'developmental state'.

In some ways this is a prospectus which again tries to explain failure on the same basis as success. But unlike Porter et al. (2000) (above), the Cowling–Tomlinson explanation of Japan's travails hinges not on the bureaucratization and state interference, or the backwardness of parts of the domestic economy, but paradoxically on the very success encountered by MITI in encouraging development in key sectors: with the rise of avowed 'national champions' in the corporate sector came pressure from these giant firms to remove impediments to the export of capital and jobs. The change is illustrated thus: in 1980, Japan's corporations held a 3 percent share in the global stock of FDI; in less than 20 years this share had risen fourfold, to 12 percent; from a 'small marginal player' in international production in the 1970s, by the mid-1990s Japan's corporations were second only to those in the US *vis-à-vis* shares in global FDI stocks (see ibid.: F359).

17. In addition to the globalizing propensities of Japanese car makers, Japanese manufacturing activity as a whole has been changing *vis-à-vis* the sourcing decisions of firms: 'Although Japanese corporations traditionally have organized sourcing of parts as geographically close to their assembly plants as possible, cost pressures have forced them to source internationally from affiliates and subcontractors abroad: Japanese firms now operate networks of production linking Europe [for example] and South East Asia' (Held et al. 1999: 263). We would tend to be chary of euphemisms here ('cost pressures') and the language of necessity, and would take a broader purview moreover of the relevant issues, but the point is clear. There is a body of econometric work that has also established that decisions on the location of foreign direct investment (at least on the relatively aggregated plane) are sensitive to wage differentials, and here Japan seems to be no exception (see Tomlinson 2002).

18. One obvious qualification must be made here: Honda, most notably, moved early towards establishing overseas operations and joint ventures despite being a relative latecomer to the Japanese car industry. This has been much commented on, and this together with its successes in the motor-cycle industry has made Honda a staple case study in courses on business strategy (for example, Mintzberg et al. 2003: 152–65). But in this regard Honda has until recently been treated as an *exception* to the Japanese rule. For example, Yonekura and McKinney (2005: 124–30), while suggesting that Honda behaved much like a 'free-standing organization' in the sense defined by Wilkins (1998: 3), namely a 'firm set up in one country for the purpose of doing business outside that country', also note that in this respect it seemed to deviate – at least until recently – from the established Japanese business model.

7. Rethinking lean thinking: substance and counterfeit

All that remains is for enough investors, managers, and employees, like the change agent heroes of these pages, and – we hope – you the reader, to create a vast movement, in North America, Europe, Japan, and every other region, which relentlessly applies lean thinking to create value and banish *muda*. (Womack and Jones 1996, 2003: 295)

7.1 INTRODUCTION

In this penultimate chapter we pause to review on the basis of our preceding arguments the book *Lean Thinking* by James P. Womack and Daniel T. Jones, published as a conceptual guide to key production concepts for lean production. This book has recently been reissued in an extended second edition, but all of the material published in the first edition has been retained and the original pagination has been left intact (a thoughtful consideration), so that more recent propositions can be separated from earlier arguments. Hence reference will be made to both editions simultaneously – to Womack and Jones (1996, 2003) – unless the material under discussion appears only in chapters added to the later edition. The book is of interest in part because it is a best-seller – with over 300,000 copies sold, according to the authors, in English alone (see Womack and Jones 2003: 5) – aimed at a practitioner audience. The significance of this work, commercial success apart, also resides in the fact that its authors comprise two-thirds of the triad who wrote *The Machine that Changed the World*, that is, Womack et al. (1990) – another best-seller and the book which first launched the idea of a 'lean' revolution in manufacture. We have already addressed the main claims in this earlier book, but its successor raises some additional points of separate interest, and it these which we now consider.

We wish to isolate two separate themes discernible in the later book. One involves a familiar set of invocations drawn around Toyota MC, of the sort to be found in any number of the books and articles written on the subject of the transformation in manufacturing practices now commonly ascribed to the company, and encountered already in our own study. The other, in a rather particular sense, is more novel, and of interest as much for what is not said as what is claimed: it manifests in the course of *Lean Thinking* through the insinuation of body metaphor into an erstwhile account of factory organization, in which work, and the 'flow' of the material items which are the objects of work, are regulated by *takt* time, the 'heartbeat' of the factory. The first is interesting because of what is assumed: the second for what is suppressed. After considering each in turn, in consecutive sections, we then briefly explore a different issue that seems to lurk just beneath the surface of much of what is written about lean production, as purportedly practiced by Toyota and its followers. For brevity we might refer to this as the 'craftwork' (or perhaps even the 'German') question: attacks on practices that might be broached under this heading have become something of a *leitmotif* in the lean literature, if by this we mean the body of writing sparked initially by the publication of Womack et al. (1990) and carried through to the present day, allowing, of course, for some internal variation. The underlying issue here is therefore what 'lean thinkers' elect to make of 'craftwork'. We consider this from the viewpoint of cultural counterfeit: we propose that 'lean thinkers' are hostile to truths which establish by their existence the falsehoods in their thinking.

7.2   LEAN THINKING

What are the key features of 'lean thinking' as posited by Womack and Jones? Their book introduces the new reader, and re-introduces the old reader, to a formidable character whom we have met before – the late Taichii Ohno. One-time Vice President of Toyota MC and self-styled founder of Toyota Production System, Ohno is here introduced as the author of a 'high level philosophic' text on the Toyota Production System, and 'the most ferocious foe of waste human history has produced' (see Womack and Jones 1996, 2003: 10, 15). From this, two immediate inferences can be drawn. Toyota, as described by Taichii Ohno, is the well-spring from which lean thinking flows, and lean thinking in turn is concerned, no less, with the elimination of all 'waste' in production, defined in this context as activity absorbing resources but creating no (corporate) value (see ibid.: 15). Much space is given over to the horrors of waste – or 'muda' – and to its progressive elimination by the application of lean thinking.[1] And the organizing concepts employed to explain the 'thought process' that comprises lean thinking, as pioneered by Ohno, are encapsulated in metaphors: *flow, pull, perfection.*

Henry Ford and his associates are accredited with being 'the first people' to realize the potential of 'flow' – a sequenced configuration of processes and a continuous movement of the materials or objects undergoing transformation through each:

Ford reduced the amount of effort required to assemble a Model T Ford by 90 percent during the fall of 1913 by switching to continuous flow in final assembly. Subsequently, he lined up all the machines needed to produce the parts for the Model T in the correct sequence and tried to achieve flow all the way from raw materials to shipment of the finished car, achieving a similar productivity leap. (Womack and Jones 1996, 2003: 22)

Hence lean thinking envisages a system of manufacture organized on the basis of the progressive flow of work through each of the successive stages of production, on which basis there is also envisaged a massive gain in resource productivity. The historical precedent supplied is the factory system of Henry Ford. At the same time, however, the Ford system was subject to an inherent limit:

But he only discovered the *special case*. His method only worked when production volumes were high enough to justify high speed assembly lines . . . In the early 1920s, when Ford towered above the rest of the industrial world, his company was assembling more than two million Model Ts at dozens of assembly plants around the world, every one of them exactly alike. (Womack and Jones 1996, 2003: 22–3, emphasis in original)

At this point the contrast is made with Ohno's 'new system':

After World War II, Taichii Ohno and his technical collaborators, including Shigeo Shingo, concluded that the real challenge was to create continuous flow in small-lot production when dozens or hundreds of copies of a product were needed, not millions. This is the *general case* because these humble streams, not the few mighty rivers, account for the great bulk of human needs. (Womack and Jones 1996, 2003: 23, emphasis in original)

Hence the Ford case was the *special* case. Where Ford achieved 'flow' for volume manufacture of a homogeneous product, replicated in identical specifications by the million, Ohno matched this for a *variety* of different specifications.

We have seen this before, and in not dissimilar terms. Womack and Jones write in ways that support – and would certainly do nothing to disturb – the view that Toyota was a prime mover in taking the world's car industry, which up to that time had been dominated by a system of the Henry Ford type, beyond the point of mass replication of identical products in enormous quantities: as with other contributions in this oeuvre, the intervening years in the West remain blank. Framed in historical or empirical terms, it would be erring on the side of understatement to say that this is problematic, but we have already rehearsed the relevant issues: in the sphere of mixed assembly, Toyota was a laggard; in the sphere of 'customization', it is more obviously distinguished by its preference for curtailing width of selection. The passing reference here to Shigeo Shingo as a chief 'collaborator' intent on meeting diverse 'human needs' is noteworthy: we saw in Chapter 2 that the Shingo Prize is frequently awarded writers who make Toyota synonymous with customization. The criticism is the same – such claims are historically and empirically counterfactual. But framed against an existing body of opinion, however, *all* the key elements are there: it is implied that Toyota's achievement *was* to sweep away Ford-like mass production, so that the 'human need' for variety *could* be met. The imagery of the 'humble stream' nicely complements the supposed ascendancy of the consumer.

It is in this context that the metaphor of 'pull' is invoked. It was noted, at an earlier stage in this study, that Ohno advanced a claim to have revolutionized car assembly by combining a just-in-time system with a new mechanism for communicating information on production requirements to the factory that could dispense with pre-planned production schedules. This is faithfully replicated in the account of Ohno's achievement given by Womack and Jones. In fact, it is quickly made explicit that the 'new system of flow management' invented by Ohno – via the progressive elimination of all impediments to continuous materials movement and processing – is the Toyota just-in-time system (see Womack and Jones, 1996, 2003: 37). The invocation of the word 'pull' is likewise a reflex to Ohno's claim to have dispensed with planned production schedules wherein 'nothing is produced by the upstream supplier until the downstream customer signals a need' (see ibid. 1996: 309; 2003: 351); again, it is a familiar claim in the literature.[2] The question that might be applied to Toyota – 'pull what?' – is not asked, since issues of comparative width in selection are broached only in ways that mislead by aggrandizing Toyota. In this sense the myths encountered in Chapter 2 of our own study are reiterated here: Ohno is taken at face value in his own assessment of his own life-achievements – he is accredited with taking the world industry beyond the Ford Model T, 'exactly alike' every one; his claim to have done so on the back of a new system of coordination that would facilitate 'flow' while 'dispensing' with production schedules is likewise repeated, without a shred of supporting evidence beyond Ohno's original assertion.

Throughout the course of their book, Womack and Jones contrast a system which achieves 'flow' with a 'batch and queue' approach to manufacture – the 'practice of making large lots of a part and then sending the batch to wait in the queue before the next operation in the production process' (see ibid. 1996: 305; ibid. 2003: 347). From this, and repeated references to 'continuous', or 'single-piece' flow, it is made clear that we must think in terms of workplace arrangements that eliminate all intra-process buffers and stocks, whether of parts or of semi-finished products. In other words, 'flow' implies no batches or queues: it is 'steady', 'continuous', 'with no wasted motions, no interruptions, no batches, and no queues' (ibid.: 352). In this context, 'flow' is simply the metaphor intended to capture the essence of Toyota-like just-in-time production. And enormous productivity gains are predicted.

For example, in a discussion of the application of lean thinking to the manufacture of bicycles, there is a lengthy description of the conversion of a 'batch and queue' system to a 'flow' system, *vis-à-vis* a change in the arrangements for processing and assembly (tube cutting, tube bending, mitering, welding, washing and painting, and final assembly) (see Womack and Jones 1996, 2003: 56–9). With the old arrangement, so it is maintained, each separate activity was organized in a separate part of the factory, and separately executed for discrete batches of parts, before the final assembly process. Under the new arrangement, the work would 'flow' in the approved manner from process to process, 'one bike at a time, with no buffer of work-in-progress in between' (ibid.: 59). In order to support this part of the discussion, a diagram is presented, in two consecutive versions, each comprised of an identical box, but with a different representation therein of factory layouts in the two cases. In each version, the box is the same size, but drawn differently so as to not only establish the different arrangement, but also a dramatic reduction in the space taken up by each arrangement. There then appears the following comment: '[although] the diagram cannot show this, the human effort needed to produce a bicycle has been cut in half as well' (ibid.: 62). No data is presented to support this, but the masterstroke is in the opening qualification, 'although the diagram cannot show this'. What, one might ask, can any diagram show, except what is intended? But the wording employed in this example is interesting nonetheless, because the 'halving' of effort derives from a formula, the same one that was first set out in the earlier Womack et al. (1990):

> Lean production . . . is 'lean' because it uses less of everything compared with mass production – half the human effort in the factory, half the manufacturing space, half the investment in tools, half the engineering hours to develop a new product in half the time. Also, it requires keeping far less than half the needed inventory on the site, results in many fewer defects, and produces a greater and ever growing variety of products. (Womack et al. 1990: 13)

At one remove, then, this is *Lean Thinking*: Toyota has reorganized the interface between factory and consumer; Toyota is massively productive; any organization realigning its processes to eliminate stock will be massively productive as well. The supporting evidence is not *in* the book, but in the precepts which inform it, which in turn provide the basis for its word associations: *flow, pull, perfection.*

And on this last:

> Perfection is like infinity. Trying to envision it (and to get there) is actually impossible, but *the effort to do so provides inspiration and direction essential to making progress along the path.* (Womack and Jones 1996, 2003: 94, emphasis in original)

Even some of the most extravagant claims are re-warmed soup. Consider the following speculation, again set out in the earlier Womack et al. (1990):

> Widespread adoption of lean production may dampen both inflation and the business cycle. If mass production is ideally suited to the survival of big companies through deep cycles in demand, it may also be cycle enhancing. That is, its penchant for massive inventories, both of in-process parts and finished units, would seem to exacerbate the cycle: As inflation builds, stocks are built up against expectations of year higher prices. This move pushes prices up further. Then, when the economy suddenly falters, the built-up stocks are worked off, deepening the slump upstream in the production system . . . Some observers have even wondered if the lack of a cyclical market in durable goods in Japan is a direct result of lean production . . . [the] system may significantly damp cyclicality. (Womack et al. 1990: 250)

The timing was perhaps unfortunate: Japan recessed shortly thereafter. But in the first edition of the later book, that is to say, in Womack and Jones (1996), a step back is taken. Despite 'several' decades of lean thinking in Japan, and dissemination elsewhere, the authors acknowledge that inventory data for America, Europe and Japan does not establish any significant change in the inventories actually held by businesses, after making due allowance for business cycle effects. But at the same time, they do not allow this judgement to challenge their basic views:

> The reason we believe, is that most applications of JIT, even in Japan, have involved Just-in-Time supply, not Just-in-Time production, and batch sizes have not reduced by much . . . one of the great prizes of the lean leap is still waiting to be claimed (Womack and Jones 1996: 88)

There is no difficulty with the theory then, it is just that the world is out of step, including, rather surprisingly given earlier speculations, Japan.

In the second edition, that is to say, in Womack and Jones (2003), while the same passage appears, there is admittedly one attempt to present some fresh evidence that looks more promising. Indices are presented using US inventory data: total domestic sales are divided through by total inventories in the manufacturing process, including raw materials, work-in-progress and finished goods, both for all manufacturing, and for the automotive industry in the US: data is presented from 1992 which seems to show proportionately smaller inventory holdings *vis-à-vis* production, most particularly for the automotive industry. In itself, this would be a less exciting development than Womack and Jones suggest: the series presented coincide with an upturn in the US economy, but there is no attempt (for example) to consider the likely consequences of this regardless of developments in manufacturing organization – they do not, contrary to their own earlier injunction, 'normalise for the business cycle'. But perhaps even worse, is the detail in the fine print: 'We use government data on inventories manufacturers hold in the United States in relation to sales in the United States' (see ibid. 2003: 374; also 310–11). The problem here, in addition to the business cycle, and of course any changes in the specification of the production-mix, is that if in this period – the 1990s – US corporations outsourced production to other countries (Mexico, say), then the parts, semi-finished goods, and work-in-progress held in those sites would *not* be included in the estimate of inventories used in the calculation of the indices employed by Womack and Jones. For this reason, and even ignoring issues like the business cycle, the data may be of little indicative value.[3]

We have run through these points not so much by way of criticism of this particular book, since in these respects Womack and Jones tread familiar territory, as to establish that what may be original must be looked for elsewhere. This takes us to a second, more interesting, theme that threads its way through *Lean Thinking*.

7.3   METAPHOR AND SUBSTANCE: '*TAKT* TIME' AND 'FLOW'

This departure, which is not wholly unique to Womack and Jones, but which is nonetheless a striking feature in their presentation, commences with the assertion that the rhythms of work in a factory should be regulated by *takt* time.

Womack and Jones define *takt* time as the available production time divided by the rate of customer demand. For example, if 200 units of a good were demand in one day, and the factory were to operate 400 minutes per day, then *takt* time would be equal to two minutes. By matching the 'pace of production' to the 'rate of customer demand', *takt* time becomes the 'heartbeat' of the lean system (see Womack and Jones 1996: 310; also Womack and Jones 2003: 352).

In this definition, 'available production time' applies to the time for which the production facility is available: the workshop, or factory. If we therefore write for available facility time AT and for required production quantity Q:

$$takt \text{ time} = \frac{AT}{Q}$$

Written like this, the ratio has no intrinsic content. It is merely one unknown divided by another. Given both, *takt* time is defined; if one changes, *takt* time changes. Consequently, without more to go on, *takt* time as such tells us nothing about the organization of a factory system. Consider 'flow', as this word is used in Womack and Jones. If what is envisaged, as seems to be the case, is a reorganization of processes to facilitate the removal of intra-process buffers from a factory process, then simply knowing the figure obtained when dividing available facility time through by a desired production quantity will provide no information on whether this is so. In other words, *takt* time can be calculated, but *takt* time itself can convey no information on the actual arrangement of processes in a factory system.

If instead the word 'flow' pertains in some sense to the *length* of time for which work is retained within the factory, then again there is no simple connection. To see this, consider a very simple assembly process comprised of *n* discrete work-points connected by a conveyor belt and with no in-process buffers of any sort. Within this type of process, 'flow' is presumably achieved by default in so far as intra-process buffers are concerned, although this has nothing to do with *takt* time. But so far as the time dimension of the process is concerned, under normal operating conditions:

$$\text{retention time} = \frac{AT}{Q} \times n \times \frac{24}{AT}$$

The constituent parts of this expression are easily understood. Looking at the right-hand side first, we have *takt* time (AT/Q) multiplied by the number of workstations in the production process (*n*) and by the maximum feasible number of operating hours divided through by available facility time ($24/AT$): the incorporation of this last term shows the effect of scheduled closure time on retention time. But from this we can see that *takt* time could change with no change in retention time, retention time could change with no change in *takt* time, and both could change together, depending on how AT and Q are each assumed to vary.[4] Possessing information on *takt* time *per se* would (even if *n* were known) tell us little about retention time.

The question which then naturally arises is this: if knowing *takt* time imparts no information on the internal organization of a factory system, or even for that matter definite knowledge of retention times for materials held as work-in-progress within that factory system, why is it significant for Womack and Jones?

Examples are given throughout the course of the book which cumulatively inveighs upon the reader the intended application of *takt* time, as a work regulator. For instance, the example is given of a factory assembling bicycles. On the assumption that 48 orders are placed with the factory, and that the factory in question operates a single 8 hour shift, *takt* time is calculated as 10 minutes per finished bicycle. The production sequence of the factory should then be run so as to match exactly the production cycle set down by the *takt* time (Womack and Jones 1996, 2003: 55–56): 'the point is always to define *takt* time precisely at a given point in time in relation to demand and to run the whole production sequence precisely to *takt* time.'

While the *takt* time itself is simply a ratio that becomes known once values are allotted to each of the two variables that define it, content is supplied with the last line in this example – the objective of the exercise is to 'run the whole production sequence precisely to *takt* time'. This implies *synchronicity* of work. In this connection Womack and Jones (1996: 381; 2003: 360) expand on the example of bicycle assembly. For instance, if for a higher volume bicycle the *takt* time is 60 seconds, then each of the individual tasks carried out on the assembly line must be completed accordingly within a matching cycle of 60 seconds (or less). This makes it a 'key task' that work-teams assisted by technical advisers learn how to 'adjust' every job accordingly. This goal is in turn to be achieved via standardization and repetition of tasks, with each task to be performed 'in exactly the same way each time'.

The system is therefore one that will combine time and motion study with a directive to synchronize each worker's *repetitive* task cycle with every other worker's. And from the viewpoint of the accompanying account of how *takt* time is intended to be perceived as a calculated time-allowance, the consumer – rather than, as is the case in reality, the employer or factory manager – is proposed as the arbiter of *pace*.[5]

On the face of things, as new 'production concepts' go, this is not promising. The literature testifying to the problems of short repetitive work cycles occasion at the point of worker satisfaction is enormous. But *Lean Thinking* is a year zero book. A type of work that a century of accumulated discussion and evidence had more or less consigned to the category 'proverbially unpleasant' is transformed into the sort of activity which workers in reality *most wish* their employers would provide:

> The types of activities which people all over the world consistently report as most rewarding – that is, which make them feel best – involve a clear objective, a need for concentration so intense that no attention is left over, a lack of interruptions and distractions, clear and immediate feedback on progress towards the objective, and a sense of challenge – the perception that one's skills are adequate, but just adequate, to cope with the task at hand. *When people find themselves in these conditions they lose their self-consciousness and sense of time.* (Womack and Jones, 1996, 2003: 65, emphasis added)

What workers want – what they really want – is to be assigned to repetitive synchronous work cycles, with no allowance even for a bounded autonomy. Even better, the happy worker is a worker who has lost 'self-consciousness' (without, one hopes, actually lapsing into unconsciousness), as well as 'sense of time'.[6] Moreover, the environment at work will then be its own reward. For example, a case is advanced against the use of incentive pay as a means of reconciling workers to their perceptions of a harder work pace in a factory organized on the basis of lean principles. Such perceptions are attributed by Womack and Jones (1996, 2003: 263) to the elimination of 'practically' all of the slack time that might otherwise afford workers a break from work, rather than any change in the actual intensity of work measured on a 'minute-to-minute' basis. But recognising that the perception of intensified work will remain Womack and Jones (ibid) recommend perseverance and 'acclimation' rather than cash rewards as the correct means of managing the workforce: rather than buy allegiance lean employers are directed to stress instead the 'positive aspects' of the new regime.

Stepping back from this, it is apparent that there is a second kind of metaphor running through the text of *Lean Thinking*: body-metaphor. It is hardly subtle. *Takt* time is variously referred to in the text as the 'heartbeat', or the 'pacemaker', of the factory, and if 'flow' pertains to the movement of work, the lean factory worker – lost in consciousness and lost in time – is the muscle that moves to the pulse. And if not exactly correct in anatomical terms, much that is odd becomes suddenly comprehensible if we rethink *Lean Thinking* in these terms. The text of this book abounds in references to ratios and dimensions that cannot easily be related if judged solely in quantitative terms – but it may be that if alternately viewed as a discourse on the factory as a body, we can see what might appeal to a certain type of manager.

And it is this, perhaps, which is the source of some of the asides running through the book: a factory needing a 'lean' refurbishment is not only a 'grimy operation' using 'old tools in old facilities', but also 'unionized'; 'lean' employers are advised to 'take action quickly' to 'remove those managers who won't give new ideas a fair trial' (see Womack and Jones 1996, 2003: 69, 260). If the lean factory is a body, does this make unions – on a par with 'grime' – and resistant managers, disease? The purpose of this chapter is not to judge such comments, or to be pejorative in any way, shape or form about the contents of this specimen book. But it interesting to speculate why this sort of thing appeals, and to whom: 'a book of great understanding, and of hope . . . an industrial world in which workers share the challenges and satisfactions of the business'; 'conveys a very human sense of managers constrained by resources'. These comments are taken from the blurbs on the dust-covers. In a book where a 'thoughtful' lean thinker is self-described, without irony, as 'Conan the Barbarian' (there is much that is puerile in *Lean Thinking*, in a proper sense), and where what workers can look forward to – if not hindered by grime, unions, resistant managers, or worse, paternalist executives – is the sinking of the self in repetitive task cycles, these are surprising epithets: 'understanding', 'hope', 'human'.

What perhaps is even more striking is that Toyota's own experiments to reorganize its assembly processes in the face of the 'crisis of work' are ignored. As observed in an earlier chapter (see Chapter 5), one of Toyota's responses has been to experiment with intra-process buffers and segmented assembly lines. The ostensible reason for this is to allow some localized bounded autonomy for operatives, or, to put the same thing differently, to allow individual operatives to depart from the rhythm set by the overall production cycle – or *takt* time – of the factory as a whole. From this we can infer an immediate point: the *image* of Toyota is important to *Lean Thinking* – riddled as this is with historical and empirical invention – with respect at least to one set of themes, encapsulated in the metaphors 'flow', 'pull', 'perfection'. But no attempt is made to connect Toyota to the second theme running through the book, that is to say, with respect to the assertions made about fulfilling work for operatives: and it is possible to surmise that this is because what Womack and Jones are asserting is inconsistent not only with the evidence on Toyota, but on what Toyota itself is prepared to admit to publicly. Instead, they opt for a discrete silence.

7.4   LEAN THINKING AS COUNTERFEIT

The issue also springs to mind in another context. It has certainly not escaped the notice of critics that 'craftwork', in all its forms, is something of a bugbear for the world's leading lean thinkers. Ulrich Jurgens, for one, has noted not only that craftwork in the making of complex products has been the past subject of 'harsh critique' by lean thinkers Womack and Jones, but that this critique has proved – unfortunately, in Jurgens' view – 'very influential' in the countries with car assemblers singled out for commination (see Jurgens 1995: 199). In this earlier body of criticism, Womack and Jones, as part of Womack et al. (1990), set out to ridicule the efforts of a quality cars producer, identified by Jurgens (ibid.: 200) in this instance as the German firm Mercedes-Benz. The relevant passages begin with a description of a factory where 'armies of technicians in white laboratory jackets labored to bring the finished vehicles up to the company's fabled quality standard':

> We politely inquired of these white-smocked workers exactly what they were doing. 'We're craftsmen, proof of our company's dedication to quality', they replied. These 'craftsmen' would have been surprised to learn that they were actually doing the work of Henry Ford's fitters in 1905 – adjusting off-standard parts, fine-tuning parts designed so as to need adjustment, and rectifying previous assembly work so that everything would work properly in the end. Certainly, these workers are highly skilled and the work they do is no doubt challenging, since every problem is different. However, from the standpoint of the lean producer this is pure *muda* – waste.

Its cause: the failure to design easy-to-assemble parts and failure to track down defects as soon as they are discovered so that they never recur.

Our advice to any company practicing 'craftsmanship' of this sort in any manu-facturing activity, automotive or otherwise, is simple and emphatic: Stamp it out. Institute lean production as quickly as possible and eliminate the need for all crafts-manship at the source. Otherwise lean competitors will overwhelm you in the 1990s. (Womack et al. 1990: 90–91)

This is 'simple and emphatic stuff' indeed; and the theme is warmed to in Womack and Jones, in a chapter dealing with the question of 'German *tech-nik*':

Perhaps the most striking feature of Porsche in the late 1980s was its craft culture, which went far beyond the norms of Mercedes and the other big German engineer-ing-based industrial firms. From the early days Porsche had stressed its craftsman-ship, and many workers with craft skills migrated to Porsche from the larger firms in reaction to the introduction of deskilled high-speed, mass-production operations with short work cycles. As a result, the skill level on the floor was truly extraordi-nary . . . workers had deep knowledge of materials and individual operations: what methods to use to fabricate aluminium, what types of machines to use to cut steel, at what speeds to run machines, and at what rate to feed parts into machines.

In the early years it was even possible for one worker to assemble a whole engine and sign it. This practice, while not the norm, continued to be the ideal for most Porsche workers. Unfortunately much of this craft work was *muda*. (Womack and Jones 1996, 2003: 193)

Again, this is simple and emphatic stuff – an 'army' of craft-workers, now blue coated, waiting in a 'vast rectification area' (see ibid.: 189). Porsche is criti-cized for having been insufficiently cost sensitive, but is then congratulated for taking its first steps to bring 'lean thinking' in, and drive craftwork out, or rather, since this is not quite how Womack and Jones put it, redefine 'craft' for a new age:

Fortunately, lean thinking carries a positive message which can redefine craft for a postcraft age . . . In short, Porsche was and still is a craft company, but the craft is becoming the new lean craft of rapid and radical continuous improvement [sic]. (Womack and Jones 1996, 2003: 207)

There are different issues involved here, ranging from the ability of workers to defend positions obtained *vis-à-vis* the quality of their working lives, to the requirements of a company keen to differentiate itself from sellers to the volume market (and perhaps intent also on doing so via manufacture of a higher quality product). What is also of some interest, however, is why Womack and Jones, and other 'lean thinkers', are so consistently hostile to arrangements in what are (relatively) small firms. And one alternative way of looking at this, is from the viewpoint of counterfeit.

We might make the point by analogy. In the study of art, a counterfeited or forged object is established by means of an assessment of materials and style. Now it so happens that the vision of Toyota which is now so popular is a fake, if judged against the discernible attributes of the real item. For example, while quality car producers like (say) BMW or Porsche do indeed place a premium on customization, for a firm like Toyota nothing could be further from its historically preferred practice. One hypothesis that might be worth considering, therefore, is that the venom directed in the direction of 'German *technik*' in the car industry, is directed at precisely those companies which by *their* practices establish the lie in the fiction. In other words, if the 'authenticity' of the received vision of Toyota requires that a fake be accepted, might not the real item be an (unconscious) source of embarrassment? By the same token, might not the dismissal of craft-work as 'muda', in a work aimed at highlighting the satisfactions for workers confined to short repetitive cycles also reflect something of the embarrassment that the real item might pose? Could it be, to push the point, that if the authenticity of 'lean thinking' requires that a culturally contextualized fake be accepted as authentic and true, the real item must then be the subject of obloquy: is the falsehood in one exposed in the truth in the other, and conversely, does the elevation of one necessitate dismissal of the other?

Attributes which are ascribed to a designated mode of thinking – 'lean thinking' – are asserted to be reflective of the particular experiences of Toyota MC, but which in fact owe little to what can be established with confidence about the company. So far as custom-led manufacture is concerned, we have already argued that it would be difficult to hard to think of a less appropriate appellation for Toyota. And so far as the organization of work in assembly operations is concerned, Toyota's own recent experiences seem to run expressly counter to what Womack and Jones recommend. Running with the theme of counterfeit, moreover, helps cast light on what might otherwise appear inexplicable: the antipathy showed to 'German craftwork'.

7.5   A LAST REMARK

Since this, in an immediate sense, involves not only the process of work but also the product produced in that process, we might close with a last observation. In this connection, consider the following telling remark:

> Meanwhile, the conventional auto industry has been focusing . . . on applying lean thinking, but only to the design and manufacture of the vehicle itself. It has done little or nothing to rethink the total product – personal mobility – which many of us want. That is why many people find today's 'post-Japanese' auto industry a very dull place and why customers frequently ask how the industry can be getting more

efficient while the cost and ease of buying and operating vehicles has hardly budged. (Womack and Jones 1996: 293)

If the 'dullness' of the industry in the throes of its 'lean revolution' is surprising enough, not least from writers keen to tell specialist niche-marketing firms how to do it better, the closing point about the 'cost' of 'buying' a car is also worth observing. At the time when the first edition of *Lean Thinking* was being penned, car industry price–cost margins had yet to feel the hammer blow of the new competitive force destined to deliver (according to Womack and Jones) the goods for the consumer. At the same time, and in this first edition, the authors remained confident: the prediction duly offered was that after Japanese firms had worked to redeploy their production networks to match their target markets while inculcating lean principles, 'fierce price competition' would result (Womack and Jones 1996: 272). In the case of North America, this was predicted to become evident by about the year 2000.

This confident assurance has certainly been followed up in the added chapters of the second addition, but only to the extent that Toyota is now congratulated for its success in *maintaining* 'higher selling prices' (see Womack and Jones 2003: 302). None of this, of course, rules out the future possibility of 'fierce price competition' – the reader is referred back to our views on contingent accommodation in Chapter 6 – but it would be a hasty individual indeed, or at least one possessing considerable *chutzpah*, who then attempted to account for this via 'lean production'.

7.6   CONCLUSIONS

A book like *Lean Thinking* is clearly in one sense about Toyota, and the inferences which close study might draw for the reorganization of other types of business. But then again, it is not about Toyota at all: it is about an *image* of Toyota, one which on one level might appeal to at least part of its business readership less from its novelty as from its familiarity – 'flexible', 'lean' and, above all else, successful. In the bigger scheme of things, and with the passage of time, it may be this rather than the shock engendered by the rapid ascendancy of the Japanese car industry in earlier decades that is now so important from the viewpoint of easy acceptance. But on close reading, one wonders if there is not something else. The point is made tentatively, but one possibility is that *Lean Thinking*, in its choice of metaphor, in its ellipses and asides, appeals to a quite different strand of the corporate psyche: the assertion that workers can indeed be satisfied – indeed, enraptured – if allowed to assume a fulfilling role as muscular cogs in a strict machine. Forms of work hitherto described even by managers as unpleasant, even degrading, are here asserted instead as the most highly desirable – and desired – organizational outcomes. And in this connection, is this at the root of the continued attacks on 'craft-work'? Or is there something in the latter that exposes more basically the counterfeit in the claims of lean thought?

NOTES

1. Indeed, at the outset of the introduction to their book readers are extolled to try out the Japanese word 'muda', because it sounds just 'awful as it rolls off your tongue' (see Womack and Jones 1996, 2003: 15). Several years ago I had the opportunity to discuss this issue with a manager who had attended a day course (organized by I know not whom) in which he was required, as part of a group, to do just that, over and over. Apparently one of the attendees was ejected for her lack of serious-mindedness: she had championed her right to an equally good word, 'nasty'. The penalties for managers, as adults, resisting incorporation into enforced infant play (about which Aldous Huxley had much to say) remains underexplored.

2. The metaphor of 'pull' is ubiquitous in Japanese accounts of Toyota Production System trans-lated for Western audiences (see, for example, Japanese Manufacturers Association 1989) and in Western textbooks on the subject: 'In JIT production only the main final build is scheduled, with all the sub-assemblies and components being pulled in as needed' (Bicheno and Elliot 1997: 470). The notion can be traced to the fact that Taichii Ohno is on record as claiming that what distinguished the Japanese car maker, under his guiding vision, was its ability to organize complex assembly *without* recourse to detailed pre-production planning schedules (see Ohno 1988: 37–80, also noted in Chapter 2, section 2.5). The implied contrast between a state of Fordist mass production, in which Western producers organized production so as to 'push' products onto consumers, and flexible manufacture of the Toyota variety in which customers lead a demand-pull system, has duly reverberated not only throughout the business management literature, but also the critical social sciences (see, for example, and perhaps in particular: Aoki 1987, 1988, 1990; and Lash and Urry 1994: chapter 4). But the implied import of the metaphor of a new type of demand-'pull' system is hardly consistent with what can be gleaned from the evidence about Toyota's actual practices *vis-à-vis* customers, as encountered in Chapter 2 (see also Chapter 3, section 3.3).

3. Indeed, Womack and Jones, in an endnote, acknowledge some quite different findings: a slightly earlier study by Richard Schonberger uses data obtained from corporate annual reports and considers worldwide inventories in relation to worldwide sales to arrive at a more or less opposite result to Womack and Jones (see ibid. 2003: 374; Schonberger 2001). While this is recognized by Womack and Jones (who cannot be faulted on this point), their reasons for thinking their own measures are unbiased by national outsourcing is left unclear.

4. The expression is not quite a tautology in that some of the magnitudes in this expression can diverge *ex post* from their expected (*ex ante*) values: for example, the facility may have to operate for longer than expected if there are unscheduled stoppages. The retention time in this expression differs from the total throughput time discussed in Chapter 5, and for this reason a different term is used to describe each: it is easy to relate the two, but not needful here.

5. Note that the bicycle example veers between an assumed 10 minute cycle and a 60 second cycle. There is no accompanying comment on what such a difference would entail for the experience of work, so it is perhaps worth noting that where *swings* in demand are explicitly discussed, in every case where there is an assumed slow-down Womack and Jones recom-mend pulling workers off the job for reassignment elsewhere: 'each of the multiskilled work-ers . . . performed several of the jobs . . . excess workers were put on other tasks' (Womack and Jones 1996, 2003: 114). But after careful reading, we have been unable to find a single contrary instance where the opposite is allowed, and an increase in demand is met by an assignment of *more* workers. This is consistent with the overall emphasis of the book: 'the constant elimination of *muda* and the movement of workers out' (ibid.: 122).

6. Lest an objection be entered at this point we should in fairness observe that Womack and
    Jones do cite what they seem to think is supporting evidence on this point. They quote the
    findings of a psychological study (see Womack and Jones 1996, 2003: 65) which finds that
    people absorbed in activities like 'rock climbing' express satisfaction: the study in question
    appears to employ the phrase 'psychological state of *flow*' to describe such experiences, and
    by analogy with their own liking for the metaphor *flow*, Womack and Jones offer *this* as their
    supporting evidence. Perhaps no further comment is needed, but being absorbed in rock-
    climbing is *not* the same thing as liking repetitive short-cycle work on an assembly line.

8. The totalizing myth: Japanese efficiency as a cultural fiction

LEAN THINKING, LEAN INITIATIVES
US Air War College Military Index to the Internet

8.1 INTRODUCTION

The opening chapter of this book commences with a proposition about a thoroughgoing non-correspondence between what is claimed on behalf of production practices purportedly developed by Toyota and other Japanese firms operating in the car manufacture and assembly sector, and what can be demonstrated. This in turn is a prelude to questions that might be summarized thus: what does this mean? In framing the issues which it has been our intent to raise in this way, we are obviously interested in more than car manufacture and assembly as a specific set of activities; but this is simply to acknowledge the peculiar status that is accorded this industry. If our purview extended no further than manufacture as such, it would still be immediately apparent to even the most casual reader of the accumulated wisdom of the past 20 or so years that the car industry has been cast in a broad role, both as a leading industry and an emblem of change in the mature industrial economies. And if our purview extends to include writers with an avowedly deeper intent – writers amongst whose ranks might be included not only representatives of the social sciences but also many self-proclaimed apostles of the lean and the flexible – it is clear that the car industry stands here also as social metaphor, a place of signs and wonders. It might certainly be observed in this connection that 'as it is now, so has it been'. But it has been the intent of this book to propose that the contrast between claim and evidence in the particular case of the ascendancy of Japan's manufacturers in the global industry is such that this in itself is a phenomenon deserving further study. If the history and substance of a major world industry undergoes systemic fictionalization in a period of ostensibly heightened scrutiny, what is made of the production fantasy?

As such, the subject matter of this book is one that clearly impinges on issues that transcend any immediate interest in the car industry, but the investigation of which must naturally first be concerned with that industry. While the individual studies of questions of process flexibility, resource productivity and the organization of work that make up some of its constituent parts can certainly be read as substantive contributions to the immediate study of the car industry, it is intrinsic to the overall spirit of this book that the issues raised are not left to rest there. In this same spirit we use this concluding chapter to reprise points already made while expanding our scope of reference to consider the 'totalizing' aspects of myth making. The chapter finishes with some speculative comments on interpretation and some brief observations on how the recent ascendancy of the lean and the flexible in the firmament of contemporary opinion is informing debate in areas as diverse as responses to global warming, the 'improvement' of the US war machine, the future of socialism.

8.2   THE MYTH OF JAPANESE EFFICIENCY: A BRIEF REPRISE

Were we to retrace steps the most intriguing item in the itinerary would perhaps be the first set in the series of points made in this book about the status of Japan's contribution to the organization of factory operations in the car industry. Views to the contrary notwithstanding, Japanese car assemblers were latecomers to the world of mixed assembly; they have typically eschewed rather than pursued marketing strategies based on customization; and the non-commensurability of their factory outputs with competitors' renders nugatory the existing case for ascribing them with possession of more 'flexible' production techniques. The sense of déjà vu experienced by anyone who takes time to compare accounts given in the 1950s and 1960s by contemporary observers of the manufacture of a mix of model specifications in the factories of Ford and General Motors, with the equally vivid but textually almost interchangeable later descriptions of the 'great transformation' in the 1970s supposedly wrought by Toyota, would be palpable. But this has not prevented a series of historical and empirical counterfactuals being asserted and accepted as fact, and by a very substantial body of commentators both within academe and without. Moreover, the emphases given, and the significance accorded this 'development', points towards much more than some mistaken details about the making and selling of cars.

In this connection we have recommended as important the observation that the past 20 or so years has seen a marked narrowing of the usage accorded the words 'mass production' in the context of manufacturing industry, a point readily supported by a comparison of commentaries in the immediate decades after World War II with those that have more recently become typical *vis-à-vis* the car industry. In further developing this theme we have been concerned to note that not only is it the case that commentaries can readily be found from the 1950s (say) which make mass production synonymous with *variety* as well as with volume; in addition, the volume production of variety by giant firms also elicited a particular kind of criticism which saw in this development the coincident death of consumer sovereignty. For this reason it is not simply a case of redating and relocating an innovation: what is required is a fundamental examination of all accompanying precepts. We should, for example, avoid the trap of supposing that the date at which a manufacturing practice appears necessarily marks the date at which it first becomes technically feasible: this would be to accept uncritically what may well be a very poorly grounded assumption. And on the question of consumer sovereignty, we must ask why the wholesale fictionalization of a period in the evolution of a much observed industry should take form in a narrative that makes the consumer ascendant *vis-à-vis* the corporation, which disallows (by construction) any recognition of a prior body of contrary opinion.

The next major item in our itinerary would undoubtedly be 'lean production'. Here it is important, indeed essential, to reiterate an observation made when first considering the data compiled in the International Motor Vehicle Programme (IMVP) research project centred at MIT, and sponsored (largely) by the car industry: lean production as a phenomenon was launched in the closing part of the 1980s, after it had already become an established view that Japanese car assemblers had revolutionized in a very fundamental way the organizing principles of car manufacture and assembly. It is necessary to be clear on this, since 'lean and flexible' are words so often now strung together in the same sentence that the sequence is easily forgotten. Indeed, the formal structure of the IMVP world productivity survey, the focus of our assessment, made no particular attempt to accommodate the story of the 'flexible' factory. We have argued that the principle claim of this survey with respect to the resource-economizing potentials of Japanese-inspired production methods is misleading. Instead of revealing the primacy of Toyota-led organizational methods over plant automation in driving down the hours of labour used to perform a set of standard operations in car assembly plants around the world, an entirely reasonable case can be made that the published data established something like the opposite: indeed, the data compiled suggests rather the tantalizing possibility that Japanese car assemblers were in fact struggling by the late 1980s to convert hours of worker time into output. The re-assessment offered in this connection gives a quite different cast to the ongoing controversy over the 'crisis of work' experienced by Toyota in the late 1980s, looked at now from the viewpoint of problems with unscheduled factory stoppages. What is as significant, however, as deficiencies in the empirical support for the 'lean' hypothesis, is that discussions of the original IMVP survey findings – hugely influential – passed rapidly from presentation to polemic, with relatively little mediating dissection.

The distinction here between the evident movement amongst an almost incredible diversity of opinion formers in the mid-1980s to reinvent the history of the world car industry as one dominated by Fordist mass production right through to the appearance on the world stage of Toyota and other Japanese assemblers, and the subsequent launch of the lean production concept via the IMVP, is important for reasons both obvious and subtle. The first movement, while certainly invoking the brilliant-preposterous claim staked by Toyota's Taichii Ohno to be credited with being the first factory organizer in the car industry to run a mix of different model specifications down a single assembly line, encompassed a swathe of writers amongst whose ranks could certainly be counted a number of radical critics of corporate capitalism, often employed in research departments operating quite independently of any direct connections with the car industry. Lean production, by contrast, emerged as the official interpretation of survey research work centred at MIT, but also disseminated via and aggressively promoted from within the corporate sector that was both its major sponsor and intended subject. We will return to this point.

Our third main stop would be to pause to consider once more the international context within which myth making about the Japanese manufacturing machine must be located if it is to be properly assessed and understood. On the side of corporate responses we highlighted the question of rivalrous asymmetries – with Japanese firms being given access to Western markets without reciprocity – and the functional role of state-mediated accommodations in mature industrial capitalism. In this connection we noted some of the political utilities of a manufacturing revolution, not only from the viewpoint of large corporations in dealing with workers and consumers but also for a state apparatus seeking to secure (amongst other things) incumbent interests. So far as the fact of one-sided encroachments by Japanese exports on Western markets is concerned, we have sympathized with commentaries that commence with the geopolitics of the global political economy: Japan was given leeway to do so as a bulwark against more pressing 'threats' – a context which has since changed.

In this last respect we note a seeming paradox. With the waning of the relative strength – that is to say, growth performance – of the Japanese domestic economy *vis-à-vis* that of its principal competitor(s) in the West, there has been a resurgent confidence in criticism of Japan's status as an economic role model. At the same time, however, the appeal of the lean and the flexible is undiminished, and it remains an article of printed faith that Japanese manufacturing methods have revolutionized the organization of production in industries like the car industry. But in this regard opinion is taking a discernible turn: Western – in particular, American – corporations are now lauded for correctly absorbing the lessons of Japanese industry at the level of the organization of manufacturing operations, but all the better to expose what are described as the inherent weaknesses of an over-managed market economy. Despite the galvanizing role still ascribed to Toyota and other Japanese firms, the associated production concepts have shown themselves readily transferred to a model of corporate capitalism divorced from any role for a regulating state. Indeed, in reviewing the 'lean thinking' of some leading 'lean thinkers' we suggested that what is most striking from the viewpoint of new departures is the emergence of a more clearly 'unitarist' model of corporate management, not only divorced from any prescribed role for the state but drifting away from any vestige of paternalism.

This is all, of course, from a Western perspective, and further work would be required to consider the same from the Japanese end. Toyota executives, it might be safely guessed, have been pleased to see their organization awarded its academy-sanctioned status as worker of miracles, a harbinger of the post-Fordist state. And it is not unlikely, and certainly possible, that Taichii Ohno's boasts responded to a need in Japan, after the catastrophe of its defeat in World War II, for some recognition for originality in industrial endeavour, as opposed to slavish imitation. We have noted, however, that the interests of Toyota and other Japanese corporations have begun to separate from those of the Japanese domestic economy, under pressures exerted from increasingly assertive Western interests seeking accommodations, and as part of the enormous growth in global significance of Japanese overseas investments. If Japan itself has not been spared swingeing criticism by observers situated in the West as its domestic economy has encountered difficulties, and as the cold-war context of earlier decades recedes into the past, it is interesting to speculate that the separation of Toyota from the fortunes of Japan's domestic economy in the realm of perception reflects its actual divorce at the level of practice *vis-à-vis* the location of production and employment in a globalizing world. At the same time, it is possible to see, in outline at least and in commentaries purportedly devoted to praise of Toyota, the emergence – or re-emergence – of a different type of occidental response to oriental competition, one based at root on a tacit contrast, to the disadvantage of the Japanese, between a mere adeptness in 'making' and real originality in 'thinking'.

8.3   THE TOTALIZING MYTH

One point to consider is that once headway is made in the construction and acceptance of a production myth amongst a sufficiently large number of appropriately placed commentators, all attendant details relating to production will come to be interpreted in ways which are consistent with the terms of that myth. Consistency in this sense can of course only be judged in relative terms, *vis-à-vis* an existing body of expectation that will shape the ancillary details of the posture adopted. A good example here might be found in the treatment of vertical ownership structures, as this pertains to what is frequently posited as one of the defining features of the industrial organization of Japanese manufacture. The example is comparatively subtle.

    The general picture typically presented of Japanese industrial organization describes large corporations which belong to a corporate group that might be broadly characterized as a horizontal conglomerate of financial and industrial interest. Production, as this would pertain to manufacture, sees intermediate goods and services vertically supplied via an extensive network of subcontracting relationships, with smaller firms at the base of a broadly pyramidal structure servicing larger firms nearer the apex: the smaller firms in such networks are typically tied in a more or less direct way to the larger firms, in the sense that it is with these particular firms that they will expect to do business. While the car industry in Japan has its own distinctive features – see, for example, Coates (2000: 178–9) on Toyota and Nissan – it is nonetheless perhaps one of the most cited examples of this form of organization with respect to vertical structure, partly because of all Japan's manufacturing sectors the car industry has the largest number of vertical (*keiretsu*) linkages. While precise numbers are less important than orders of magnitude, Coffey and Tomlinson (2003: 124) present and assess some illustrative data for the Japanese car assembly sector compiled by market researchers in the second half of the 1990s: this found more than 10,000 smaller producers supplying some 1400 component suppliers supplying less than a dozen assemblers, through vertical production structures of this kind. This vertical fragmentation, however, is complicated by complex ownership structures: assemblers hold substantial equity holdings in their component part suppliers, are closely involved with appointments at senior level to the management hierarchy of these firms, and hold contracts with and pursue sourcing strategies *vis-à-vis* these firms that would tend to imply a high degree of vertical control. Similarly, both the assemblers and their large component suppliers hold ownership stakes in smaller companies further down the chain – yielding top-down influence. This influence naturally extends to foreclosing competition, and blocking outside interests:

> When the American raider, T. Boone Pickens, bought a 24.6% share stake in Koito Manufacturing, the country's second largest maker of car lights and a member of the Toyota group, he became its largest single shareholder, but he failed to obtain a seat on the board. Toyota, with a 6% stake has three board members. Pickens' had to get a court order to see the [company's] books . . . could not find a Japanese accountant willing to explain them . . . gave up and sold his stake. (Reading 1993: 227)

Our interest in structures of this kind is not in their efficacy: whether they are best viewed as effective mechanisms for technological transfers and mutual support, or as anti-competitive structures perpetuating a form of elite government by oligarchy, is not a question which it is our intent to consider, important though this question is. The question which we would like to ask is this: how should an observer describe the degree of vertical integration apparent in an industrial structure of this type?

If we take Cusumano (1985) as a benchmark we find comparisons being made between vertical ownership structures in Toyota and Nissan on the one hand, and General Motors, Ford and Chrysler on the other. Cusumano, always careful with figures, observes that the comparative degree of vertical integration as measured by the data employed is sensitive to the ownership thresholds (for assemblers) in suppliers' equity selected by the analyst. When a 50 percent minimum threshold was selected (non-minority ownership), the American firms were more integrated, but when this was lowered to 20 percent the rankings were reversed, with Toyota and Nissan the most vertically integrated units. On this basis, Cusumano duly concluded that the Japanese producers were 'far more' vertically integrated organizations than their North American comparators (see ibid.: 188–90). This in itself is not a conclusion to surprise: it is consistent, for example, with the conclusion of the landmark Berle and Means book (1932) that a 20 percent threshold of ownership is a sufficient basis for effective control by a firm with a stake in other members of an identifiable interest group (a condition satisfied for Toyota and Nissan). And indeed, it is not difficult to find examples of Japanese economists publishing at about this time who, even while noting that a large part of the work undertaken in the manufacture of the components assembled into cars in Japanese factories was via contracted suppliers, nonetheless took care to stress the closeness of the ties; the 'quasi-integration' of the structure (see Kono 1984: 122–8). An assessment of more recent data, in Coffey and Tomlinson (2003: 123–35), suggests that much the same conclusion as that reached by Cusumano still obtains: if a lower but controlling ownership threshold is selected, these are highly integrated units. But more often than not – and despite exceptions (see, for example, Dicken 2003: 380) – this is not how the issue is today typically presented, and it is now more common to see emphasis run the other way: Toyota is noted for a de-integrated structure (Fujimoto 1999: 100), the Japanese car assembler *sui generis* is a 'vertically de-integrated entity' (Ruigrock and Van Tulder 1995: 39, 51–54).

One possible reason for this shift in emphasis may be that the extent to which Japanese car assembly is perceived to be more de-integrated vertically is closely linked to the extent to which the same writers also believe it to be more 'flexible'. The logic informing this position (to the extent that it is thought through) could hinge on the supposed specificity-in-use of the investments which are made in machinery and tooling for purposes of manufacturing component parts. If these investments are highly dedicated in purpose (that is to say, the range of alternative uses to which the equipment can be put is narrowly circumscribed) then an 'independent' supplier might balk at accepting this business from an assembler because of the attendant risk in the post-investment situation: no willing suppliers will be found. If the investments are in machinery and tooling of more general purpose, the problem will not arise in the same way, and subcontracting becomes a more feasible option. Someone who believed that the car industry was in transition, from a state characterized by investments in 'Fordist' factories to factories capable of catering to the production of a mix of model-specifications, might also believe for this same reason that the newer forms of production would (in likelihood) be more de-integrated. And in this connection the association between Japanese car assemblers, cast in their role as harbingers of post-Fordist manufacture, and vertically de-integrated procurement structures, might seem to be an entirely natural one. Thus, for example, the following view, from two leading economists, Paul Milgrom and John Roberts (1990: 118): 'manufacturing today is undergoing a fundamental transition, from mass production of a standardized product to flexible production of diversified products . . . [and] to the degree to which use of flexible general-purpose equipment increases, the necessity of vertical integration decreases'.[1] To what extent this type of rationale can be extended to account for a shift in perspectives with respect to vertical ownership structures is hard to say, but the shift is a discernible one. In this context, it is by no means unreasonable to ask if more recent reviewers of the evidence on vertical structures in the car industry are (unconsciously) filtering out of their reading of the data inferences that sit less well with initial precepts about 'flexibility'.

8.4   THE EXPANDED VISION

It is for such reasons that the suggestion was offered at the outset of this book that the studies presented within raise issues that might best be broached not by the economist or the engineer, the business consultant or human resource specialist, nor perhaps even by the industrial sociologist, but rather by the cultural anthropologist. When planning the architecture of this book the present writer happened upon a commentary intended for another context but which nonetheless contains observations that seem peculiarly apt in this connection: 'human-made objects reflect, consciously or unconsciously, directly or indirectly, the beliefs of the individuals who commissioned, fabricated, purchased, or used them and, by extension, the beliefs of the larger society to which these individuals [belong]' (Prown 1993: 1). The subject which these comments specifically address is the study of material culture: the words are in fact from an illuminating expository essay by Jules David Prown on the study of artifacts as a contribution to cultural anthropology and cultural history, part of an absorbing collection on this theme intended to develop this branch of study as a cross-disciplinary endeavour. The proposal is that insights into culture can be obtained through the apprehension and analysis of material things (artifacts): the form of material things can throw light on the underlying attitudes or 'mind' of a society, and the form of material things is also liable to change in response to stresses in that society. What particularly draws attention is the view that artifacts can be appropriated as fictions, amenable to understanding as unconscious representations of reflections on the world, a window to the world of belief: 'Mind, whether individual or cultural, does not reveal itself fully in overt expression: it hides things from itself, and it hides things from others'. And since cultural 'mind' can express itself in 'complex' or 'elliptical' ways, an analogy can usefully be drawn between artifacts and dreams, as 'expressions of subconscious mind': 'artifacts may reveal deeper cultural truth if interpreted as fictions rather than history' (ibid.: 3–4).

Something like this might also be an appropriate analogy by which to consider stories of transformation and change grown up around the organization of production and the interface between factory and market in the car industry, and with a wider purview than the particular role of Japanese manufacturers and assemblers. Viewed as a construct, the contrast between Fordist mass production and a flexible manufacturing form that is a point of departure repeatedly informing discussion of recent developments in the organization of production is obviously an 'account' with material existence: it exists in books, articles, and other recorded forms. It presumably exists too, as a way of capturing a real event, in the minds of its proponents. And while it might be going (perhaps) too far to suggest that this construct be treated as an artifact and hence part of material culture as described by Prown, it is nonetheless a fiction in the most literal sense of the term, and one which when posited as a basis for understanding changes in industrial society writ large employs all of the accompanying devices of fiction that Prown highlights as the starting point for cultural investigation – simile, metonymy, synecdoche and metaphor (ibid.: 4).

In proposing that there is material here of a type requiring cultural investigation what we have in mind is in one sense a natural progression from existing studies of technology and culture, as these relate to factories, products and people. The anthropology of the car is, moreover, increasingly a significant area of study. Daniel Miller, an anthropologist and editor of a recent collection on the car as an object in material culture, could observe as recently (at the time of writing) as just five years ago that whereas 'in the case of every other aspect of material culture with an equivalent presence in the world the literature seemed to be at least to some degree commensurate with the importance of the object' – clothing or housing, say – 'it was as if it [the car] had not yet been made legitimate as a topic to focus upon', notwithstanding the importance frequently attached to the car by anthropologists in the course of their fieldwork (see Miller 2001: ix). But this is a situation which is quickly changing: Sarah Jain, for example, who has published original work on the production of injury in American commodity capitalism, and the role of tort law therein as a mechanism for distributing inequalities and wounding in an already unequal society, has broached the question of commodity violence in the US *vis-à-vis* the car as an object of consumption (see Jain 2004, 2006; also 2005).

The premise that a state of 'Fordist mass production' has only recently given way under the impetus of Japanese pressure in the car industry to more flexible arrangements invokes at the outset a changed status for the consumer. And the accompanying shifts in precepts, attendant upon the construction of this fiction, are evidently both deep and subtle. The myth is a two-sided one: it is not simply what is claimed for Japan's car assemblers, it is what is simultaneously denied *vis-à-vis* the previous evolution of Western industry. Lyddon (1996: 80), whom we previously consulted in this connection in Chapter 2, observes that Raymond Williams, in his well known study *Keywords* (1988), considers the evolving usage of the words 'mass production' in a way which makes no assumption that what is entailed involves volume production or consumption of *identically*-specified goods. Williams' study, intended to investigate the language of cultural transformation via an historically aware study of changes in the meaning of words, was of course written prior to the recently narrowed usage explored by Lyddon. But an update to the Raymond Williams study, recently published as *New Keywords*, deals with these words as if self-evidently implying 'standardized' 'cultural goods' (see Bennett et al. 2005: 208, compare with Williams ibid.: 195; and see also Lyddon ibid.); and a few pages earlier, and with no hint of doubt, historical, cultural, or otherwise, reference is made to the impact of the 'break-up of Fordism' circa the 1970s. This example is particularly apt from the viewpoint of demonstrating the pervasiveness of a phenomenon of reconstructed memory, since the whole point of Williams' initial study was to encourage historical sensitivity to a shift in precepts of this kind, as a means of deepening both understanding and awareness of cultural change. Similarly pervasive, and again apparently unconscious and unwitting, shifts are equally evident when one also considers the attendant associations established in this context – as for example where the blankness (homogeneity) of the consumed product in the invented state of Fordist mass production is made a counterpart to a particular status for the worker, as if such a connection were a manifestly self-evident thing.

A study drawn by analogy with the interpretation of artifacts as fictions would require sensitivity to two things. First, and commencing with the relationship between consumer and factory, we have a construct that invites a contrast between one world characterized by production that is unresponsive to the individual consumer and another in which the consumer's individualized needs are paramount. But added to this are a series of related propositions concerning other dimensions of the organization of production – as for example on the status of the worker – again typically presented dichotomously as reflections upon the two sides of a changed state, but in a manner which simply assumes an obvious connection with the change being asserted at the level of the relationship between consumer and producer. Such connections, if believed attendant upon and integral to the assumed transformation in production potentials in mature industrial economies, must also be scrutinized. The assertion that there *must* be a link (to retain the example) between the flexibility of a manufacturing process *vis-à-vis* the number of product specifications, and the quality and nature of the experience of working within it, jars with the precepts of earlier industrial commentaries – this assertion is *part* of the phenomenon.[2]

A study of this type would be both about and not about the car industry, in the same way that it would be both about and not about Japanese manufacturing practices. The car industry is the vehicle for fictions about production: close study of that industry and its historiography would be a prerequisite to understanding the terms of that fiction. But while the question *why* the car industry is an interesting one, it would be ancillary to the main purpose of this type of study: what does this express about stresses in the wider society within which this fiction is written. And in this respect the starting point must also be to ask why a *production* fantasy. Is it because the act of production encompasses here a particular type of dual interface – between the producer–employer and the consumer–worker in a capitalist-system – or are there deeper connections to the emotive role of production in industrial society? Insight would follow not from the faithfulness of commentaries on the transition from a hitherto dominant state of Fordist mass production to more flexible and productive organizational regimes (in manufacture) in capturing observations on the empirical world, but rather from the form of the suppressions, omissions and departures implied by the invention and projection of the contrast drawn between these states.

There are other layers too to consider. Nationalisms are certainly involved, but not in any simple sense. The transfer to Japan of the historical proprietorship for types of industrial activity not only with an earlier provenance in the West but previously also boasted about by Western corporations, a transfer expressed moreover in almost textually interchangeable word-forms, does not invoke a simple type of nationalism – this aspect is by no means simple. Susceptibility on the part of the recipients to claims broadcast by corporations might also play a role: witness the frequency to which mere statements by firms on the efficacy of their organizational reforms *vis-à-vis* 'Japanese' production methods, even statements by struggling firms, have been taken up even by erstwhile critics. But again, this aspect is by no means a simple one: advertising campaigns of an earlier period that contradict the terms of the emerged 'truth' about the era of Fordist mass production – '*YOU end up with a car that has the features you decided to have . . . That's the whole point of our policy of offering so many cars and so many options*' – appear readily wiped from memory. It is in this connection that we might recall again the view of Jules Henry considered in respect of our discussion of globalization (Chapter 6): the modern psychology is one marked by an essential plasticity of thought, an inability to retain a view of the world.

The same period over which the myth (or myths) of a great transformation in the fundamental organization of production *vis-à-vis* the rise of Japan as an industrial power gathered pace in the West coincided with other developments: it hardly requires a subtle imagination to note that the 'market', as social metaphor, rode higher in the firmament; North American involvement in Japan, as with Japanese penetration of Western product markets, was in part a Cold-War involvement, and upon reflection the period in which a particular fantasy about Japanese manufacturing prowess gained ascendancy in the West is also one marked by the dissipation of the 'communist threat', the rolling back of social welfare programmes and the weakening of labour movements. If the issues are bigger than the car industry, considerations other than the disturbances caused by the aggressive entry of Japan into world markets hitherto the domain of Western corporations may also be central: looked at from another angle, it may be that ascribing wonders to 'Japan' – via projection into and through a particular industry, and indeed (via Toyota) a particular firm – has represented a means by which to reconcile the irreconcilable across a wider plane. In this respect, our opening proposal in this book, that the 'lean and the flexible' might shed light less on the manufacturing innovations of Japanese car makers than on some of the attendant stresses of globalization may be adequate only as a first step in a different kind of study, one oriented towards the potential for a wider purview. It is for this reason that we recommend the area as one requiring study by investigators at least open to the possibility that the investigation of an apparently limited question – how a car is manufactured and sold – might expand to encompass bigger things.

With this in mind we close the book with two last sections, each providing an example that illustrates what seem like relevant issues. We have been at pains to differentiate the initial emergence of a narrative concerning the emergence of a more flexible and consumer oriented type of manufacture – an initial proposition that quickly gained ground in the early to middle part of the 1980s – from the subsequent launch of the concept of lean production, based on the IMVP projects. Chronology aside, and crudely put, the first movement is potentially distinguishable from the second by the degree of active corporate sponsorship and promotion: accordingly, and without wishing to over-simplify unduly, the first examples are chosen because they point to an association between 'lean thinking' and an untrammelled capitalism. The second example is chosen, however, to underscore the need for nuance in the investigation of the phenomenon that is the subject matter of our book. Fittingly, perhaps, the corporate bodies invoked in the first example are US bodies, the region that bore the main brunt of Japanese export penetration, the first major moves towards industrial accommodation and the most aggressive promotion of the 'lean'. The second example, by contrast, looks to Europe, and a revivified socialism. We conclude therefore with global warming, military procurements, and Andre Gorz.

8.5 COMMERCE AND UTOPIA

The first of these issues impinges on a topic that could hardly loom larger in current political discourse; so it is with global warming that we start. Taken at face value, the essential judgement invoked in this connection would appear to be the great leap forward in resource productivity – and an attendant elimination of 'waste' – achievable by means of 'lean thinking' in the workplace.

Consider the following comment, three years old at time of writing:

> After Kyoto and Johannesburg, only an idiot would say that it is easy to save the planet, wouldn't they? But the dizzying irony is that it is. All the posturing at political level ignores a prosaic truth. Every company in the world would directly benefit – in lower costs and higher profits – by doing its bit for the earth. And it would cost nothing except the energy to shift office furniture or a few machines around . . . In *Lean Thinking*, Dan Jones and James Womack suggest that if for a given activity you haven't cut effort in half . . . within a week, you're doing something wrong. (Caulkin 2002)

This summary judgement, which appeared in the pages of a leading liberal British broadsheet in a business opinion column, is stark in its simplicity: it is, after all, easy to save the planet, provided that one has absorbed the tenets of 'lean thinking'.

Compare now with the following passage, selected from an internationally best-selling book, *Natural Capitalism* by Paul Hawken and Amory B. and L. Hunter Lovins, dealing with the future of the global environment more broadly. It commences with a paean to Taichii Ohno, late Vice President of Toyota MC:

> Ohno-sensei [sic] was the father of the Toyota Production System, which is the conceptual foundation of the world's premier manufacturing organization, and one of the pivotal innovators in industrial history. His approach, though adopted successfully by Toyota, remains rare in Japan. However, it has shown remarkable results in America and elsewhere in the West, and is poised for rapid expansion now it has been systematized by industrial experts Dr. James Womack and Professor Daniel Jones. With their kind permission, we gratefully quote and paraphrase their book, *Lean Thinking*, in the hope that more business leaders will read it in full . . . For the first time, we can plausibly and practically imagine a more rewarding and less risky economy whose health, prospects and metrics reverse age-old assumptions about growth: an economy where we grow by using less and less, and become stronger by being leaner. (Hawken et al. 1999: 125, 143)

The authors of this passage are leading advocates of business-friendly corporate reforms *vis-à-vis* environmentally sound practices.[3] Like the preceding commentator they put great store by the merits of 'lean thinking', again as expounded by James Womack and Dan Jones, as pointing the way ahead. The book from which the excerpt is taken exemplifies the view that environmental pressures as well as other social problems can be resolved via what are essentially technological solutions within an existing market framework: 'natural capitalism', as Hawken et al. call it, is to be founded on a new industrial revolution, based on a series of step-changes in economic organization combined with investment in so-called 'natural capital' – natural resources in need of constant renewal. On the question of the combination of inputs to provide outputs in production processes, Hawken et al. (1999: 127) are explicit on the way to deal with environmentally damaging and socially expensive commercial 'waste': 'The nearly universal antidote to such wasteful practices is what Womack and Jones call 'lean thinking'. Again, the proposition is stark in its simplicity: there is a 'nearly universal' antidote.

The last passage is taken from a current web-based publication, namely the 'Lean Manufacturing and the Environment' homepage of the US Environmental Protection Agency (EPA), a body recently much taken by the possibilities of lean thinking:

> By definition, lean manufacturing is the systematic elimination of waste from all aspects of an organization's operations, where waste is viewed as any use or loss of resources that does not lead directly to creating the product or service a customer wants when they want it. In many industrial processes, such non-value added activity can comprise more than 90 percent of a factory's total activity . . . Lean manufacturing – also known as lean, agile manufacturing, or Just-in-Time production – was originally developed by the Toyota Motor Company in Japan based on concepts pioneered by Henry Ford. (www.epa.gov/lean/thinking/index.htm)

The site is both as well-constructed and as expansive as one might expect. On another page further details are given as to the implications of 'lean trends' for the regulatory agencies and voluntary programmes of the EPA: in June 2003, that is to say, relatively recently, a steering committee (the 'Lean and Environment Steering Committee') was formed for purposes of guidance. The website describes this committee as including 'representatives from multiple Offices across the agency as well as several EPA Regional Offices and state environmental agencies': its intent is to assist both the EPA and state environmental programmes to 'leverage lean trends to improve environmental performance' (www.epa.gov/lean/activity.htm). It is envisaged that this will help environmental agencies 'understand the environmental benefits of reducing regulatory "friction" around lean implementation' – further detail on what these regulatory frictions entail, while doubtless interesting, is not given – as well as assisting the EPA itself, and 'other state agencies', to use 'lean techniques'.[4]

There are some obvious issues here that might merit further assessment. To what extent, for example, does the relatively recent but manifestly thorough conversion of the US Environmental Protection Agency reflect an earlier decision to back away from environmental considerations *vis-à-vis* the regulation of industry in favour of market-based solutions that look to 'best practice' in corporate organization?[5] There are independently important questions arising too from what businesses actually do in this respect, quite apart from flag-waving about lean production practices. If we refer back to the thesis of the emergence of a new 'natural capitalism', while it is readily apparent that the car industry looms large as a preferred source of evidence, not all of this hinges on the viability of lean thinking as a production concept: for example, and in the sphere of product consumption and use, ultra-light car bodies and hybrid-electric engines are invoked as instances of how improvements in product technology for a major pollutant (cars) can be employed to solve environmental problems.[6] What is required for criticism here is separate from a criticism of lean production. But of immediate interest, however, is the use made of the view that the liberation of production potentials achieved by Toyota in the car industry will help transform industrial capitalism in a way that will satisfy environmental concerns. The passage cited above, for example, refers to a high level of 'non-value added activity', but the only evidence attached to this page of the EPA website is a reference back to a single source – namely the same article by Simon Caulkin as is also cited above.

In this way one begins to get a sense of the loop within which this world is defined: the EPA cites Caulkin, who (like Hawken et al.) cites Womack and Jones, who draw sustenance from the received interpretation of the IMVP world productivity survey carried out in the 1980s, and a fictionalized version of manufacturing history. But the sense of an 'agreed' vision supported by acts of corporate-congratulation is also palpable – the EPA website, for instance, delivers the following item, as news:

On May 20, 2004, EPA received the prestigious 2004 Shingo Prize for Research that fosters Excellence in Manufacturing Business. The Prize – dubbed the Nobel Prize for Manufacturing – recognizes and promotes awareness of research on lean manufacturing processes in the United States, Canada and Mexico. Lean manufacturing is a business model and a collection of manufacturing methods that emphasize continuous improvements to speed up production times, deliver high quality, low-cost products, and eliminate waste.

We have met Shingo Prize winners before, but readers unaware of just how important the 'lean thinking' nexus of visionaries now is should take stock of the pleasure afforded the US Environmental Protection Agency in being awarded one. Equally, if not more, striking, is the current enthusiasm for 'lean thinking' for the organization of the procurement of military equipment for the US air-force and army: space precludes a survey of what in itself might make a substantial chapter in this book, but the reader still doubtful as to the recent explosion of lean thinking activity could do worse than to consult the linkages helpfully supplied, as per the citation at the outset of this chapter, by the home page of the US Air War College (via its Index to the Internet). The example is in no real sense a different one, polemical appeal aside: in each case, whether the site consulted is the EPA site, or the Air War College site, great weight is given in the referenced pages to the same (alleged) breakthroughs in the organization of manufacturing activities on the side of product supply broadly defined; and in each, the same corporate players loom large. The EPA's principal case study illustration, for example, is Lockheed Martin, 'the world's largest defense contractor'.

The explosion in lean thinking ventures in the US does not mean that there is substance after all to the concept, any more than it implies that there is no substance whatsoever to the steps taken by corporations under the rubric of lean thinking. This would be to confuse the issues which are relevant under each heading. But what this does illustrate – perhaps more dramatically so in the US than in Europe – is the extent to which corporate-led activities are now pursued under this banner. At the risk of taking speculation one step too far, does 'lean' in this connection equate with 'liberty' – liberty for commerce, to the smell of victory on the morning wind?

8.6 TOYOTA AND THE NEW MODEL WORKER

Our last stop might seem the most unlikely, given what we have previously suggested about the creeping authoritarianism and industrial unitarism of 'lean thinkers'. But consider the following passage, taken from the launch of the lean programme:

[W]e believe that once lean production principles are fully instituted, companies will be able to move rapidly in the 1990s to automate most of the remaining tasks in auto assembly – and more. Thus by the end of the century we expect that team-assembly plants will be populated almost entirely by highly skilled problem-solvers whose task will be to think continually of ways and means to make the system run more smoothly and productively. The great flaw of neocraftsmanship is that it will never reach this goal, since it aspires to go in the other direction, back toward an era of handcrafting as an end in itself. (Womack et al. 1990: 102)

The future predicted at this time, for lean plants at least, would be one of increasingly automated factories especially in car assembly, a desirable goal that could only be blocked by attempts to inculcate worker satisfaction through craft-work. We have, in the preceding chapters, set out the basis for point-by-point disputation, and it is not needful at this juncture that we go back over all of the issues again. But consider now the following comment, by two not uncritical writers, on the same passage:

It remains to be seen . . . how far this optimism might be justified. Paradoxically, this lean production dream . . . resembles the old Marxist dream of abolishing the distinction between mental and manual labour and turning all workers into skilled knowledge workers who would enjoy work as a necessity rather than as a burden. (Freeman and Soete 1999: 157)

And if this association between the 'old Marxist dream' and the 'lean produc-tion dream' seems an incongruous one, achieving by means of corporate capi-talist expediency that which revolutionary socialists used to aspire to, it has to be admitted at this juncture that the sentiment – cautiously expressed – has found its echo in the committed radical press. Andre Gorz wrestles with the thorny question of whether a post-Fordist organization of manufacture in the car industry points to a (possible) 'reappropriation of work by the workers', or a 'regression towards a total subjugation and quasi-vassaldom of the very person of the worker' (Gorz 1999: 32). The context for this speculation is the purported transformation wrought by Toyota in the organization of production in the car industry towards more 'flexible forms', taken as indicative of a (possible) fundamental change in the nature of work. Again, there is no need at this juncture to revisit our previous assessments of relevant points. Rather, we should ponder the hopes and fears set forth by Gorz in this connection:

Whereas for Taylorism, the self-organization, ingenuity and creativity of the work-ers were to be combated as the source of all dangers of rebellion and disorder, for Toyotism these things were a resource to be developed and exploited . . . The work-ers must understand what they are doing. Indeed, they must (in theory) come to grasp the complete manufacturing process and system as an intelligible whole. They must 'own' that system, control it and feel in command of its workings. They must think about ways of improving and rationalizing product design. They must reflect on possible improvement to procedures and to the overall organization of the system. To this end, they must consult and engage in discussion; they must be able to express themselves and listen; they must be ready to question their own assumptions, to learn, and to develop continually. The worker, writes Benjamin Coriat, must become simultaneously 'manufacturer, technologist and manager'. (Gorz 1999: 30)

It is perhaps noteworthy that Gorz not only assumes that all of these things are prerequisites to 'flexibility in production', the changed relationship between consumer and factory reflecting the changing status of the worker in the factory, but that nothing is said of the reorganization of work at Toyota occasioned by what the company itself has defined as a response to labour problems.[7] Like corporate bodies in the US today, lobbying for business and freedom to do business in state-bothered areas, Gorz is much taken by the liberating potentials of the lean-revolution:

> According to Womack, the Western adaptation of the Toyota system ought to make it possible to manufacture the same volume of products with half as large a workforce, half as much capital, and premises half as large, in half the time. The time required for designing and developing new products ought also to be reduced by half, as should the working hours of the research department. (Gorz 1999: 48)

But at the same time:

> Japanese official surveys show that between two-thirds and three-quarters of final assembly workers in the car industry complain of chronic fatigue and exhaustion at the end of the working day. The big companies move these workers to less strenuous posts at the age of 30. Instance of people dying from overwork (*karoshi*) are not exceptional. (ibid.: note 8)

To watch Gorz wrestle with the embryonic soviet of Toyota factory life – at least as envisaged from the perspective of the great transformation from 'Fordism' – versus the alleged deaths of workers from work stress in Japan, makes it abundantly clear that there is more to consider here than some misconceptions about an industry.

8.7   CONCLUSIONS

In the introduction to this book we observed that its intent was neither to challenge the intrinsic interest of detailed investigations into comparative manufacturing practices, or to doubt the importance of the Japanese impact on the world car industry, or to deny that a great deal of valuable information has been carefully collected: what it is concerned to do is to make the case robustly, through a series of connected studies, for abandoning as wholly untenable any suggestion that it has been the historic contribution of Toyota and other Japanese firms to usher in a 'new' type of production characterized either by a superior manufacturing flexibility or a great leap forward in resource productivity, to be compared and contrasted on this basis with a previously existing organizational form ('Fordist mass production') in the West; and it does so as a necessary prelude into an investigation as to why a myth of this kind should hold such extraordinary appeal in the face of manifestly contrary evidence. In this last chapter we have given freer rein than elsewhere to critical speculation: in doing so, we hope to press the case for a different type of study, that necessarily includes close scrutiny of industrial developments but with a broader purview, intent on gauging not only the forms but also the meanings of fictions about production understood in their historical and societal context, fictions understood as production fantasies.

NOTES

1. An argument cited approvingly, for example, by Asanuma (1994: 118). The Milgrom–Roberts paper raises a number of interesting points which we hope to explore in another work: it sets out a formal analysis intended to 'capture' the essential features of the assumed transition from Fordist mass production to more flexible modes of manufacture (for examples of how this attempt has been received, see Boyer (1999: 31), or Kuenne (2000)). Our basic point of departure, however, would be to consider what might be made of this type of formalism in light of the views developed in our book of the attendant 'data'.

2. In the decades before the re-invention of the post-World War II history of the Western car industry factory observers could not only take it for granted that one of the principal areas affecting the assignment of workers to car assembly was the number of different models which the track was expected to accommodate, but were frequently also at pains to emphasize the 'flexibility' of workers required to handle 'non-standard' parts and subject to the 'almost weekly' 'changes and modifications of jobs and components' suffered by 'most' popular models 'throughout' their production lives (Turner et al. 1967: 40, 169). At the same time, the attendant assumptions made about the experience of work in such environments could hardly be more different from those which are currently popular, an observation which raises a number of issues that we again hope to consider in proper detail in a future study.

3. Two of the authors are in fact founders of the Rocky Mountain Institute, sufficiently well-known, in the US at least, to be cited in undergraduate textbooks as a leading centre of industrial innovation: 'The Rocky Mountain Institute, an innovative think tank located in Colorado, has taken the approach that a powerful way of encouraging energy efficiency is to demonstrate clear and unambiguous financial benefits from the adoption of energy efficient strategies. The Institute has become so well known that staff members are employed as energy efficient consultants to businesses around the United States. In tracking the consequences of energy efficient design, the Institute has uncovered a latent consequence of energy efficient design: increases in workplace productivity' (Stover et al. 1999: 314).

4. We might observe parenthetically at this point that in the passage cited above the closing lines indicate that the words 'agile manufacturing' and 'lean manufacturing' are employed interchangeably. Some writers in fact attempt to distinguish the two: for example, Christopher (2005: 118–19, see also Chapter 3 section 3.4) suggests that 'agile' production be invoked only in situations in which 'demand for variety is high', implying that this is not so for lean

production. For most writers, however, the words 'lean and flexible' are inextricably linked, so that in this regard the EPA usage is most in keeping with the popularly held view.

5. One might note, for instance, that this enthusiasm postdates the decision of the US government under the Bush administration to withdraw from obligations under the Kyoto treaty. The case is not cut-and-dried: Hawken et al. (1999: 244–46), for example, while equally as enthusiastic as the copy-writers of the EPA website for 'lean thinking', are nonetheless also notable for their endorsement of Kyoto, positing international regulation and business-friendly organizational reform as mutually complementary practices. At the very least, however, it might be reasonably proposed that the assertion that 'lean thinking' vitiates the need for 'posturing' at a 'political level' (the words are Caulkin's, above) is hardly calculated to be confrontational in a political context that rejects treaties of this kind.

6. The key breakthroughs here are dated to the 1990s: lighter cars (it is said) will make hybrid-electric motors more viable (see Hawken et al. 1999: 22–47). We do not possess sufficient technical knowledge of the relevant areas of product engineering to offer judgement on what the authors describe as a 'forward-looking' projection of existing industry trends. For the UK, Professor Garel Rhys (2005) is relatively downbeat on hybrid technologies. An enthusiastic account of Toyota's hybrid car programme is given in Itakazi (1999).

7. A sympathetic introduction to Andre Gorz is provided by Geoghegan (1987); for a broader discussion of some of the issues raised in this last section see Coffey and Thornley (2006a).

References

Abegglen, J. and Stalk, G. (1985) *Kaisha: The Japanese Corporation*, New York: Basic Books.

Abelshauser, W. (1995) 'Two Kinds of Fordism: On the Differing Roles of Industry in the Development of the Two German States', in H. Shiomi and K. Wada (eds), *Fordism Transformed: The Development of Production Methods in the Automobile Industry*, Oxford: Oxford University Press, pp. 269–96.

Abernathy, W.J. (1978) *The Productivity Dilemma*, Baltimore: Johns Hopkins University Press.

Abernathy, W.J., Clark, K.B. and Kantrow, A.M. (1983) *Industrial Renaissance*, New York: Basic Books.

Abernathy, W.J., Harbour, J.B. and Henn J.M. (1981) 'Productivity and Comparative Cost Advantages: Some Estimates for Major Automotive Producers', Draft Report to the Department of Transportation, Washington, DC: Transportation Systems Centre.

Aglietta, M. (1976) *Regulation et Crises du Capitalisme*, Calmann-Levy.

Aglietta, M. (1987) *A Theory of Capitalist Regulation: The US Experience*, London and New York: Verso.

Allen, G.C. (1981) 'Industrial Policy and Innovation in Japan', in C. Carter (ed.), *Industrial Policy and Innovation*, London: Heinemann, pp. 68–87.

Altshuler, A., Anderson, M., Jones, D., Roos, D. and Womack, J. (1984) *The Future of the Automobile*, Cambridge: MIT Press

Aoki, M. (1987) 'Horizontal vs vertical information structure of the firm', *American Economic Review*, **76**, December, 971–83.

Aoki, M. (1988) *Information, Incentives, and Bargaining in the Japanese Economy*, Cambridge: Cambridge University Press.

Aoki, M. (1990) 'Toward an economic model of the Japanese firm', *Journal of Economic Literature*, **28** (1), 1–27.

Appelbaum, E., Bailey, T., Berg, P. and Kalleberg, A.L. (2000) *Manufacturing Advantage: Why High Performance Work Systems Pay Off*, Ithaca and London: Cornell University Press.

Arnowitz, S. (1973) *False Promises: the Shaping of American Working Class Consciousness*, New York: McGraw-Hill Co.

Arrighi, G. (1994) *The Long Twentieth Century: Money, Power and the Origins of our Times*, London and New York: Verso.

Asanuma, B. (1994) 'Co-Ordination between Production and Distribution in a Globalizing Network of Firms: Assessing Flexibility Achieved in the Japanese Automobile Industry', in M. Aoki and R. Dore (eds), *The Japanese Firm: Sources of Competitive Strength*, Oxford: Oxford University Press, pp. 117–53.

Bannock, G. (1973) *The Juggernauts: The Age of the Big Corporation*, Harmondsworth, England: Penguin Books Ltd.

Baran, P. and Sweezy, P. (1966) *Monopoly Capitalism: An Essay on the American Economic and Social Order*, New York: Monthly Review Press.

Barrow, M. and Wagstaff, A. (1995) 'Efficiency measurement in the public sector: an appraisal', *Fiscal Studies*, **10** (1), 72–96.

Basu, R. and Wright, J.N. (1997) *Total Manufacturing Solutions*, Butterworth/Heinemann.

Baumol, W.J. (1994) 'Multivariate Growth Patterns: Contagion and Common Forces as Possible Sources of Convergence', in W.J. Baumol, R.R. Nelson and E.N. Wolff (eds), *Convergence of Productivity: Cross-national Studies and Historical Evidence*, Oxford: Oxford University Press, pp. 62–85.

Benders, J. and Morita, M. (2004) 'Changes in Toyota Motors' operations management', *International Journal of Production Research*, **42** (3), 433–44.

Bennett, T., Grossberg, L. and Morris, M. (eds) (2005) *New Keywords: A Revised Vocabulary of Culture and Society*, Oxford: Blackwell Publishing.

Berggren, C. (1992) *The Volvo Experience: Alternatives to Lean Production in the Swedish Auto Industry*, Houndmills, Basingstoke: The Macmillan Press Ltd.

Berggren, C. (1993) 'Is lean production the end of history?', *Work, Employment and Society*, **7** (2), 163–88.

Berle, A.A. and Means, G.C. (1932) *The Modern Corporation and Private Property*, New York: Macmillan.

Bernstein, J.S. (1997) 'Toyoda Looms and Toyota Automobiles', in T.M. McCraw (ed.), *Creating Modern Capitalism: How Entrepreneurs, Companies and Countries Triumphed in Three Industrial Revolutions*, Cambridge, MA: Harvard University Press, 398–38.

Best, M.H. (1990) *The New Competition: Institutions of Industrial Restructuring*, Cambridge, UK: Polity Press.

Best, M.H. (2001) *The New Competitive Advantage: The Renewal of American Industry*, Oxford and New York: Oxford University Press.

Beynon, H. (1973) *Working for Ford*, Harmondsworth: Middlesex, Penguin Books Ltd.

Bicheno, J. and Elliot, B. (1997) *Operations Management: An Active Learning Approach*, Blackwell Business Approach, Blackwell Business.

Blumenstein, R. (1997) 'GM is building plants in developing nations to woo new markets', *Wall Street Journal*, August 4.

Boyer, R. (1999) 'Hybridization and Models of Production: Geography, History and Theory', in R. Boyer, E. Charron, U. Jurgens and S. Tolliday (eds), *Between Imitation and Innovation: The Transfer and Hybridization of Productive Models in the International Automobile Industry*, Oxford and New York: Oxford University Press.

Bradley, H., Erickson, M., Stephenson, C. and Williams. S. (2000) *Myths at Work*, Oxford and Malden, MA: Polity Press.

Brady, C. and Lorenz, A. (2001) *The End of the Road: BMW and Rover – A Brand Too Far*, London: Financial Times–Prentice Hall.

Braverman, H. (1974) *Labour and Monopoly Capitalism: the Degradation of Work in the 20th Century*, New York: Monthly Review Press.

Brecher, J. (1972) *Strike!* San Francisco: Straight Arrow.

Carroll, L. (1998) Alice's Adventures in Wonderland and Through the Looking Glass, London and New York: Penguin Classics (edited by H. Haughton).

Carter, C.F. and Williams, B.R. (1957) *Industry and Technical Progress: Factors Governing the Speed of Application of Science*, London: Oxford University Press.

Caulkin, S. (2002) 'Waste Not, Want Not', *Observer*, September 8 (also available on www.leaninstitut.nl/publications/waste-not-want-not.pdf).

Christopher, M. (1998) *Logistics and Supply Chain Management: Strategies for Reducing Cost and Improving Service*, Financial Times: Pittman Publishing.

Christopher, M. (2005) *Logistics and Supply Chain Management: Creating Value-Adding Networks* (3rd edition), Harlow: Financial Times–Prentice Hall.

Church, R. (1994) *The Rise and Decline of the British Motor Industry*, Houndmills, Basingstoke, Hampshire and London: The Macmillan Press Ltd.

Coates, D. (2000) *Models of Capitalism: Growth and Stagnation in the Modern Era*, Oxford and Malden, MA: Polity Press.

Coates, D. (2006) 'The rise and fall of Japan as a model of "progressive capitalism"', in D. Bailey, D. Coffey and P.R. Tomlinson (eds), *Crisis or Recovery: State and Industry in Japan*, Cheltenham, UK and Northampton, MA, USA: Edward Elgar (forthcoming).

Coffey, D. (1995) 'Turning Virtue into Vice: Does "Lean" Make Sense', Centre for Industrial Policy and Performance, University of Leeds, Bulletin no. 7 (Spring 1995), pp. 10–12.

Coffey, D. (2003) 'Best Practice Manufacture as Industrial Policy: Lean Production, Competitiveness and Monopoly Capitalism', in D. Coffey and C. Thornley (eds), *Industrial and Labour Market Policy and Performance: Issues and Perspectives*, London and New York: Routledge, pp. 45–61.

Coffey, D. (2005a) 'Delineating comparative flexibility in car assembly: the problem of wide selection', *International Journal of Automotive Technology and Management*, **5** (1), 18–31.

Coffey, D. (2005b) 'Lock-ins and lead times: interpreting strategic matching in car assembly', *International Journal of Automotive Technology and Management*, **5** (3), 320–35.

Coffey, D. and Thornley, C. (eds) (2003) *Industrial and Labour Market Policy and Performance: Issues and Perspectives*, London and New York: Routledge.

Coffey, D. and Thornley, C. (2006a) 'Automotive assembly: automation, motivation and lean production reconsidered', *Assembly Automation*: The International Journal of Assembly Technology and Management, **26**, (2), pp. 98–103.

Coffey, D. and Thornley, C. (2006b) 'Changes in Toyota Motors' operations management further considered: line-stoppage frequencies and theoretical cost efficiencies', mimeo.

Coffey, D. and Thornley, C. (2006c) 'Can Japan Compete Reconsidered: Globalisation and Transformation in the Japanese Industrial Crisis', in D. Bailey, D. Coffey and P.R. Tomlinson (eds), *Crisis or Recovery: State and Industry in Japan*, Cheltenham, UK and Northampton, MA, USA: Edward Elgar (forthcoming)

Coffey, D. and Thornley C. (2006d) *New Labour and the Abject State*, mimeo.

Coffey, D. and Tomlinson, P.R. (2003) 'Globalization, vertical relations, and the J-mode firm', *Journal of Post Keynesian Economics*, **26** (1), Fall, 117–44.

Cole, R.E. (ed.) (1981) *The Japanese Automobile Industry: Model and Challenge for the Future?*, Michigan Papers in Japanese Studies, no. 3, Ann Arbor: Centre for Japanese Studies at the University of Michigan.

Collins, P. and Stratton, M. (1993) *British Car Factories from 1896: A Complete Geographical, Architectural and Technological Survey*, Dorset: Veloce Publishing plc.

Coriat, B. (1997) 'Globalization, Variety and Mass Production: The Metamorphosis of Mass Production in the New Competitive Age', in J.R. Hollingsworth and R. Boyer (eds), *Contemporary Capitalism: The Embeddedness of Institutions*, Cambridge: Cambridge University Press, pp. 240–64.

Cowling, K. (1982) *Monopoly Capitalism*, London and Basingstoke: The Macmillan Press Ltd.

Cowling, K. and Tomlinson, P.R. (2000) 'The Japanese crisis – a case of strategic failure?', *Economic Journal*, **110** (464), F358–F381.

Cowling, K. and Tomlinson, P.R. (2003) 'Industrial Policy, Transnational Corporations and the Problem of "Hollowing Out" in Japan', in D. Coffey and C. Thornley (eds), *Industrial and Labour Market Policy and Performance: Issues and Perspectives*, London and New York: Routledge, pp. 62–82.

Cusumano, M.A. (1985) *The Japanese Automobile Industry: Technology and Management at Nissan and Toyota*, Cambridge, MA, and London: Harvard University Press.

Delbridge, R. and Oliver, N. (1991a) 'Just-in-time or just the Same? Developments in the auto industry – the retailers' view', *International Journal of Retailing and Distribution Management*, **19** (2), 20–26.

Delbridge, R. and Oliver, N. (1991b) 'Narrowing the gap? Stock turns in the Japanese and Western car industries', *International Journal of Production Research*, **29** (10), 2083–95.

Dicken, P. (2003) *Global Shift: Reshaping the Global Economic Map in the 21st Century*, (4th edition), London: Sage Publications Ltd.

Drucker, P. (1955) *The Practice of Management*, London: Heinemann.

Dubois, P. (1976) *Le Sabotage dans l'industrie*, France: Calmann-Levy.

Dubois, P. (1979) *Sabotage in Industry*, Harmondsworth: Penguin Books.

Dunnett, P.J.S. (1980) *The Decline of the British Motor Industry*, London: Croom Helm.

Eberts, R. and Eberts, C. (1995) *The Myths of Japanese Quality*, Upper Saddle River, NJ: Prentice Hall Publishers.

Edwards, R. (1979) *Contested Terrain: The Transformation of the Workplace in the 20th Century*, New York: Basic Books.

El-Agraa, A.M. (1997) 'UK competitiveness policy vs. Japanese industrial policy', *The Economic Journal*, **107**, September.

Fisher, F., Griliches, Z. and Kaysen, C. (1962) 'The costs of automobile model changes since 1949', *American Economic Review*, **LXX** (5), May, 433–50.

Foreman-Peck, J., Bowden, S. and McKinlay, A. (1995) *The British Motor Industry*, Manchester and New York: Manchester University Press.

Freeman, C. and Soete, L. (1999) *The Economics of Industrial Innovation*, (3rd edition, Reprint Issue), London and Washington: Pinter.

Freyssenet, M. (1995) 'The Origins of Teamwork at Renault', in A. Sandberg (ed.), *Enriching Production: Perspectives on Volvo's Uddevalla plant as an alternative to lean production*, Aldershot: Avebury, pp. 293–307.

Friedmann, G. (1953) *Ou va le travail humain?*, (2nd edition), Paris: Gallimard.

Fujimoto, T. (1999) *The Evolution of a Manufacturing System at Toyota*, Oxford and New York: Oxford University Press.

Fuss, M.A. and Waverman, L. (1992) *Costs and Productivity in Automobile Production: the Challenge of Japanese Efficiency*, Cambridge: Cambridge University Press.

Geoghegan, V. (1987) *Utopianism and Marxism*, London and New York: Methuen.

Giddens, A. (2001) *Sociology* (4th edition), Cambridge, UK: Polity Press.

Gilpin, R. (2000) *The Challenge of Global Capitalism: The World Economy in the 21st Century*, Princeton and Oxford: Princeton University Press.

Gilpin, R. (2001) *Global Political Economy: Understanding the International Economy Order*, Princeton and Oxford: Princeton University Press.

Gordon, R.B. (1993) 'The Interpretation of Artifacts in the History of Technology', in S. Lubar and W.D. Kingery (eds), *History from Things: Essays on Material Culture*, Washington and London: Smithsonian Institution Press, pp. 74–93.

Gorz, A. (1999) *Reclaiming Work: Beyond the Wage-Based Society*, Cambridge, UK: Polity Press (translated by C. Turner).

Greenhalgh, C. and Kilmister, A. (1993) 'The British Economy, the State and the Motor Industry', in T. Hayter and D. Harvey (eds), *The Factory and the City: The Story of the Cowley Automobile Workers in Oxford*, London: Mansell, pp. 26–46.

Gronning, T. (1995) 'Recent Developments at Toyota Motor Co.', in A. Sandberg (ed.), *Enriching Production: Perspectives on Volvo's Uddevalla Plant as an Alternative to Lean Production*, Aldershot: Avebury, pp. 405–25.

Groover, M.P. (1987) *Automation, Production Systems, and Computer Integrated Manufacturing*, London: Prentice-Hall (UK) International Ltd.

Hartley, J. (1977) 'The changing scene in car manufacture', *Automotive Engineer*, April/May, 14–19.

Hawken, P., Lovins, A.B. and Hunter-Lovins, L. (1999) *Natural Capitalism: The Next Industrial Revolution*, London: Earthscan Publications Ltd.

Hayter, T. (1993) 'Local Politics', in T. Hayter and D. Harvey (eds), *The Factory and the City: The Story of the Cowley Automobile Workers in Oxford*, London: Mansell, pp. 161–85.

Hayter, T. and Harvey, D. (1993) *The Factory and the City: The Story of the Cowley Automobile Workers in Oxford*, London: Mansell.

HC (1999–2000a) *BMW, Rover and Longbridge*, House of Commons, Session 1999–2000, Trade and Industry Committee, Eighth Report (HC 383).

HC (1999–2000b) *Government Observations on the Eighth Report of Session 1999–2000*, House of Commons, Session 1999–2000, Eighth Special Report (HC 634).

HC (2000–2001) *Vehicle Manufacturing in the UK: Report, Together with the Proceedings of the Committee, Minutes of Evidence, and Appendices*, House of Commons, Session 2000–01, Trade and Industry Committee, Third Report (HC 128).

Held, D., McGrew, A., Goldblatt, D. and Perraton, J. (1999) *Global Transformations: Politics, Economics and Culture*, Cambridge: Polity Press.

Henle, P. (1974) 'Economic Effects: Reviewing the Evidence', in J.M. Rosow (ed.), *The Worker and the Job: Coping with Change*, Englewood Cliffs, NJ: Prentice Hall, Inc.

Henry, J. (1968) 'Social and Psychological Preparation for War', in D. Cooper (ed.), *The Dialectics of Liberation*, Harmondsworth: Penguin Books Ltd, pp. 50–71.

Higdon, H. (1966) 'The Big Auto Sweepstakes', *New York Times Magazine*, May 1.

Holweg, M. and Oliver, N. (2005) 'Who Killed MG Rover?' A Special Report from the Cambridge–MIT Institute's Centre for Competitiveness and Innovation (CCI), Centre for Competitiveness and Innovation, University of Cambridge, April 2005.

Howes, D. (1998) 'GM, Ford play for keeps abroad', *The Detroit News*, March 8, 1998.

Itakazi, H. (1999) *The Prius That Shook the World: How Toyota Developed the World's First Mass-Production Hybrid Vehicle*, Tokyo: The Kikkan Kogyo Shimbun Ltd. (translated by A. Yamada and M. Ishidawa).

Jain, S. (2004) 'Dangerous Instrumentality': the bystander as subject in auto-mobility', *Cultural Anthropology*, **19** (1), 61–94.

Jain, S. (2005) *Injury: Design and Litigation in the United States*, Princeton University Press.

Jain, S. (2006) *Commodity Violence: American Automobility*, Duke University Press.

Japanese Manufacturers Association (eds) (1989) *Kanban: Just-in-Time at Toyota*, Cambridge, MA: Productivity Press (translated by D.J. Lu).

Johnson, C. (1982) *MITI and the Japanese Miracle: The Growth of Industrial Policy 1925–75*, Stanford: Stanford University Press.

Jurgens, U. (1995) 'Group Work and the Reception of Uddevalla in German Car Industry', in Sandberg, A. (ed.), *Enriching Production: Perspectives on Volvo's Uddevalla Plant as an Alternative to Lean Production*, Aldershot and Vermont: Avebury, pp. 199–213.

Jurgens, U., Malsch, T. and Dohse, K. (1993) *Breaking from Taylorism: Changing Forms of Work in the Automobile Industry*, Cambridge: Cambridge University Press.

Kaplinsky, R. (1988) 'Restructuring the capitalist labour process: some lessons for the car industry', *Cambridge Journal of Economics*, **12**, 451–70.

Katzner, D.W. (1999) 'Western economics and the economy of Japan', *Journal of Post Keynesian Economics*, **21** (3), Spring, 503–22.

Katzner, D.W. (2006) 'The Workings of the Japanese Economy', in D. Bailey, D. Coffey and P.R. Tomlinson (eds), *Crisis or Recovery: State and Industry in Japan*, Cheltenham, UK and Northampton, MA, USA: Edward Elgar (forthcoming).

Kawahara, A. (1998) *The Origin of Competitive Strength: Fifty Years of the Auto Industry in Japan and the U.S.*, Tokyo: Springer-Verlag.

Keegan, R. (ed.) (1998) *Benchmarking Facts: A European Perspective*, European Benchmarking Forum/European Commission.

Kenney, M. and Florida, R. (1993) *Beyond Mass Production: The Japanese System and Its Transfer to the US*, Oxford and New York: Oxford University Press.

Kinch, N. (1995) 'The Road from Dreams of Mass Production to Flexible Specialization: American Influences on the Development of the Swedish Automobile Industry, 1920–39', in H. Shiomi and K. Wada (eds), *Fordism Transformed: The Development of Production Methods in the Automobile Industry*, Oxford: Oxford University Press, pp. 107–36.

Kono, T. (1984) *Strategy and Structure of Japanese Enterprises*, London: Macmillan.

Krafcik, J.F. (1988a) 'Complexity and Flexibility in Motor Vehicle Assembly: A Worldwide Perspective', IMVP International Policy Forum, Cambridge, MA: MIT, May.

Krafcik, J.F. (1988b) 'A Methodology for Assembly Plant Performance Determination', IMVP Research Affiliates, Cambridge, MA: MIT, October.

Krafcik, J.F. (1989) 'A Comparative Analysis of Assembly Plant Automation', IMVP International Policy Forum, Cambridge, MA: MIT, May.

Krafcik, J.F. and Womack, J.P. (1987) 'Comparative Manufacturing Practice: Imbalances and Implications', IMVP Working Paper, Cambridge, MA: MIT, May.

Krugman, P. (1994) 'Competitiveness: a dangerous obsession', *Foreign Affairs*, March/April, 28–44.

Kuenne, R.E. (ed.) (2000) *Readings in Applied Microeconomic Theory: Market Forces and Solutions*, Oxford and Massachusetts: Blackwell Publishers Ltd.

Lash, S. and Urry, J. (1994) *Economies of Signs and Space*, London: SAGE Publications, Ltd.

Liker, JK. (2004) *The Toyota Way: 14 Management Principles From the World's Greatest Car Manufacturer*, New York: McGraw Hill.

Lyddon, D. (1996) 'The myth of mass production and the mass production of myth', *Historical Studies in Industrial Relations*, 1, March, 77–105.

Mair, A. (1994) *Honda's Global Local Corporation*, Houndmills, Basingstoke: The Macmillan Press Ltd.

Mandel, E. (1968) *Marxist Economic Theory*, London: Merlin Press.

Mather, H. (1985) *Competitive Manufacturing*, Prentice Hall Trade.

Maxcy, G. and Silberston, A. (1959) *The Motor Industry*, London: Allen and Unwin.

McCracken, P.W. (1981) 'The Government, Business and Labor Perspective', in D. Cole (ed.), *The Japanese Automobile Industry: Model and Challenge for the Future?*, Michigan Papers in Japanese Studies, no. 3, Ann Arbor: Centre for Japanese Studies (The University of Michigan).

Menge, J.A. (1962) 'Style change costs as a market weapon', *Quarterly Journal of Economics*, 76.

Milgrom, P. and Roberts, J. (1990) 'The economics of modern manufacturing: technology, strategy and organization', *American Economic Review*, **80**, 511–28.

Miller, D. (ed.) (2001) *Car Cultures*, Oxford and New York: Berg.

Mintzberg, H., Lampel, J., Quinn, J.B. and Ghosal, S. (2003) *The Strategy Process: Concepts, Contexts, Cases, Pearson Education International*, Pearson: Prentice Hall.

Monden, Y. (1998) *Toyota Production System: An Integrated Approach to Just-in-Time*, (3rd edition), Norcross, GA: Engineering and Management Press.

Murakami, Y. (1996) *An Anticlassical Political–Economic Analysis: A Vision for the Next Century*, Stanford, CA: Stanford University Press.

Nove, A. (1965) *The Soviet Economic System: An Introduction*, London: George Allen and Unwin, Ltd.

Ohno, T. (1978) *Toyota Seisan Hoshiki: Datsu Kibo no Keiei wo Mezashite* (The Toyota Production Method: How Can We Overcome The Management Philosophy of Scale Economies), Tokyo: Diamond Sha.

Ohno, T. (1988) *Toyota Production System: Beyond Large Scale Production*, Cambridge, MA: Productivity Press.

Oliver, N. and Wilkinson, B. (1992) *The Japanization of British Industry: New Developments in the 1990s*, (2nd edition), Oxford and Cambridge, MA: Blackwell.

Pine, B.J. (1999) *Mass Customization: The New Frontier in Business Competition*, Boston, MA: Harvard Business School Press (paperback edition).

Piore, M.J. and Sabel, C.F. (1984) *The Second Industrial Divide: Policies for Prosperity*, New York: Basic Books.

Porter, M.E., Takeuchi, H. and Sakakibara, M. (2000) *Can Japan Compete?*, Hampshire and London: Macmillan Press Ltd.

Prown, J.D. (1993) 'The Truth of Material Culture: History or Fiction', in S. Lubar and W.D. Kingery (eds), *History from Things: Essays on Material Culture*, Washington and London: Smithsonian Institution Press, pp. 1–19.

Rae, J.B. (1965) *The American Automobile: A Brief History*, The University of Chicago and London: University of Chicago Press.

Reading, B. (1993) *Japan: The Coming Collapse*, London: Orion Books, Ltd.

Reeves, R. (1961) *Reality in Advertising*, New York MacGibbon and Kee.

Rhys, D.G. (1972) *The Motor Industry: An Economic Survey*, London: Butterworth & Co (Publishers) Ltd.

Rhys, D.G. (2005) 'Competition in the auto sector: the impact of the interface between supply and demand', *International Journal of Automotive Technology and Management*, **5** (3).

Rosow, J.M. (ed.) (1974) *The Worker and the Job: Coping with Change*, Englewood Cliffs, NJ: Prentice Hall, Inc.

Ruigrock, W. and Van Tulder, R. (1995) *The Logic of International Restructuring*, London and New York: Routledge.

Salpukas, A. (1974) 'Unions: A New Role?' in J.M. Rosow (ed.), *The Worker and the Job: Coping with Change*, Englewood Cliffs, NJ: Prentice Hall, Inc.

Samuelson, P.A. (1976) *Economics*, (10th edition), New York: McGraw Hill, Inc.

Sandberg, A. (1995) *Enriching Production: Perspectives on Volvo's Uddevalla Plant as an Alternative to Lean Production*, Aldershot, England and Brookfield, VT: Avebury.

Schonberger, R.J. (1982) *Japanese Manufacturing Techniques: Nine Hidden Lessons in Simplicity*, New York: The Free Press, Macmillan Publishing Co., Inc.

Schonberger, R.J. (2001) *Let's Fix It!*, New York: Free Press.

Shingo, S. (1989) *A Study of the Toyota Production System*, Cambridge, MA: Productivity Press.

Shiomi, H. (1995) 'The Formation of Assembler Networks in the Automobile Industry: The Case of Toyota Motor Company (1966–1980)', in H. Shiomi and K. Wada (eds), *Fordism Transformed: The Development of Production Methods in the Automobile Industry*, Oxford: Oxford University Press, 28–48.

Simon, H. (1991) 'Organisations and markets', *Journal of Economic Perspectives*, Spring, **5** (2), 25–44.

Simonian, H. (1997) 'GM hopes to turn a corner with new Astra', *Financial Times*, November 29.

Sinclair, S.W. (1983) *The World Car: The Future of the Automobile Industry*, Euromonitor Publications, London.

Stover, R.G., Lichty, M.L. and Stover, P.W. (1999) *Industrial Societies: An Evolutionary Perspective*, New Jersey: Prentice Hall.

Strauss, G. (1974) 'Workers: Attitudes and Adjustments', in J.M. Roson, (ed) *The Worker and the Job: Coping with Change*, Englewood Cliffs: N.J. Prentice Hall, Inc.

Tabb, W.K. (1995) *The Postwar Japanese System: Cultural Economy and Economic Transformation*, Oxford: Oxford University Press.

Thurow, L. (1992) *Head to Head: the Coming Economic Battle between Japan, Europe and America*, London: Brealey Publishing.

Tolliday, S. and Zeitlin, J. (1986) 'Introduction: Between Fordism and Flexibility', in S. Tolliday and J. Zeitlin (eds), *The Automobile Industry and its Workers: Between Fordism and Flexibility*, Oxford: Polity Press, pp. 1–25.

Tomlinson, P.R. (2002) 'The real effects of transnational activity upon investment and labour demand within Japan's machinery industries', *International Review of Applied Economics*, **16** (2), 107–29.

Tomlinson, P.R. (2005) 'The overseas entry patterns of Japanese automobile assemblers 1960–2000: globalization of manufacturing capacity and the role of strategic contingency', *International Journal of Automotive Technology and Management*, **5** (3), 284–304.

Turner, H.A., Clack, G. and Roberts, G. (1967) *Labour Relations in the Motor Industry: A Study of International Unrest and an International Comparison*, London: George Allen & Unwin Ltd.

Walker, C., Guest, R. and Turner, A. (1956) *The Foreman on the Assembly Line*, Cambridge, MA: Harvard University Press.

Whipp, R. and Clark, P. (1986) *Innovation and the Auto Industry: Product, Process and Work Organization*, London: Frances Pinter (Publishers) Limited.

Whisler, T.R. (1999) *The British Motor Industry 1945–1994: A Case Study in Industrial Decline*, Oxford: Oxford University Press.

White, L.J. (1971) *The Automobile Industry Since 1945*, Cambridge MA: Harvard University Press.

Wilkins, M. (1998) 'The Free-Standing Economy Revisited', in M. Wilkins and H.G. Schroter (eds), *The Free-Standing Company in the World Economy, 1830–1996*, Oxford and New York: Oxford University Press.

Wilks, S. (1984) *Industrial Policy and the Motor Industry*, Manchester: Manchester University Press.

Williams, K., Williams, J. and Haslam, C. (1987) *The Breakdown of Austin Rover*, Leamington Spa: Berg Publishers Ltd.

Williams, K., Haslam, C., Williams, J., Cutler, T., Adcroft, A. and Johal, S. (1994) *Cars: Analysis, History, Cases*, Oxford: Berghahn.

Williams. R. (1988) *Keywords: A Vocabulary of Culture and Society*, (3rd edition), London: Fontana.

Willman, P. and Winch, G. (1985) *Innovation and Management Control: Labour Relations at BL Cars*, Cambridge: Cambridge University Press

Womack, J. and Jones, D.T. (1996) *Lean Thinking: Banish Waste and Create Wealth in Your Corporation*, (1st edition), Bath: Simon and Schuster.

Womack, J. and Jones, D.T. (2003) *Lean Thinking: Banish Waste and Create Wealth in Your Corporation*, (2nd edition), Bath: Simon and Schuster.

Womack, J., Jones, D.T. and Roos, D. (1990) *The Machine That Changed the World*, New York: HarperCollins.

Woodley, T. (2000) 'Minutes of Evidence Taken Before The Trade and Industry Committee, 24th October', in HC (2000–2001) *Vehicle Manufacturing in the UK: Report, Together with the Proceedings of the Committee, Minutes of Evidence, and Appendices*, House of Commons, Session 2000–01, Trade and Industry Committee, Third Report (HC 128).

Woollard, F.G. (1954) *Principles of Mass and Flow Production*, London: Iliffe and Sons, Ltd.

Yonekura, S. and McKinney, S. (2005) 'Innovative Multinational Forms: Japan as a Case Study', in A.D. Chandler, Jr. and B. Mazlish (eds), *Leviathans: Multinational Corporations and the New Global History*, Cambridge: Cambridge University Press, pp. 105–31.

Zimbalist, A. (ed.) (1979) *Case Studies on the Labor Process*, New York and London: Monthly Review Press.

Index